Women and Slavery in America

Women and Slavery in America

A Documentary History

EDITED BY
CATHERINE M. LEWIS AND J. RICHARD LEWIS

The University of Arkansas Press
Fayetteville
2011

ISBN-10: (cloth) 1-55728-957-3
ISBN-13: (cloth) 978-1-55728-957-5

ISBN-10: (paper) 1-55728-958-1
ISBN-13: (paper) 978-1-55728-958-2

15   14   13   12   11   5   4   3   2   1

Designed by Liz Lester

⊗ The paper used in this publication meets the minimum requirements of the
American National Standard for Permanence of Paper for Printed Library Materials
Z39.48-1984.

LIBRARY OF CONGRESS CATALOGING-IN-PUBLICATION DATA

Women and slavery in America : a documentary history / edited by Catherine M.
    Lewis and J. Richard Lewis.
        p.   cm.
    Includes bibliographical references and index.
    ISBN 978-1-55728-957-5 (cloth : alk. paper) -- ISBN 978-1-55728-958-2 (pbk. :
alk. paper)
        1. Women slaves—United States—History—Sources. 2. Slavery—United
States—History—Sources. 3. Women—Southern States—History—Sources.
4. African American women—Southern States—History—Sources. I. Lewis,
Catherine M. II. Lewis, J. Richard, 1967–
    HT1048.W66   2011
    306.3'620820973—dc22
                                                        2010047822

For Emma Lewis Companiotte,
who arrived just in time

CONTENTS

ACKNOWLEDGMENTS

Like all books, this one has been a collaborative endeavor, depending on many dedicated and generous colleagues and friends. We would like to begin by thanking Larry Malley, Julie Watkins, Brian King, Shay Hopper, Michael W. Bieker, and Thomas Lavoie at the University of Arkansas Press. Their enthusiasm for and support of this project, the third in a series of documentary collections, inspired us throughout the writing and research.

We would like to thank Erin Cortner and Allison Lester, both fine public historians, who helped type many of the documents and prepare the manuscript. The staff at the Kenan Research Center at the Atlanta History Center helped us in innumerable ways throughout the process, and we are grateful for their knowledge of this important archive.

There are numerous individuals who helped us secure permissions to use many of the documents included in this volume: Christine Beauregard at the New York State Archives; Jeff Bridgers at the Library of Congress; Mike Millner and Matthew Turi at the Wilson Library at the University of North Carolina at Chapel Hill; Mitch Fraas at the Rare Books, Manuscript, and Special Collections Library at Duke University; Alanna J. Patrick at the Mississippi Department of Archives and History; Chris Kolbe at the Library of Virginia in Richmond; Edwina D. Ashie-Nikoi at the Schomburg Center for Research in Black Culture at the New York Public Library; Elaine Grublin and Peter Drummey at the Massachusetts Historical Society; Thomas Haggerty at the Bridgeman Art Library in New York; Ronald A. Lee at the Tennessee State Library and Archives; Beth M. Howse at Fisk University Special Collections; Sylvia Cyrus and Daryl Michael Scott at the Association for the Study of African American Life and History; Thomas Knoles at the American Antiquarian Society; Ken Barr, Rebecca Gregory, Nancy Duprea, and especially Dr. Norwood Kirk of the Alabama State Archives; the staff at the John Pace Library at the University of West Florida; and the staff at the Florida State Archives in Tallahassee.

We would like to extend a warm thanks to Dr. Ouida Dickey for her valuable edits to the introduction as we were completing the manuscript. Dr. Jennifer Dickey deserves special recognition for her assistance with editing the introduction and for her useful comments on documents to consider. She is a gifted public historian and delightful colleague. Many others at Kennesaw State University deserve recognition, especially Dr. Howard Shealy, Dr. Tom Keene, Dr. David Parker, Dr. Bill Hill, Dr. Wesley K. Wicker, Dr. Randy Hinds, Lori Meadows, Dr. Lana Wachniak, Dr. Anne Sinkey, Patricia Mosier, Anna Tucker, and Tony Howell for their encouragement and patience as we finished this manuscript. Dr. Sarah Robbins at Texas Christian University deserves special mention for her good cheer and encouragement.

Catherine owes a special debt to Dr. Leslie Schwalm and Dr. Linda Kerber at the University of Iowa, who have guided her through the study of U.S. women's history. Their wisdom and curiosity have helped shape a generation of scholars.

We would like to thank Betty Lewis and John Companiotte, who have supported and assisted us throughout the research and writing of this book. They have remained patient and encouraging, as we spent many hours searching for new documents to enhance this collection. There are few ways to express our gratitude. Finally, we would like to dedicate this book to Emma Lewis Companiotte, who came into our lives as a daughter and granddaughter in the midst of this project. There are not words enough to express our great love for you.

INTRODUCTION

Over the past four decades, women's history has grown into a vibrant field of study focused on recovering and documenting the details of women's lives. Interest in women's history has brought attention to areas that have been ignored and has encouraged the development of new methods for reinterpreting topics that have mainly focused on the experiences of men. The most influential and significant scholarship on the history of slavery has followed this pattern. Early works, such as Ulrich B. Phillips's *American Negro Slavery,* Kenneth Stampp's *The Peculiar Institution,* and Stanley Elkins's *Slavery: A Problem in American Institutional and Intellectual Life,* used men's experiences as the norm.[1] A second generation of scholars, led by John Hope Franklin's *From Slavery to Freedom,* John Blassingame's *The Slave Community: Plantation Life in the Antebellum South,* and Herbert Gutman's *The Black Family in Slavery and Freedom, 1750–1925,* followed a similar patter. Later works by Catherine Clinton, in *The Plantation Mistress;* Jacqueline Jones, in *Labor of Love, Labor of Sorrow;* Elizabeth Fox-Genovese, in *Within the Plantation Household;* and Sally McMillen, in *Southern Women: Black and White in the Old South,* focused on how gender helped order relationships in Southern society and challenged the omission of women. More recent scholarship such as Jennifer Morgan's *Laboring Women: Reproduction and Gender in New World Slavery* and Patricia Morton's edited collection, *Discovering the Women in Slavery,* examine how the nexus of gender, race, class, region, religion, sexuality, and other mediating factors account for the experiences of American women, often placing women's experiences in a global context.[2] As Morton argues in her introduction, "In short, it becomes clear that placing women in slavery history brings new perspectives to the past. These are perspectives that both emancipate women's history from slavery's silencing of women's voices and also emancipate American slavery history from the stifling exclusion of half the population, in a way that frees us all to raise and examine a host of new questions."[3]

Women and Slavery: A Documentary History offers readers an opportunity to examine the establishment, growth, and evolution of slavery in the United States as it impacted women—enslaved and free, African

American and white, wealthy and poor, Northern and Southern. As Peter Parish writes in his 1989 volume *Slavery: History and Historians,* "There can be no greater mistake than to regard slavery as monolithic . . . Slavery was a system of many systems, with numerous exceptions to every rule."[4] His observations presented a special challenge for the editors of this volume. Because of our focus on slavery in the United States, a nuanced analysis of slavery throughout the Atlantic world is not possible. Historians estimate that between 1450 and 1850, more than ten million enslaved men and women were forcibly brought from Africa, yet less than 5 percent ended up in the United States. At the same time, by 1825, the Southern states of the United States had the largest enslaved population in the New World—more than one-third of the total.[5] So our main focus is on the United States, but we have included several documents that extend beyond those borders and have included recent scholarship in this area in the annotated bibliography. Readers interested in this topic will find the edited volume *Women and Slavery: The Modern Atlantic* especially useful.[6]

The primary documents included in our volume (newspapers, broadsides, cartoons, pamphlets, excerpts from oral histories and memoirs, speeches, photographs, and editorials) are organized thematically and represent cultural, political, religious, economic, and social perspectives on this dark and complex period in American history. Some documents focus specifically on a single woman's experience; others, such as legal proceedings and laws, do not mention women but influenced their daily lives in important ways. Women did not always have to be present or even named to be impacted.

As the historian Peter Parish argues, "For all the harsh lines of status and class, race and color, which divided owners and slaves, both were caught up in a complex web of compromise, adjustment, inconsistency, ambiguity, and deception."[7] This very fact makes generalizations difficult, as American slavery is notable for its sheer variety. On the eve of the Civil War in the fifteen slave states, there were nearly 4 million slaves out of a population of 12.3 million. Half of the slave owners had no more than five slaves; only 12 percent of the owners had twenty or more slaves. Three-quarters of white families in the South owned no slaves at all; and the largest slave owners (mainly sugar or rice planters) comprised barely one-half of 1 percent of all Southern white families.[8] Yet, their power was far disproportionate to their numbers, and they often left the most complete and detailed records and are thus the most widely discussed by historians.

This introduction functions as an overview of the main issues, followed by five chapters that include numerous documents that provide multiple perspectives on women and slavery. The brief head notes introduce each document, offering readers important background information in which to evaluate it. We have remained faithful to the original sources without changing spelling or grammar. Many of the documents are excerpted, which is noted in the individual head notes. The appendix includes a "Timeline" and "Annotated Bibliography," as well as "Questions for Consideration" and "Classroom and Research Activities" to aid readers in grappling with the complex nature of slavery in America and women's myriad roles in it.

Law, Custom, and Tradition: A Comparative Perspective

Before being partially dismantled by the Emancipation Proclamation in 1863 and finally by the Thirteenth Amendment in 1865, American slavery was among the most repressive institution of its kind in modern history. It did not begin as such. From the seventeenth century to the eve of the Civil War, slavery continually evolved. When the twenty or so African "Negars" were brought to Jamestown in 1619 by a Dutch trading ship, their status was ambiguous because Virginia had neither laws nor customs governing the condition of slaves. Many were regarded as indentured servants, and thus enjoyed some opportunity to gain their freedom after a set period of service. Certainly some did, like Anthony Johnson who married, acquired property, and indentured servants of his own.[9] Such ambiguity was short lived; by 1630 laws were passed in Virginia and other colonies that restricted their labor, movement, freedom, and progeny.[10] In 1857, the status of the American slave, male or female, was firmly codified. Chief Justice Roger Brook Taney wrote in *Scott v. Sanford* in 1857 (commonly known as the Dred Scott decision) that "people of African descent are not and cannot be citizens of the United States, and cannot sue in any United States Court" and "he is declared to be an inferior and degraded being, having no rights which white men are bound to respect."[11]

French, English, Spanish, Dutch, and Portuguese slavery shared many of the cruelties and injustices of American slavery, but moderating forces such as the church, law, and custom created a brand of slavery in Peru, Brazil, and the Caribbean Islands that was notably different from what would later emerge in the United States. For example, France had a kingdom-wide maxim that "all persons are free in this kingdom, and as soon as a slave has arrived at the borders of this place, [the slave] is free." Unfortunately, this law was modified in 1716 and 1738 to allow slaveholders to bring slaves for religious or training purposes for a maximum of three years. By 1777, various laws known as the *Police de Noirs* (in chapter 1) dramatically reduced the civil liberties of all blacks, free and enslaved. Certain restrictions, on interracial intercourse for instance, were rarely enforced. However, some courts simply freed any slave who protested his or her condition. It was not until 1848 that slavery was finally abolished in France and her colonies.[12] Although initiating slavery in her American colonies and dominating the slave trade internationally, England had a strong abolitionist movement, and the 1772 landmark *Somersett* decision signaled the end of slavery there. Although England led the world in abolishing the slave trade, starting in 1807, it was not until 1834 that the slave trade was abolished in the English colonies.[13]

As early as 1265 the Spanish Crown issued a legal code, *Las Siete Partidas* (in chapter 1) governing the practice of slavery. Based on the premise that slavery was contrary to nature and liberty, this early code restricted slave owners regarding punishment and provided pathways to freedom, rights of free blacks, prohibitions on separating families, laws forbidding prostitution, and rules for coartacion (the ability to purchase one's freedom). Despite legislative efforts to ameliorate the worst injustices, Spanish colonies such as Cuba, Puerto Rico, and Santo Domingo (later Haiti) saw especially harsh conditions for slaves as sugar production soared in the nineteenth century.[14]

As with Spain, Portugal had a long tradition of slavery and laws controlling it, such as the 1603 *Ordenacoes Filipinas*. Believing also that slavery was foreign to the natural state of man, Portugal placed some limits on the power of masters, including the provisions for emancipation, achieved by a letter of liberty, the declaration in wills, and by baptism, as well as provisions for self-purchase. Ending in 1867 in Portugal itself, slavery flourished in its colonies, with Brazil finally abolishing slavery in 1888, the last country to do so in the Atlantic world. Every one of these restrictions on slave owners in all these countries and their colonies were at some time or another ignored or violated, seldom with resulting punishment for the offender; but they did exist, and they sometimes reduced the worst abuses of the system.

Regrettably, almost none of the moderating forces present in France, Spain, or Portugal were present in American slavery, or they disappeared after a short time, especially as large-scale agricultural production became profitable. Except in the North, neither law, nor custom, nor church did much to lift the burden on the enslaved during the heyday of the eighteenth and nineteenth centuries.

How did much of America, built on the principles of liberty and equality, persuade itself that slavery was just? The historians John Hope Franklin and Alfred A. Moss provide a useful rationale for the thinking of the times. Many reasoned that indentured servants were expensive and temporary, while African slaves were bound for life and easily recognizable should they try to escape. Cast as the "other," enslaved men and women were often deemed subhuman and non-Christian.[15] Mainly, however, slavery's benefits to whites were just too great to resist, and slave owners quickly developed multiple rationales—religious, scientific, and social—for the defense of their actions. Southern whites, as Winthrop Jordan points out in *White Over Black,* often argued that "slavery and liberty were inextricably intertwined; indeed, their conception of the latter depended upon the preservation of the former."[16] Documents detailing these justifications are included in chapter 1. There were certainly dissenting voices that recognized that the ideals of the Founding Fathers were at odds with the practice of slavery. Abigail Adams wrote, "It always appears a most iniquitous scheme to me to fight ourselves for what we have been robbing and plundering from those who have as good a right to freedom as we have."[17] The ever-caustic Dr. Samuel Johnson scathingly asked how it was "that we hear the loudest *yelps* for liberty among the drivers of Negroes."[18] It is intriguing to reflect on the thinking of most of our Founding Fathers, who were unwilling to suffer the abuses of the mother country in terms of taxes and tariffs, the quartering of soldiers, limited control over the rights to legislate, and other abuses they felt directed toward them by England, but were willing to doom almost a million persons of color to a life of unremitting toil, rape and sexual abuse, destruction of family, physical mutilation, and brutal punishment sometimes resulting in death.

Their objections to the abuses of British rule, which pale in comparison to the lot they inflicted on blacks, seem almost trivial. More voices of protest are included in chapter 4.

A Double Burden: Enslaved Women's Work and Daily Life

One challenge historians face when uncovering the experiences of enslaved women is illustrated by the story of Angela, the first African woman believed to have been brought to the American colonies in 1619. Almost nothing is known about her background or fate, as she left no surviving record behind. As with so much of women's history, her story and the story of thousands of other enslaved women has to be gleaned or teased from other sources. This results in an incomplete record, a puzzle with many missing pieces. But as scholars continue to mine the sources available, a more complete picture of American slavery emerges.

By 1662, slavery was firmly established in Virginia, with other colonies to follow. The nature of slavery in America was distinctly gendered, and that year all children, regardless of patrimony, born to enslaved women were declared "held in bond or free only according to the conditions of the mother." As the historian Darlene Clark Hine argued, "Other colonies followed suit, reversing traditional British law and patriarchal custom that prescribed a child's status according to his or her father."[19] Coming mainly from the west coast of Africa and representing diverse ethnic groups, African women arrived in the colonies after being torn from their families, often with the complicity of African traders, where they had been agriculturalists, weavers, warriors, and leaders. Most were brought to slave forts (barracoons) before being shipped to the Caribbean and then onto North America. The Middle Passage across the Atlantic was often the most terrifying portion of the journey, as women were crammed into the slave ships with men and children, forced to wallow in their own feces, urine, blood, and vomit for sometimes three-month voyages.[20] Though often in the minority, African women joined men in acts of resistance against traders and the crews, albeit with limited success.[21] The historian John Blassingame noted that from 1699 to 1845, fifty-five mutinies were documented, and many involved women.[22]

In the early years of colonial slavery, male slaves far outnumbered females because masters believed that their greater strength made them superior agricultural workers. By the time of the American Revolution, women were imported in greater numbers to the northern, middle, and southern colonies. When the slave trade was abolished in America in 1809, and slaves became scarcer and more expensive, women became especially valuable for their ability to bear children, thereby dramatically increasing the wealth of their masters. In the first century of slavery, African women who were torn from family and community networks had difficulties reproducing them in America, as they were largely isolated on small farms or in urban settings. Such spatial isolation offered few social networks with fellow slaves. They did share a common fate with indentured servants, and cross-racial friendships emerged out of necessity. Laws from this early period suggest that interracial sexual relationships required attention and control, making antimiscegenation laws throughout the colonies common. Enslaved women were defined, like men, primarily as laborers, and their daily lives were shaped mainly by work, conditions that bred illness, and violence. As a result, fertility rates were relatively low in this early period.[23]

The economies of the middle and northern colonies were far more diversified than those in the South, so enslaved women's experiences were different. They often lived on smaller farms and engaged in a wide range of tasks that were not necessarily gendered. While they helped care for children and the elderly, they also butchered livestock and farmed. Some had the opportunity to work as midwives, seamstresses, or weavers and were occasionally permitted by their masters to hire themselves out to earn extra money. In the South, most enslaved women worked in agriculture, an area in which they had some familiarity in West Africa. Some women brought other skills with them, such as basket weaving, that were highly prized by masters because their production made them more valuable. The rhythm of daily life for enslaved women in the South was mainly shaped by the crop they tended—tobacco, rice, or indigo, as shown in several documents included in chapter 2.

By the end of the colonial period, slavery was mainly concentrated in the American South, and several factors changed the nature of slavery. Eli Whitney's cotton gin patent (1793) helped make the processing of cotton more profitable. The Louisiana Purchase in 1803, the purchase of Florida from Spain in 1819, and the annexation of Texas (1845) expanded slavery into these new territories. As a result, the slave population shifted from the Upper South to the Lower South, often dividing families.[24] The historian Jacqueline Jones illustrates an important feature of plantation slavery, "A compact, volatile, and somewhat isolated society, the slave-holder's estate represented in microcosm, a larger drama in which physical force combined with the coercion embedded in the region's political economy to sustain the power of whites over blacks and men over women."[25]

Women's experiences as a slave in the antebellum period depended on numerous variables. While most were field hands, a much smaller percentage, estimated by the historian Eugene Genovese at 5 percent, served as domestic servants.[26] Both positions had their advantages. Only in the largest plantations were women confined to the household; in most cases they worked both indoors and out. The promise of better rations and less physically demanding work in the household was balanced by frequent contact with masters and mistresses that isolated them from their families and made them more prone to physical and sexual violence. Work in the fields was physically demanding, but also allowed for some degree of autonomy when the work was finished. Regardless of an enslaved woman's work assignment, a decade before the Civil War, 90 percent of all female slaves over sixteen years old worked an average of twelve hours a day, 261 days per year.[27]

All slaves were subject to abuse and violence, but women suffered additionally from rape and sexual coercion, often at an early age (see chapter 2).[28] Although there is some evidence that a small number of men suffered similar abuses, this was a particular burden of women. The reality of this violence was further complicated by the common stereotype that whites, in the North and the South, held about black women as lascivious Jezebels. Thomas Jefferson was persuaded black women mated with anything, including orangutans, certain that this animal preferred "the black woman over those of his own species."[29] This image of Jezebel, starkly contrasted to the ideal southern lady, provided a rationale for many white men's sexual behavior. Some white women even blamed enslaved women for luring their husbands, not recognizing their common sisterhood. The historian Deborah Gray White argued, "The choice put before many slave women was between miscegenation and the worst experiences that slavery had to offer. Not surprisingly, many chose the former, though they were hardly naïve. Many expected and often got something in return for their sexual favors. There was no reason for them to believe that even freedom could not be bought for the price of their bodies. Some women, therefore, took the risk involved and offered themselves. When they did so, they breathed life into the image of Jezebel."[30] Slave mothers struggled to prepare their daughters for such abuse, but they could do little to ameliorate it. In fact, masters often saw miscegenation as yet another way to increase their profits.

Marriage, in the face of such abuse, was difficult and tenuous, especially since it was entirely without the benefit of law. Largely controlled by whites, slave marriages were sometimes forced upon slaves as a way to increase the population. Some were born of love, but few were without the complications of bondage. There were less common forms of marriage, even a few that were interracial. One particularly intriguing story is that of the mulatto woman Amanda America Dickson, daughter of a slave mother (Julia Francis Lewis Dickson) and a wealthy Georgia planter (David Dickson), who, despite enormous impediments, lived as a white woman, married a white man, and was identified as "the wealthiest black woman in Georgia, or the southeast, or the world." Her story is certainly not typical.[31]

The much-romanticized quadroons of New Orleans were some of the most fortunate products of black and white liaisons. Relatively little is known about them, since they left almost no records, but "what is known about the quadroons is that there was a significant community of free women of color in New Orleans from the earliest days; that some of these women became mistresses of French men; that they could not marry their French lovers due to the ban on miscegenation; that some of these women were given houses, property, and financial support by their French lovers; that children were frequently born to these liaisons; that these children usually received their father's French surname and, in some cases, were educated and received indirect inheritances from their father; that some of these quadroons never married but were faithful to their French lover long after he had taken a French wife; that the French wife was often aware of her husband's quadroon mistress; that the quadroon system ended with the Civil War."[32] Quadroon balls and other events surrounding the lives of these women provide a window into the complex world of interracial sex (see chapters 1 and 3).[33]

Some women earned their freedom by various means—pleasing a master, developing a familial relationship with those who owned them, performing an exceptional act, or, very rarely, buying their freedom. The historian Suzanne Lebsock presents the most detailed experience of freed-women in her book *The Free Women of Petersburg.*[34] However they earned it, freedmen and women, numbering over a hundred thousand in 1810, were seen largely as an unwanted population because they were not fully under the control of whites. Prior to the Civil War, laws similar to the Black Laws later passed during Reconstruction restricted manumission, employment, freedom of movement, and even personal relationships between and among free blacks.[35] Still, freedwomen managed to earn a living, establish families, build community institutions, and even possess private property. However, some found it so difficult to survive in a racist society that constantly chipped away at their freedom that they even requested to be returned to slavery. The 1859 petition of Lucy Andrews (in chapter 1) documents one such extraordinary case.

Building Community Under Slavery

Despite a brutal and unjust system, backbreaking labor, and great suffering, enslaved men and women sought to create communities apart from the influence of masters and mistresses. Women's work on behalf of their own families had a specific irony—such labor also helped sustain the masters' workforce and made slavery even more profitable. Additionally, Jacqueline Jones explains, "Under slavery, blacks' attempts to sustain their family life amounted to a political act of protest against the callousness of owners, mistresses, and overseers. In defiance of the slaveholders' tendencies to ignore gender differences in making assignments in the fields, the slaves whenever possible adhered to a strict division of labor within their own households and communities."[36] Slaves were denied opportunities to own land, become literate, marry or worship freely, but there were times when they had some measure of control over their lives—mainly on Sundays and Christmas, evidenced in the *Narrative of Solomon Northurp* (in chapter 3). During these rare moments, women made, mended, or washed clothes or tended small garden plots. A small minority was hired out to make extra money, as John Edward Bruce's "A Sketch of My Life" (in chapter 3) suggests. In those cases, they often used those funds to purchase the freedom of their loved ones. During these free times, other enslaved women attended church services, illustrating the important role of religion in their lives. Though often controlled and mediated by whites, religion was another area where enslaved men and women sought self-determination. *The Memoir of Mrs. Chloe Spear, The Religious Experience and Journal of Mrs. Jarena Lee, The Narrative of Bethany Veney,* and *The Life of Mary F. McCray* (in chapter 3) document the role of faith in slavery.

The nature of slavery required that both field and house slaves who comprised the broader community cooperate in important ways. Child rearing is one important example. While slavery separated husbands and wives, sisters and brothers, and parents and children, slave communities often embraced the notion of "fictive kin," establishing family relationships with unrelated persons to build social networks and simply for survival.[37] Infant mortality rates were extremely high—two out of three black children survived to the age of ten by 1850—and women who worked as midwives were respected members of the society.[38] Elderly women were similarly honored in the slave community, as were conjurors, who often were feared by whites. Child socialization often depended on these powerful female networks, as mothers, sisters, or "aunts" helped educate daughters or nieces about courting rituals or sexual violence from whites.

The existence of a tight-knit slave community does not diminish the fond and sometimes loving relationships that emerged between whites and blacks, shown in this documentary collection in the exchange of letters between Vilet Lester and Patsey Patterson (in chapter 3), a result of the complex nature of slavery. The letter from J. W. Loguen to Mrs. Sarah Logue published in *The Liberator* in 1860 (in chapter 3) counters such a fond memory. The example of the octoroons (also featured in chapter 3) reveals yet another area in which miscegenation created an entire class of women in New Orleans who enjoyed some degree of autonomy of affection.

Slavery's Impact on White Women

While slavery was devastating for African American women, it also affected the lives of white women to varying degrees. Yeoman women, often the most impoverished group in the South, suffered from the effects of slavery as it permeated all aspects of Southern social and economic life. Almost all political and economic power in the antebellum South was concentrated in the hands of slaveholders, who comprised one-fourth of the population. The remaining three-fourths, with the exception of a small professional and merchant class, were largely isolated from the financial rewards reaped from the trafficking in human labor. The historian Orville Vernon Burton argues, "For all the brave promises that slaveholders made that King Cotton would raise up whites to common prosperity and cultural progress, doubts lingered and resentments festered. In spite of high cotton prices and booming output during the 1850s, increasing numbers of nonslaveholders slipped down into the ranks of unpropertied tenant farmers and wage workers."[39] Men and women who were not part of the "master class" were often forced to work small farms or hire out their own labor to survive. They found themselves outside the social network that was controlled by those who had amassed power and wealth from slavery. Women helped earn a hardscrabble living by assisting their husbands on small, often impoverished farms, or occasionally teaching or nursing children of wealthy planters and merchants. These women were too often regarded as little more than "white trash" by both the men and women who held sway over their lives. Yeoman women left few documents detailing their own lives and even fewer commenting on slavery. Because of the scope of this collection, the editors did not focus on these women, but their stories are nonetheless important in understanding slavery as an economic and social system. They are well documented in Stephanie McCurry's article, "The Politics of Yeoman Households in South Carolina."[40]

Slaveholding women often fared better than their yeoman sisters, but their fate depended on many variables. Women in the slave-owning aristocracy seldom benefited from the bounty realized by the enslavement of others in the same ways as Southern men. Women faced a legal, economic, and social system that was constrained and limiting. The myth of the "Southern belle" was based on the assumption that white Southern women were not like other humans; instead, they were perceived to be virtuous, honorable, and above human error and must entirely depend on men to defend them. As the social theorist and slavery advocate George Fitzhugh argued, "In truth, women, like children, have but one right, and that is the right to protection. The right to protection involves the obligation to obey. A husband, a lord and master, whom she should love, honor and obey, nature designed for every woman, for the number of males and females is the same. If she be obedient, she is in little danger of mal-treatment: if she stands upon her rights, is coarse and masculine, man loathes and despises her, and ends up abusing her."[41] Women had a clear place in Southern society, yet it was a liminal space below white men and above slaves.[42]

The historians Catherine Clinton and Elizabeth Fox-Genovese have best analyzed the lives of white slaveholding women. Clinton argues in *The Plantation Mistress* that many white women of the elite classes were educated at home by tutors and enjoyed their happiest times as unmarried "belles." Upon marriage, they assumed the position of plantation mistress, a profession that, because of lack of training, they were almost wholly ill equipped to handle. If she were the wife of a prosperous planter with a large estate, she was not only charged with all the demands of a new husband, especially for providing him with multiple heirs, but also with the distribution of food, not only for her own kitchen, but for the slaves owned by the family, as well.[43] She helped preserve foodstuffs, participated in the annual hog killing, made sausage, and processed lard. She helped make clothing for both her family and slaves, made candles, gathered goose down, and often served as a nurse to all on the plantation.[44] While many had household help from family members or slaves, they still had to deal with the frequent absence of their husband, which was complicated by the fact that they had no legal standing in the community and were unable to travel freely without being accompanied by a male relative. Many inexperienced white women surely turned to household slaves for assistance and guidance, which often resulted in a complex relationship that combined affection and domination, made more complex by the fact that all real authority rested with the master. Many white women of the South remember these relationships nostalgically, often referring to enslaved women as members of their family. Their enslaved counterparts likely presented a very different view. They were often forced away from their own families to serve white masters and mistresses, even suckling their children. Clinton concludes that the white slaveholding woman was "trapped within a system over which she had no control, one from which she had no means of escape. Cotton was King, white men ruled, and both white women and slaves served the same master."[45] Jacqueline Jones interprets the relationship between mistresses and their female slaves in this manner, "On a more immediate level, slavery rubbed raw the wounds of white women's grievances in two specific ways—first, it added greatly to their household responsibilities, and second, it often injected irreconcilable conflicts into the husband-wife relationship."[46] She argues that such tensions many times resulted in mistresses punishing their female slaves and even seeking divorce, especially when sexual liaisons were involved, as the 1845 petition from Ruthey Ann Hansley (in chapter 1) illustrates.

Elizabeth Fox-Genovese presents a different view from that of Clinton, noting the considerable leisure time that was available to the slaveholding women. She makes important distinctions between women who lived on large, rural plantations engaged in agricultural production and those women who lived in towns and villages. The latter had much more time for visiting, reading, and churchgoing. Even the former were sometimes removed from the backbreaking labor of farm life. Mary Boykin Chestnut, the wife of Senator James Chestnut Jr., spent much of her married life in the home of her in-laws and had little or no responsibilities for the plantation household. While Louisa S. McCord had some experience with the duties of the plantation mistress, she spent the majority of her life in intellectual pursuits as an essayist, poet, playwright, and political commentator. Another problem in understanding the labor of slaveholding women is the way they wrote about it. They often mentioned labor as if they performed the work themselves rather than work that was actually done by their slaves, either male or female. While some slaveholding women led busy and demanding lives, they had freedoms not enjoyed by those over whom they ruled.

The vast majority of white Southern women actively supported slavery, sharing the paternalism of their husbands and fathers. Louisa S. McCord, daughter of an aristocratic South Carolina planter, believed slavery mandatory "not only for her own well-being and upkeep, but also for the improvement of people of African descent and for the maintenance of peaceful relations between classes and races."[47] Others refused to speak out because they profited so handsomely from the peculiar institution. Mary Boykin Chestnut penned a diary during the Civil War that made connections between the plight of women of all races. One entry noted, "You know how women sell themselves and are sold in marriage from queens downward, eh? You know what the Bible says about slavery—and marriage. Poor women. Poor slaves." This was little more than an observation sympathetic to married women, since she made little or no attempts to help her sisters in bondage.[48] Chestnut condemns the actions of slaveholding men who people their homes with mulatto children and also laments women's refusal to recognize their husbands' responsibility for those children, but her main concern is that his pure and beautiful wives and daughters are made to suffer the presence of mulatto children; those "countrywomen (who) are as pure as angels, tho' surrounded by another race who are the social evil."[49] Fox-Genovese states, "And, despite all attempts to interpret Mary Chestnut's occasional outbursts out of context, her life demonstrated nothing so much as certainty that her world, however flawed, was on balance the best available."[50]

Other Southern women expressed much the same sentiments. Caroline Lee Hentz wrote a paean to slavery, *The Planter's Northern Bride*. The diarists Anna Matilda Page King and Keziah Brevard both blamed slaves for much of the difficulties of their lives. Elizabeth Meriwether claimed long after the Civil War to have opposed slavery but kept a slave nevertheless. Gertrude Thomas, active in the suffragist movement after the war, was silent on the issue of freedom of bondsmen and -women.[51]

Resisting Slavery

Resistance from both enslaved men and women took many forms. Large slave rebellions—Stono River (South Carolina 1739), Gabriel (Prosser) (Virginia 1800), Denmark Vesey (South Carolina 1822), and Nat Turner (Virginia 1831)—were not common, but they did have a broad impact on the institution of slavery. The successful overthrow of government forces by slaves in Haiti (1791–1803) sent shock waves of terror throughout America and caused many states to pass even more restrictive laws. Individual acts of resistance were far more common. Work slowdowns, poisoning food, burning crops, learning to read, conjuring, feigning illness, running away, and refusing to bear children for a cruel master were all strategies employed by women; many are included in chapter 4. These acts were inventive and effective, if even for a short period of time, but often earned severe punishment.

Enslaved women who lived in close proximity to whites often used psychological techniques as a form of resistance. Elizabeth Fox-Genovese argues in *Within the Plantation Household,* "Impudence and 'uppityness,' which derived from intimate knowledge of a mistress's weak points, demonstrated a kind of resistance and frequently provoked retaliation out of all proportions to the acts, if not the spirit. Because the mistress lacked the full authority of the master, her relations with her servants could easily lapse into a personal struggle. When servants compounded sauciness and subtle disrespect with a studied cheerful resistance to accomplishing the task at hand, the mistress could rapidly find herself losing control—of herself as well as her servant."[52]

Enslaved women sometimes used their sexuality to their advantage, thereby receiving more humane treatment. Some granted sexual favors to those who had power over them to gain whatever benefits they could. Additionally, the arrival of the menarche provided young women with the opportunity to obtain special consideration for real or imagined health problems, often relieving them from hard labor. Pregnancies (and sometimes pretended pregnancies) usually, but not always, were times when women might receive easier treatment and duties and better rations. When forced into multiple pregnancies, some women practiced birth control or abortion. Some disfigured themselves to become less attractive or desirable. Others practiced infanticide, refusing to allow their children to become slaves. Margaret Garner of Kentucky (featured in chapter 4) killed one of her children and tried to kill others before she and her husband were discovered by slave hunters, in an effort to prevent them from suffering under this inhumane system.[53]

As with men, women often attempted to escape from slavery, but their experiences were shaped by their gender. While enslaved men were more likely to be hired out and have the opportunity to travel, women were more likely confined on farms or on larger plantations. As the primary caregivers for children, women were less likely to flee alone. When they did try to escape, family members often traveled with them. There were extraordinary cases. In 1857, one young woman enclosed herself in a box and mailed herself to Philadelphia. Although nearly killed by the experience, she managed to escape to Canada.[54] In 1848, William and Ellen Craft escaped Georgia slavery when Ellen disguised herself as a white master with William as her slave (see chapter 4). Harriet Tubman, one of the most prominent conductors on the Underground Railroad, was a key figure in helping slaves escape. Over a decade, she made nineteen trips South to lead more than three hundred slaves to freedom. Elizabeth Fox-Genovese argues that resistance was not just a strategy women employed; it was an identity they embraced:

> Resistance was woven into the fabric of slave women's lives and identities. If they defined themselves as wives, mothers, daughters, and sisters within the slave community that offered them positive images of themselves as women, they were also likely to define themselves in opposition to the images of the slaveholders for whom their status as slave ultimately outweighed their identity as women. The ubiquity of their resistance ensured that its most common forms would be those that followed the patterns of everyday life: shirking, running off, taking, sassing, defying. The extreme forms of resistance—murder, self-mutilation, infanticide, suicide— were rare. But no understanding of slave women's identities can afford to ignore them, for, if they were abnormal in their occurrence, they nonetheless embodied the core psychological dynamic of all resistance. The extreme forms captured the essence of self-definition: You cannot do that to me, whatever the price I must pay to prevent you.[55]

Resistance by enslaved women, blatant or subtle, violent or pacific, was ever present, and a constant cause of fear for their white masters.

The abolitionist movement had, almost from the time of the institutionalization of slavery, been active in America and widely supported by women. Although many churches, such as the Baptist and Methodist, eventually split into northern and southern branches due to disagreements over slavery, the Quakers were distinctive. They first objected to slavery in a petition in 1688, and after a time censured and expelled slave-holding members, lobbied for antislavery legislation, and formed or contributed to abolitionist societies.[56] The abolitionist meetings became places where

African American and white women could find their voice, function with some autonomy in public life, and build a career during a time where their roles were circumscribed and limited. Abolitionists were present in the North and South in the early years of slavery, but found few adherents as cotton became king in the South. Opponents of slavery in the region were subject to social pressure, ostracizism, and sometimes violence. The writings of pro-slavery advocates such as John C. Calhoun, Edmund Ruffin, the Reverend A. T. Holmes, and George Fitzhugh were widely distributed and enormously popular. Laws were passed forbidding the possession of abolitionist literature. Interference with the postal service was commonplace, with United States postmasters confiscating and sometimes burning such writings, and even violence directed toward the mail, as occurred in Charleston in 1835, when mobs broke into the post office and burned abolitionist literature and hanged figures of prominent abolitionists.[57] The vast majority of white women in the South were either enthusiastic supporters of slavery or remained largely silent (see chapters 2 and 5).

In the North, antislavery women found a much more hospitable climate with important figures supporting their cause, such as William Lloyd Garrison (founder of *The Liberator* in 1831, the most prominent abolitionist newspaper and founder of the American Anti-Slavery Society), Theodore Weld (an associate of Garrison's and a riveting orator), and Frederick Douglass (a former slave, lecturer, and publisher of *The North Star*). Documents detailing their perspectives are included in chapter 4. Northern women, such as Lucretia Mott (a Quaker minister and one of the founders of the Philadelphia Female Anti-Slavery Society) and Elizabeth Cady Stanton (a vigorous abolitionist and suffragist) were equally active. Maria Weston Chapman (active in the Boston Female Anti-Slavery Society, lieutenant to Garrison, and editorial assistant for *The Liberator*) added her voice and writings to those of other white women. Two of the most interesting and influential women, partly because of their unique background, were Sarah and Angelina Grimké. Born to a prominent Protestant French family in Charleston, South Carolina, they saw firsthand the abuses of slavery within their own slave-owning family. Gradually, and under the influence of the evangelical Christianity of the "Second Great Awakening," both women began to react more strongly to the abuses of slavery. They became prominent lecturers, given particular credibility because of their Southern pedigree. Free women of color, such as Maria Stewart, minister and lecturer, and Sara Forten, daughter of a prominent black abolitionist and active in the Philadelphia Female Anti-Slavery Society, rose to positions of responsibility. Women who escaped slavery, such as Harriet Jacobs and Sojourner Truth, became powerful voices within this movement.

Conflict arose among abolitionists over the proper role of women, shown in the documents by Angelina Grimké and Catharine Beecher (in chapter 4), many feeling that women exceeded their proper role by their actions. This was especially true among religious leaders, most of whom did not support abolition before the Civil War and who also feared that they were losing control over female congregants. Congregational leaders published a pastoral letter, warning "those who encourage females to bear an obtrusive and ostentatious part in measures of reform, and countenance any of that sex who so far forget themselves as to itinerate in the character of public lectures and teachers."[58] Tensions escalated between those who supported women's rights and those who felt either that women should not participate, or that the focus on women's rights diluted the focus on slavery. Between 1838 and 1840, Garrison's American Anti-Slavery Society split into several groups, some denying membership to women. Many African American women shared the fear of losing focus on slavery. Others, like Sojourner Truth, with her famous "Ar'n't I a Woman?" speech, also recognized the need for greater rights for all women. The Negro Convention Movement in 1848 gave this issue a particularly warm reception.[59]

The Meaning of Freedom

As early as the seventeenth century, enslaved men and women sought their freedom using myriad strategies. A petition from 1661 in New Netherlands (in chapter 3) demonstrates legal remedies that were sometimes successful. There are other stories of families seeking to purchase husbands, wives, and children. Freedom was more commonly something achieved by brave action—such as those taken by Sojourner Truth and Harriet Tubman (in chapter 4) on the Underground Railroad. The shape and meaning of freedom dominated the national conversation with the start of the Civil War. Shortly after it began on April 14, 1861, enslaved women and men, often whole families, fled the plantations, seeking refuge among Union forces. It was especially galling to masters and mistresses when those they considered family members left "without provocation" or "without the slightest notice."[60] Many whites believed their slaves to be loyal to their family and incapable of independent thought and action, illustrated by one Florida woman who wrote, "I hardly know how to tell it, my dear black Mammy has left us . . . I feel lost, I feel as if someone is dead in the house. Whatever will I do with out my Mammy? When she was going she stopped on the doorstep and, shaking her fist at Mother [with whom she had had an altercation], she said: I'll miss you—the Lord knows I'll miss you—but you'll miss me too,—you see if you don't."[61]

Former slaves who reached Union lines did not always find the Promised Land they had anticipated; sometimes they were given provisions and work. More often, they were left to fend for themselves. The Union soldiers were not equipped to handle an influx of civilians, and rarely shared a desire to see them free. The historian Deborah Gray White argues, "Union soldiers were unpredictable and unsympathetic to blacks, whom they blamed for the war. Hardly eager liberators, they left both blacks and whites homeless and hungry when they destroyed plantation property, raided both the big house and slave quarters for food and supplies, and seized black men for involuntary service in the Union army. 'Us all thought the Yankees some kin' of debils an' we was skeered to death of 'em,' recalled Mollie Williams, who was just a child during the war. Indeed they had reason to be." When a Union soldier stole her quilts, a black woman called after him, "'Why, you nasty, stinking rascal,' she shouted, 'you say you come down there to fight for the niggers, and now you're stealing from 'em.' His response no doubt reflected the feelings of most white Union soldiers, especially those who were drafted. 'You're a goddamm liar,' he retorted, 'I'm fighting for $14 a month and the Union.'"[62] Women often faced rape, brutality, and theft; and the destruction of homes and temporary shelters blacks had constructed for themselves were all too commonplace, especially during the first years of the war.

Although initially Lincoln was reluctant to address slavery, he authorized the Confiscation Act of August 6, 1861, that classified slaves as "contraband" to be seized and used by federal forces. When African American men were denied the right to serve the Union in the army, they repeatedly petitioned government, even forming ad hoc military units. Over 93,000 black men from southern states joined the Union when the policy was changed in July 1863; an additional 87,000 from the North eventually served. Twenty-three African American men earned the Medal of Honor.[63] Women, too, served the Union. Sojourner Truth, a former slave, assisted the war effort by recruiting black troops and working among freed slaves at a government refugee camp in Virginia while employed by the Freedmen's Bureau; and she may have provided intelligence to Union forces. Harriet Tubman, the most famous conductor of the Underground Railroad, continued with these efforts up until 1861, then served as a cook, nurse, scout, and spy during the Civil War. She provided information for Colonel Robert Gould Shaw during the battle of Fort Wagner in South Carolina and even led the raid on the Combahee River, freeing about seven hundred slaves. Susie King Taylor worked as a laundress, nurse, and teacher for black children in Union camps. Charlotte Forten taught newly freed children on St. Helene's Island in South Carolina (see chapter 4). Countless other women served in less exceptional roles, but many of them contributed substantially to the success of the Union. The Emancipation Proclamation of January 1, 1863, declared slaves free in those parts of the Confederacy unoccupied by Union troops, and the Thirteenth Amendment in 1865 ended slavery in America.

The end of slavery in 1865 and the beginning of Reconstruction often brought hardship and uncertainty for former slaves, but also the symbolic and real power of freedom. For many, it promised an opportunity to reunite families, control their own labor, become literate, marry a spouse of their choice, leave the South, and raise their children without the interference of whites. Jacqueline Jones argues, "Control over one's labor and one's family life represented a dual gauge by which true freedom could be measured."[64] One woman named Patience was reluctant to leave her master in South Carolina, but concluded, "I must go, if I stay here I'll never know I'm free."[65] Not all women knew they were free, including Hannah, a rural Kentucky woman, who remained enslaved until the mid-1880s.[66] Regrettably, freedom sometimes resulted in increased violence against women. Northern indifference or outright hostility to former slaves, combined with Southern anger at the loss of the war, property, and prestige, partly explained this spike in violence. The founding of the Ku Klux Klan in 1866 began a reign of terror that directly shaped black women's lives. The historian Deborah Gray White argues that violence at polling places prompted women in South Carolina to carry "axes or hatchets in their hands hanging down on their sides, their aprons or dresses half-concealing the weapons."[67] During and after Reconstruction, lynching was widespread, but not limited to men. Between 1882 and 1927, seventy-six African American women were lynched, with fifteen between 1888 and 1889 alone. Rape, however, was far more common and victims faced few remedies. White argues, "From emancipation through more than two-thirds of the twentieth century, no Southern white male was convicted of raping or attempting to rape a black woman, yet the crime was widespread."[68]

Clothing became a powerful symbol by which African American women asserted their freedom during and after Reconstruction. Many rejected homespun and the drab clothing of slavery, favoring instead bright colors and expensive materials. One Freedmen's Bureau agent stationed in North Carolina in 1865 observed that "the wearing of black veils by the young Negro women have given great offense to the young white women."

Freedom also brought new opportunities for women. During the Civil War, many Northern women, both African American and white, came south to teach in schools for newly freed children and adults. Charlotte Forten describes her experience on the Sea Islands in a letter published in *The Liberator* (in chapter 5). Formerly enslaved women frequently turned to the Freedmen's Bureau to help negotiate wage-labor agreements with whites, in some cases their former owners. Established as the Bureau of Refugees, Freedmen, and Abandoned Lands by the War Department in 1865, the Freedmen's Bureau (in chapter 5) provided food and clothing, hospitals, temporary housing, educational opportunities, and legal and employment assistance. While some women found limited assistance from the short-lived bureau, others struggled on their own as seamstresses, washerwomen, or nurses. Some perished. Many joined their husbands as sharecroppers. By 1870, most formerly enslaved women (more than 90 percent) lived in rural areas, were illiterate and poor, and faced declining fertility rates.[69] Despite these challenges, they found great comfort in reassembling their families and engaged in community building, often through associations and churches. Many women faced freedom with courage and built lives of their own; some achieved remarkable success. Others were victimized by violence, poverty, or even their own vice. The difference was that what they became was, for the most part, the result of their own decisions, not those controlled by master or mistress.

Irene Robertson, at age seventy-four, told a Federal Writers' Project interviewer in the mid-1930s, "Mama and papa spoke like they was mighty glad to get set free. Some believed they'd get freedom and others didn't. They had places they met and prayed for freedom. They stole out in some houses and turned a washtub down at the door. Another white man, not Alex Rogers, tole mama and papa and a heap of others out in the field working [that they were free]. She say they quit and had a regular bawl in the field. They cried and laughed and hollered and danced. Lot of them run offen the place soon as the man tole 'em. My folks stayed that year and another year."[70] Freedom meant a new life for some; for others little changed. It meant the promise and then the failure of Reconstruction. Freedom eventually gave way to the anguish of segregation and violence under Jim Crow. But enslaved men and women were free and would make their own way.

Notes

1. See U. B. Phillips, *American Negro Slavery: A Survey of the Supply, Employment and Control of Negro Labor as Determined by the Plantation Regime* (New York: D. Appleton, 1918); Kenneth Stampp, *The Peculiar Institution: Slavery in the Ante-Bellum South* (New York: Knopf, 1956); and Stanley Elkins, *Slavery: A Problem in American Institutional and Intellectual Life* (New York: Grosset and Dunlap, 1963).

2. See John Hope Franklin, *From Slavery to Freedom: A History of American Negroes* (New York: Knopf, 1947); John Blassingame, *The Slave Community: Plantation Life in the Antebellum South* (New York: Oxford University Press, 1972); Herbert Gutman, *The Black Family in Slavery and Freedom, 1750–1925* (New York: Pantheon, 1976); Catherine Clinton, *The Plantation Mistress: Woman's World in the Old South* (New York: Pantheon, 1982); Jacqueline Jones, *Labor of Love, Labor of Sorrow: Black Women, Work and the Family from Slavery to the Present* (New York: Basic Books, 1985); Elizabeth Fox-Genovese, *Within the Plantation Household: Black and White Women of the Old South* (Chapel Hill: University of North Carolina Press, 1988); Sally McMillen, *Southern*

Women: Black and White in the Old South (Arlington Heights, IL: Harlan Davidson, 1992); Jennifer L. Morgan, *Laboring Women: Reproduction and Gender in New World Slavery* (Philadelphia: University of Pennsylvania Press, 2004); and Patricia Morton, ed., *Discovering the Women in Slavery: Emancipating Perspectives on the American Past* (Athens: University of Georgia Press, 1996).

    3. Morton, 13.

    4. Peter J. Parish, *Slavery: History and Historians* (New York: Harper and Row, 1989), 3–6.

    5. Parish, 12.

    6. See Gwyn Campbell, Suzanne Miers, and Joseph Miller, eds., *Women and Slavery: The Modern Atlantic,* vol. 2 (Athens: Ohio University Press, 2008).

    7. Parish, 1.

    8. Parish, 26–27.

    9. Edward Countryman, *How Did American Slavery Begin?* (Boston: Bedford/St. Martin's, 1999), 3.

    10. Franklin, 76, 93.

    11. Herbert Aptheker, *The Negro People of the United States,* vol. 1 (New York: Citadel Press, 1951), 392–93.

    12. Sue Peabody and Keila Grinberg, eds., *Slavery, Freedom, and the Law in the Atlantic World: A Brief History with Documents* (Boston: Bedford/St. Martin's, 2007), 8–10.

    13. Peabody and Grinberg, 12–13.

    14. In 1890, a law passed ten years earlier—the Law for the Suppression of Slavery and Patronage (in Cuba), Madrid—came into full effect and ended slavery in Spain.

    15. See Orlando Patterson, *Slavery and Social Death: A Comparative Study* (Cambridge, MA: Harvard University Press, 1985).

    16. Parish, 3. See Winthrop D. Jordan, *White over Black: American Attitudes toward the Negro, 1550–1812* (Chapel Hill: University of North Carolina Press, 1968), 80–82.

    17. John Hope Franklin and Alfred Moss, *From Slavery to Freedom: A History of African Americans* (New York: Knopf, 2000), 70.

    18. Samuel Johnson quoted in Edward Countryman, *How Did American Slavery Begin?* (New York: Bedford/St. Martin's, 1999), 4.

    19. Darlene Clark Hine, *Black Women in America: An Historical Encyclopedia* (Brooklyn: Carlson, 1993), 1045–46.

    20. See August Meier and Elliott Rudwick, *From Plantation to Ghetto: An Interpretive History of American Negroes* (New York: Hill and Wang, 1966), quoted in Hine, 1047.

    21. Hine, 1047.

    22. See Blassingame.

    23. Hine, 1048–49. Jennifer Morgan offers a nuanced discussion of sex ratios during slavery, suggesting an early concern for the purchase of female slaves.

    24. Hine, 1053.

    25. Jones, 11.

    26. See Eugene Genovese, *Roll, Jordan, Roll: The World the Slaves Made* (New York: Vintage, 1976).

    27. Jones, 18. Thavolia Glymph's *Out of the House of Bondage: The Transformation of the Plantation Household* (Cambridge: Cambridge University Press, 2008) thoroughly documents the challenges of household labor.

28. Hine, 1062.

29. Merrill D. Peterson, ed., *The Portable Thomas Jefferson* (New York: Viking, 1973), 187.

30. Deborah Gray White, *Ar'n't I a Woman? Female Slaves in the Plantation South* (New York: Norton, 1999), 34.

31. Kent Leslie in Virginia Bernhard, Elizabeth Fox-Genovese, and Theda Perdue, eds., *Southern Women: Histories and Identities* (Columbia: University of Missouri Press, 1992), 72.

32. Mary Gehman, "Toward an Understanding of the Quadroom Society of New Orleans, 1780–1860," in *Southern Women*, ed. Caroline Dillman Matheny (New York: Hemisphere Publishing Company, 1988), 26.

33. For a more thorough examination of slavery in New Orleans, see Jennifer M. Spear, *Race, Sex, and Social Order in Early New Orleans* (Baltimore: Johns Hopkins University Press, 2009).

34. Suzanne Lebsock, *The Free Women of Petersburg: Status and Culture in a Southern Town, 1784–1860* (New York: W. W. Norton, 1985).

35. David Brion Davis, *Inhuman Bondage* (New York: Oxford University Press, 2006), 104. See also, Spear.

36. Jones, 12–13.

37. Jones, 31.

38. Jones, 35.

39. Orville Vernon Burton, *The Age of Lincoln* (New York: Hill and Wang, 2007), 89.

40. Stephanie McCurry, "The Politics of Yeoman Households in South Carolina," in *Divided Houses: Gender and the Civil War,* ed. Catherine Clinton and Nina Silber (New York: Oxford University Press, 1992), 36–37. See also, Keith L. Bryant, "The Role and Status of the Female Yeomanry in the Antebellum South: The Literary View," *Southern Quarterly* 18 (winter 1980): 73–88; and D. Harlan Hagler, "The Ideal Woman in the Antebellum South: Lady or Farmwife?" *Journal of Southern History* 46 (August 1980): 405–18.

41. George Fitzhugh, *Sociology for the South, or the Failure of a Free Society* (New York: Burt Franklin, 1965), 214–15.

42. Thomas R. Dew, *Pro-Slavery Arguments* (Philadelphia: Lippincott, Grambo and Co., 1853), 287–90.

43. Clinton, 20.

44. Clinton, 28–29.

45. Clinton, 35.

46. Jones, 25.

47. Leigh Fought, *Southern Womanhood and Slavery: A Biography of Louisa S. McCord, 1810–1879* (Columbia: University of Missouri Press, 2003), 43.

48. Fox-Genovese, 343, 348.

49. Fox-Genovese, 353.

50. Fox-Genovese, 345.

51. Fox-Genovese, 370

52. Fox-Genovese, 308.

53. Hine, 1058.

54. Gerda Lerner, *Black Women in White America: A Documentary History* (New York: Vintage Books, 1972), 59.

55. Fox-Genovese, 329.

56. Franklin and Moss, 302.

57. Kathryn Kish Sklar, *Women's Rights Emerges within the Antislavery Movement, 1830–1870* (Boston: Bedford/St. Martins, 2000), 14.

58. Sklar, 32.

59. Sklar, 65.

60. White, 168.

61. White, 168.

62. White, 163–64.

63. See National Park Service, African American Medal of Honor Recipients, http://www.itd.nps.gov/cwss/history/aa_medals.htm (accessed February 11, 2010).

64. Jones, 46.

65. Patience quoted in Orville Vernon Burton, "Ungrateful Servants? Edgefield's Black Reconstruction: Part I of the Total History of Edgefield County, South Carolina" (Ph.D. diss., Princeton University, 1976), 136. Quoted in Jones, 51.

66. Quoted in George P. Rawick, ed., *The American Slave: A Composite Autobiography,* 19 vols., Series 1 (Westport, CT: Greenwood Press, 1972). Also quoted in Jones, 47.

67. White, 188.

68. White, 188.

69. Jones, 62.

70. Peggy Bulger, *Slave Narratives from the Federal Writers' Project, 1936–38, Arkansas* (Washington, D.C.: Bedford, n.d.), 9.

CHAPTER 1

Law, Custom, and Tradition

The documents in this first section examine the changing legal codes (federal, state, and local) and religious, cultural, and scientific theories that contributed to the establishment and expansion of slavery, with a particular focus on women.

DOCUMENT 1:
Las Siete Partidas (The Seven Sections), 1265.

This Spanish legal code, issued by King Alfonso X, was the foundation of slavery legislation for Spanish colonies. Many of the laws address the status of women broadly; Law 4 focuses on women who were freed if forced into prostitution by their masters. In comparison to the British, the Spanish laws were quite liberal in the areas of manumission and perceptions of liberty and affected slaves in Spain's colonies in the New World.

TITLE XXII. ON LIBERTY
All creatures of the world naturally love and desire liberty, especially men who have authority over others and, for the most part, those who are of noble heart.

Law 1. What is liberty, who can give it and to whom and in what manner? Liberty is the power that every man has by nature to do what he wants, except in those areas where the power or right of law restrains him. And a lord can give this liberty to his slave in the church or outside of it, or before a judge, or in some other way, or in a will, or without a will, or by letter. But he must do this himself personally, and not through a representative, except if he orders it to be done by his descendants or those who are related through the same direct lineage. . . .

Law 3. Concerning the ways a slave may become free for doing good deeds; even if the lord does not desire it. At times slaves deserve to be freed for the good things that they do, even though their lords do not benefit. And this may occur for four reasons. The first is when a slave makes it known to the king or to a judge that some man raped a virgin woman. The second is when he reports a man who makes counterfeit money. The third is when he discovers that someone who is placed as [military] leader on the frontier or in some other place so ordered by the King, who deserts or abandons them without the consent of the King. . . . The fourth is when he accuses someone who had killed his lord, avenges him or informs upon a treasonous plot against the King or the Queen.

Law 4. How a female slave can gain her freedom when her lord puts her into prostitution to make money from her. As to the putting of one's slaves into prostitution in [any] place wherein men give money, we establish that for such ill will as this the lord must lose his female slaves, and that they be henceforth freed. . . .

Law 8. On how one is freed must honor the one who freed him and his woman, and his children, and in what ways the freedmen are obliged to acknowledge the good deed and to thank his former master so that he can pay him reverence. Since liberty is one of the most honored and dearest things in the world; therefore those who receive it are very obliged to obey and love and honor those who free them. And since he wants men to know about the good deed and thank those from whom he receives it, there is no way to do other than this. For servitude is the vilest thing on earth, there is no worse sin, and therefore the former master and his children are due much honor. . . .

DOCUMENT 2:
Statutes from the State of Virginia, 1630–1691. From William Waller Hening, ed., *The Statutes at Large: Being a Collection of All the Laws of Virginia, from the First*

Session of the Legislature in the Year 1619, 13 vols. (Richmond, 1809–23).

Slavery is not mentioned in colonial Virginia law until 1661; prior to that date the term "Negro" is commonly used. The 1630 and 1640 decisions reprinted here were passed by the Governor and his Council, who served as a court. The Assembly passed the other statutes; especially important is the 1662 statute about children born to an enslaved woman. Many of these laws show the complicated relationships that emerged between men and women across racial lines and the unusual status of Native Americans.

[1630] September 17th, 1630. Hugh Davis to be soundly whipped, before an assembly of Negroes and others for abusing himself to the dishonor of God and shame of Christians, by defiling his body in lying with a negro, which fault he is to acknowledge next Sabbath day. *Statutes* I:146

[1640] Robert Sweet to do penance in church according to laws of England, for getting a negroe woman with child and the woman whipt. *Statutes* 1:552

[1662] Act XII. Negro womens children to serve according to the condition of the mother.
Whereas some doubts have arrisen whether children got by any Englishman upon a negro woman shall be slave or ffree, *Be it therefore enacted and declared by this present grand assembly,* that all children borne in this country shalbe held bond or free only according to the condition of the mother, *And* that if any christian shall committ ffornication with a negro man or woman, hee or shee soe offending shall pay double the ffines imposed by the former act. *Statutes* 2:170

[1670] Act XII. What tyme Indians to serve.
Whereas some dispute have arisen whither Indians taken in warr by any other nation, and by that nation that taketh them sold to the English, are servants for life or terme of yeares, *It is resolved and enacted* that all servants not being christians imported into this colony by shipping shalbe slaves for their lives; but what shall come by land shall serve, if boyes or girles, until thirty years of age, if men or women twelves yeares and no longer. *Statutes* 2:283

[1691] Act XVI. An act for suppressing outlying Slaves.

. . . And for prevention of that abominable mixture and spurious issue which hereafter may encrease in this dominion, as well by negroes, mulattoes, and Indians intermarrying with English, or other white women, as by their unlawfull accompanying with one another, *Be it enacted . . .* that . . . whatsoever English or other white man or woman being free shall intermarry with a negroe, mulatto, or Indian man or woman bond or free shall within three months after such marriage be banished and removed from this dominion forever . . . *And be it further enacted . . .* That if any English woman being free shall have a bastard child by any negro or mulatto, she pay the sume of fifteen pounds sterling, within one moneth after such bastard child shall be born, to the Church wardens of the parish . . . and in default of such payment she shall be taken into the possession [of] the said Church wardens and disposed of for five yeares, and the said fine of fifteen pounds, or whatever the woman shall be disposed of for, shall be paid, one third part to their majesties . . . and the other third part to the use of the parish . . . and the other third part to the informer, and that such bastard child be bound out as a servant by the said Church wardens untill he or she shall attaine the age of thirty yeares, and in case such English woman that shall have such bastard child be a servant, she shall be sold by the said Church wardens, (after her time is expired that she ought by law to serve her master) for five yeares, and the money she shall be sold for divided as is before appointed, and the child to serve as aforesaid.

DOCUMENT 3:
The Code Noir, March 1685.

The Code Noir, a French legal code written under Louis XIV and prepared specifically for "the Islands of French America," March 1685, would later serve as a model for Spain and the Netherlands. Several groups contributed to the code, including colonial officials, missionaries, and royal officials in Versailles. The passing of slavery from mother to child resembles a similar provision in the 1662 Virginia law above. The codes, which envisioned a society of enslaved blacks and free whites, are excerpted below to include those articles focused on slavery and the status of women.

Article 9. Free men who sire one or more children during with slaves out of wedlock, together with the masters who permitted this, will each be condemned to a fine of two thousand pounds of sugar. And if they are the masters of the slave by whom they have had the said children, we wish that, in addition to the fine, they be deprived of the slave and the children, and that she and they be confiscated for the profit of the [royal] hospital, without ever being manumitted. Nevertheless we do not intend for the present article to be enforced if the man was not married to another person during his concubinage with his slave, and if he marries the said slave according to the church's formalities. She, then, by this means will be manumitted and the children rendered free and legitimate.

Article 12. Children who are born of a marriage between slaves will be slaves and will belong to the master of the women slaves, and not to those of their husbands, if the husband and wife have different masters.

Article 13. We wish that if a slave husband has married a free woman, the children, both male and female, follow the condition of their mother, and be free like her, in spite of the servitude of their father; and that if the father is free and the mother is enslaved, the children will likewise be slaves.

Article 19. We also forbid them from displaying for sale at the market or from carrying to private houses for sale any kind of commodity—even fruits, vegetables, firewood, grasses for feeding animals, and their crafts—without express permission of their masters. . . .

Article 27. Slaves who are infirm by age, sickness, or otherwise . . . will be fed and maintained by their masters. And in the case when they are abandoned, the slaves will be awarded to the hospital, to which the masters will be required to pay sixpence per day, for their nourishment and maintenance of each slave.

Article 28. We declare that slaves can own nothing that does not belong to their masters. And everything that comes to them—by their own industry, by the generosity of others, or otherwise—. . . be acquired in full property to their masters, without the slaves' children, their fathers and mothers, their relatives or any others, being able to claim anything of it by inheritance, donations inter vivos, or because of death. We declare such dispositions null, together with any promises and obligations that they have made, as being made by people incapable of disposing and contracting on their own initiative.

Article 59: We grant to manumitted slaves the same rights, privileges and liberties enjoyed by persons born free. We wish that they merit this acquired liberty and that it produce in them, both for their persons and for their property, the same effects that the good fortune of natural liberty causes in our other subjects.

Versailles, March 1685, the forty second year of our reign.
Signed LOUIS,
and below the King.
Colbert, visa, Le Tellier.
Read, posted and recorded at the sovereign council of the coast of Saint Domingue, kept at Petit Goave, 6 May 1687, Signed Moriceau.

DOCUMENT 4:
Title Page, James Sommersett Case.

Courtesy Library of Congress, LC-USZ62–90721

DOCUMENT 5:
Excerpt, "The Case of James Sommersett, a Negro, on a Habeas Corpus, King's Bench: 12 George III, A.D. 1771–72," reprinted in Thomas Bayly Howell, *A Complete Collection of State Trials,* vol. 20, 1771–1777 (London: T. C. Hansard, 1814): columns 23–82.

British abolitionist Granville Sharp defended James Sommersett against Charles Stewart, a Boston customs official who purchased him in London. After several years, Sommersett escaped, and Stewart sought to have him recaptured. The decision was a victory for antislavery activists and had broad implications for both male and female slaves. It supported the notion that slaves were permitted their freedom once they had reached free soil. The following excerpt is Chief Justice William Murray's final judgment.

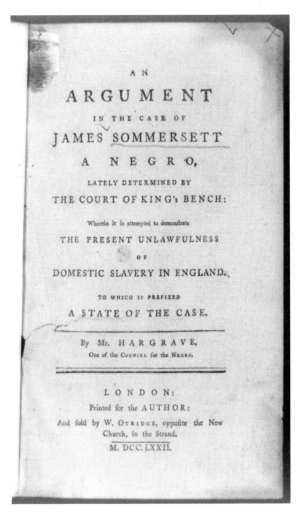

A N

ARGUMENT

IN THE CASE OF

JAMES SOMMERSETT

A   N E G R O,

LATELY DETERMINED BY

THE COURT OF KING's BENCH:

Wherein it is attempted to demonstrate

THE PRESENT UNLAWFULNESS

OF

DOMESTIC SLAVERY IN ENGLAND.

TO WHICH IS PREFIXED

A STATE OF THE CASE.

By Mr. HARGRAVE,
One of the COUNSEL for the NEGRO.

LONDON:
Printed for the AUTHOR:
And sold by W. OTRIDGE, opposite the New
Church, in the Strand.
M. DCC. LXXII.

Document 4

Chief Justice William Murray, Earl of Mansfield, Decision, June 22, 1792

The only question before us is, whether [Stewart is legally justified in detaining Sommersett]. If [he] is, the negro must be remanded [returned to Stewart's custody]; if not, he must be discharged. Accordingly, the [documents from Somerset's lawyers] state that the slave departed and refused to serve; whereupon he was kept, to be sold abroad. So high an act of dominion must be recognized by the country where it is used.

The power of a master over his slave has been extremely different in different countries. The state of slavery is of such a nature, that it is incapable of being introduced on any reasons, moral or political; but only by positive law, which preserves its force long after the reasons, occasion, and time itself from whence it was created, is erased from memory. It is so odious that nothing can be suffered to support it but positive law. Whatever inconveniences, therefore, may follow from a decision, I cannot say this case is allowed or approved by the law of England; and therefore the black man must be discharged.

DOCUMENT 6:
Proposed Spanish Slave Codes in the Americas, 1784–1789.

Slave codes illustrated the expansion of slavery in the Americas, in this case those areas under Spanish rule. They are an extension and expansion of the Las Siete Partidas included in this chapter. Spanish King Carlos IV requested that the governor of Santo Domingo prepare a code to control the behavior, labor, and movement of slaves. This particular excerpt focuses on slave dwellings. Planters resisted the measures because it also limited free blacks, so it was replaced with a less-restrictive code five years later.

Colonial Government of Santo Domingo, Draft Legal Code for the Moral, Political, and Economic Governance of the Negroes of the Island of Hispaniola (The Carolina Black Code), December 14, 1784.

INTRODUCTION
The lamentable decadence that the island of Hispaniola has suffered for more than two centuries, the old abuses of its constitution and the small number of freed slaves and negroes that it possesses, whose shameful idleness, independence and pride, and the continuous robberies and disorder that they commit in the countryside and on the ranches have reduced it to poverty and the most deplorable situation, presenting a dry and limited subject for the legislator who is to propose the governmental system for its improvement. . . .

But the happy dawn of the glorious reign of our august sovereign,

Carlos IV (whom may God keep safe), over the Island of Hispaniola . . . offers a new career to its industry and navigation, through the cultivation of its fertile plains, and still more considerable treasures that it produces daily in the land, populated . . . by a great multitude of settlers and negro farmers, extracted directly from the coasts of Africa, and made available to be purchased by the landowners, which will accelerate the island's return to the operations and progress of Agriculture, which should in a short time elevate Hispaniola to its zenith of prosperity and wealth. . . .

The ministers and officials must apply themselves to: the useful and regular employment of the free negroes and the slaves in its cultivation of products, so greatly needed in the metropole, and to the appropriate division of classes and races; to the perfect subordination and respect of the workers for the magistrates, their masters and, generally for every white person; the incentives and rewards for good service and conduct.

CHAPTER 18: ON SLAVE DWELLINGS
One of the major incentives for the faithfulness and good service of the slave should be the granting that, through his lord, the slave may have the power to acquire a modest amount of property on his own behalf, which will never exceed one quarter of his value . . . or by distributing to him a small portion of land for his own private cultivation, or giving him permission to raise birds and animals, or by earning a daily wage, his lords making appropriate payments.

Law 1: The good services and conduct of the slave will be the just means for the increase in the granting of land, the amount of which will grow accordingly; but it will be agreed that there be a limit, so that the slave will remain dependent upon his owner—since he will otherwise think of throwing off the yoke that oppresses him and so that he will look only to his owner for his needs.

Law 2: So that they might be worthy of the property given them by their virtue, the slaves will lose these prerogatives and rewards after they have committed any offense. . . .

Law 3: In spite of the law's harsh strictness—that the children of slaves may not inherit anything from the parents—nor from their relations nor from [slaves belonging to another master] the slave who maintains and preserves his virtue and good services until his death, may dispose of his property in favor of his children and his wife, even if they are not slaves of the same lord.

Law 4: Those who marry with a woman of another owner may leave only half of his holdings to her, and the remainder he may leave to the hospital and for the good of his soul, the penalty being so that he may prefer to marry negro women owned by his master, in the interest of the public welfare.

Law 5: The single man or widower without children may dispose of half of his property to the same establishment, and the rest for the good of his soul, it being just that, since while alive he could not enjoy the fruits of his labors, he will succeed in that way after his death, for his good services and loyalty.

DOCUMENT 7:
Constitution of the United States of America, 1787.

As early as 1776, the U.S. Continental Congress declared "no slave shall be imported to any of the thirteen United Colonies." Eleven years later, the delegates from Georgia and South Carolina to the Constitutional Convention refused to allow the Constitution to oppose slavery. The various articles (excerpted below) were seen as a compromise between abolitionists and proslavery activists. By the time the document was signed, two northern states had already abolished slavery.

Article I, Section 2
. . . Representatives and direct Taxes shall be apportioned among the several States which may be included within this Union, according to their respective Numbers, which shall be determined by adding to the whole Number of free Persons, including those bound to Service for a Term of Years, and excluding Indians not taxed, three fifths of all other Persons.)

Article I, Section 8
The Congress shall have Power To lay and collect Taxes, Duties, Imposts and Excises, to pay the Debts and provide for the common Defence and general Welfare of the United States . . . [t]o provide for calling forth the Militia to execute the Laws of the Union, suppress Insurrections and repel Invasions. . . .

Article 1, Section 9

The Migration or Importation of such Persons as any of the States now existing shall think proper to admit, shall not be prohibited by the Congress prior to the Year one thousand eight hundred and eight, but a tax or duty may be imposed on such Importation, not exceeding ten dollars for each Person.

Article IV, Section 2

. . . *No Person held to Service or Labour in one State, under the Laws thereof, escaping into another, shall, in Consequence of any Law or Regulation therein, be discharged from such Service or Labour, but shall be delivered up on Claim of the Party to whom such Service or Labour may be due.)*

Article IV, Section 4:

The United States shall guarantee to every State in this Union a Republican Form of Government, and shall protect each of them against invasion; and on Application of the Legislature, or of the Executive (when the Legislature cannot be convened) against domestic Violence.

DOCUMENT 8:

Fugitive Slave Act, 1793. *Proceedings and Debates of the House of Representatives of the United States at the Second Session of the Second Congress, Begun at the City of Philadelphia, November 5, 1792.* Annals of Congress, 2nd Congress, 2nd Session (November 5, 1792 to March 2, 1793): 1414–15.

Although Article 4 of the U.S. Constitution stated that runaway slaves must be returned to their owners, it did not make any provisions for enforcement. This law held that slaves could be recaptured in any state or U.S. territory, as well as children born to enslaved women. It also made it a crime for anyone to help a fugitive. It was passed in February 1793 and signed by President George Washington. With its weak enforcement, it spawned the Fugitive Slave Act of 1850 (see Documents 14 and 15), which divided the nation.

An Act respecting fugitives from justice, and persons escaping from the service of their masters.

Be it enacted, &c., That, whenever the Executive authority of any State in the Union, or of either of the Territories Northwest or South of the river Ohio, shall demand any person as a fugitive from justice, of the Executive authority of any such State or Territory to which such person shall have fled, and shall moreover produce the copy of an indictment found, or an affidavit made before a magistrate of any State or Territory as aforesaid, charging the person so demanded with having committed treason, felony, or other crime, certified as authentic by the Governor or Chief Magistrate of the State or Territory from whence the person so charged fled, it shall be the duty of the executive authority of the State or Territory to which such person shall have fled, to cause him or her arrest to be given to the Executive authority making such demand, or to the agent when he shall appear; but, if no such agent shall appear within six months from the time of the arrest, the prisoner may be discharged: and all costs or expenses incurred in the apprehending, securing, and transmitting such fugitive to the State or Territory making such demand, shall be paid by such State or Territory.

SEC. 2. *And be it further enacted,* That any agent appointed as aforesaid, who shall receive the fugitive into his custody, shall be empowered to transport him or her to the State or Territory from which he or she shall have fled. And if any person or persons shall, by force, set at liberty, or rescue the fugitive from such agent while transporting, as aforesaid, the person or persons so offending shall, on conviction, be fined not exceeding five hundred dollars, and be imprisoned not exceeding one year.

SEC. 3. *And be it also enacted,* That when a person held to labor in any of the United States, or in either of the Territories on the Northwest or South of the river Ohio, under the laws thereof, shall escape into any other part of the said States or Territory, the person to whom such labor or service may be due, his agent or attorney, is hereby empowered to seize or arrest such fugitive from labor, and to take him or her before any Judge of the Circuit or District Courts of the United States, residing or being within the State, or before any magistrate of a county, city, or town corporate, wherein such seizure or arrest shall be made, and upon proof to the satisfaction of such Judge or magistrate, either by oral testimony or affidavit taken before and certified by a magistrate of any such State or Territory, that the person so seized or arrested, doth, under the laws of the State or Territory from which he or she fled, owe service or labor to the person claiming him or her, it shall be the duty of such Judge or magistrate to give a certificate thereof to such claimant, his agent, or attorney, which shall be sufficient warrant for removing the said fugitive from labor to the State or Territory from which he or she fled.

SEC. 4. *And be it further enacted,* That any person who shall knowingly and willingly obstruct or hinder such claimant, his agent, or attorney, in so seizing or arresting such fugitive from labor, or shall rescue such fugitive from such claimant, his agent or attorney, when so arrested pursuant to the authority herein given and declared; or shall harbor or conceal such person after notice that he or she was a fugitive from labor, as aforesaid, shall, for either of the said offences, forfeit and pay the sum of five hundred dollars. Which penalty may be recovered by and for the benefit of such claimant, by action of debt, in any Court proper to try the same, saving moreover to the person claiming such labor or service his right of action for or on account of the said injuries, or either of them.

Approved [signed into law by President George Washington], February 12, 1793.

DOCUMENT 9:
Excerpt, Thomas Jefferson, *Notes on the State of Virginia* (Philadelphia: Mathew Carey, 1794).

First published privately and anonymously, *Notes on the State of Virginia* was written in response to questions by the French government about Jefferson's home. As governor of Virginia, this volume focuses on the colony's natural resource, as well as laws and constitution. While focused on issues of liberty, Jefferson grapples with the problem of slavery and the extermination of native peoples. He is writing largely for a European audience and bases his opposition to slavery on the fact that it had a negative impact on the owners. Jefferson's theory of racial inferiority was reflective of the late eighteenth century. As a slaveowner himself, he strongly advocated colonization of free blacks, believing the two races could not coexist.

Query XVIII.

The particular customs and manners that may happen to be received in that state?

It is difficult to determine on the standard by which the manners of a nation may be tried, whether *catholic*, or *particular*. It is more difficult for a native to bring to that standard the manners of his own nation, familiarized to him by habit. There must doubtless be an unhappy influence on the manners of our people produced by the existence of slavery among us. The whole commerce between master and slave is a perpetual exercise of the most boisterous passions, the most unremitting despotism on the one part, and degrading sub-missions on the other. Our children see this, and learn to imitate it; for man is an imitative animal. This quality is the germ of all education in him. From his cradle to his grave he is learning to do what he sees others do. If a parent could find no motive either in his philanthropy or his self-love, for restraining the intemperance of passion towards his slave, it should always be a sufficient one that his child is present. But generally it is not sufficient. The parent storms, the child looks on, catches the lineaments of wrath, puts on the same airs in the circle of smaller slaves, gives a loose to his worst of passions, and thus nursed, educated, and daily exercised in tyranny, cannot but be stamped by it with odious peculiarities. The man must be a prodigy who can retain his manners and morals undepraved by such circumstances. And with what execration should the statesman be loaded, who permitting one half the citizens thus to trample on the rights of the other, transforms those into despots, and these into enemies, destroys the morals of the one part, and the amor patriae of the other. For if a slave can have a country in this world, it must be any other in preference to that in which he is born to live and labour for another: in which he must lock up the faculties of his nature, contribute as far as depends on his individual endeavours to the evanishment of the human race, or entail his own miserable condition on the endless generations proceeding from him. With the morals of the people, their industry also is destroyed. For in a warm climate, no man will labour for himself who can make another labour for him. This is so true, that of the proprietors of slaves a very small proportion indeed are ever seen to labour. And can the liberties of a nation be thought secure when we have removed their only firm basis, a conviction in the minds of the people that these liberties are of the gift of God? That they are not to be violated but with his wrath? Indeed I tremble for my country when I reflect that God is just: that his justice cannot sleep for ever: that considering numbers, nature and natural means only, a revolution of the wheel of fortune, an exchange of situation, is among possible events: that it may become probable by super-natural interference! The Almighty has no attribute which can take side with us in such a contest.—But it is impossible to be temperate and to pursue this subject through the various considerations of policy, of morals, of history natural and civil. We must be contented to hope they will force their way into every one's mind. I think a change already perceptible, since the origin of the present revolution. The spirit of the master is abating, that of the slave rising from the dust, his condition mollifying, the way I hope preparing, under the auspices of heaven, for a total emancipation, and that this is disposed, in the order of events, to be with the consent of the masters, rather than by their extirpation.

DOCUMENT 10:
U.S. Congress, "An Act to Prohibit the Importation of Slaves, 1807–1808."

The importation of slaves was the key to slavery's success in both the United States and the Caribbean, because slaves could always be replaced. Two events—the Northwest Ordinance in 1787 and the invention of the cotton gin in 1793—increased the demand for cotton, which required larger numbers of slaves. This prohibition on the importation of slaves, passed on March 2, 1807, and signed into law by President Thomas Jefferson, dramatically affected the lives of women, who quickly became essential to reproducing property for slave owners. The act went into effect on January 1, 1808.

An Act to Prohibit the Importation of Slaves into any Port or Place Within the Jurisdiction of the United States, From and After the First Day of January, in the Year of our Lord One Thousand Eight Hundred and Eight.

Be it enacted by the Senate and House of Representatives of the United States of America in Congress assembled, That from and after the first day of January, one thousand eight hundred and eight, it shall not be lawful to import or bring into the United States or the territories thereof from any foreign kingdom, place, or country, any negro, mulatto, or person of colour, with intent to hold, sell, or dispose of such negro, mulatto, or person of colour, as a slave, or to be held to service or labour.

SECTION 2. And be it further enacted, That no citizen or citizens of the United States, or any other person, shall, from arid after the first day of January, in the year of our Lord one thousand eight hundred and eight, for himself, or themselves, or any other person whatsoever, either as master, factor, or owner, build, fit, equip, load or otherwise prepare any ship or vessel, in any port or place within the jurisdiction of the United States, nor shall cause any ship or vessel to sail from any port or place within the same, for the purpose of procuring any negro, mulatto, or person of colour, from any foreign kingdom, place, or country, to be transported to any port or place whatsoever, within the jurisdiction of the United States, to be held, sold, or disposed of as slaves, or to be held to service or labour: and if any ship or vessel shall be so fitted out for the purpose aforesaid, or shall be caused to sail so as aforesaid, every such ship or vessel, her tackle, apparel, and furniture, shall be forfeited to the United States, and shall be liable to be seized, prosecuted, and condemned in any of the circuit courts or district courts, for the district where the said ship or vessel may be found or seized.

SECTION 3. And be it further enacted, That all and every person so building, fitting out, equipping, loading, or otherwise preparing or sending away, any ship or vessel, knowing or intending that the same shall be employed in such trade or business, from and after the first day of January, one thousand eight hundred and eight, contrary to the true intent and meaning of this act, or any ways aiding or abetting therein, shall severally forfeit and pay twenty thousand dollars, one moiety thereof to the use of the United States, and the other moiety to the use of any person or persons who shall sue for and prosecute the same to effect.

SECTION 4. And be it further enacted, If any citizen or citizens of the United States, or any person resident within the jurisdiction of the same, shall, from and after the first day of January, one thousand eight hundred and eight, take on board, receive or transport from any of the coasts or kingdoms of Africa, or from any other foreign kingdom, place, or country, any negro, mulatto, or person of colour, in any ship or vessel, for the purpose of selling them in any port or place within the jurisdiction of the United States as slaves, or to be held to service or labour, or shall be in any ways aiding or abetting therein, such citizen or citizens, or person, shall severally forfeit and pay five thousand dollars, one moiety thereof to the use of any person or persons who shall sue for and prosecute the same to effect; and every such ship or vessel in which such negro, mulatto, or person of colour, shall have been taken on board, received, or transported as aforesaid, her tackle, apparel, and furniture, and the goods and effects which shall be found on board the same, shall be forfeited to the United States, and shall be liable to be seized, prosecuted, and condemned in any of the circuit courts or district courts in the district where the said ship or vessel may be found or seized. And neither the importer, nor any person or persons claiming from or under him, shall hold any right or title whatsoever to any negro, mulatto, or person of colour, nor to the service or labour thereof, who may be imported or brought within the United States, or territories thereof, in violation of this law, but the same shall remain subject to any regulations not contravening the provisions of this act, which the legislatures of the several states or territories at any time hereafter may make, for disposing of any such negro, mulatto, or person of colour.

SECTION 5. And be it further enacted, That if any citizen or citizens of the United States, or any other person resident within the jurisdiction of the same, shall, from and after the first day of January, one thousand eight hundred and eight, contrary to the true intent and meaning of this act, take on board any ship or vessel from any of the coasts or kingdoms of Africa, or from any other foreign kingdom, place, or country, any negro, mulatto, or person of colour, with intent to sell him, her, or them, for a slave, or slaves, or to be held to service or labour, and shall transport the same to any port or place within the jurisdiction of the United States, and there sell such negro, mulatto, or person of colour, so transported as aforesaid, for a slave, or to be held to service or labour, every such offender shall be deemed guilty of a high misdemeanor, and being thereof convicted before any court having competent jurisdiction, shall suffer imprisonment for not more than ten years nor less than five years, and be fined not exceeding ten thousand dollars, nor less than one thousand dollars.

SECTION 6. And be it further enacted, That if any person or persons whatsoever, shall, from and after the first day of January, one thousand eight hundred and eight, purchase or sell any negro, mulatto, or person of colour, for a slave, or to be held to service or labour, who shall have been imported, or brought from any foreign kingdom, place, or country, or from the dominions of any foreign state, immediately adjoining to the United States, into any port or place within the jurisdiction of the United States, after the last day of December, one thousand eight hundred and seven, knowing at the time of such purchase or sale, such negro, mulatto or person of colour, was so brought within the jurisdiction of the Unified States, as aforesaid, such purchaser and seller shall severally forfeit and pay for every negro, mulatto, or person of colour, so purchased or sold as aforesaid, eight hundred dollars; one moiety thereof to the United States, and the other moiety to the use of any person or persons who shall sue for and prosecute the same to effect: Provided, that the aforesaid forfeiture shall not extend to the seller or purchaser of any negro, mulatto, or person of colour, who may be sold or disposed of in virtue of any regulation which may hereafter be made by any of the legislatures of the several states in that respect, in pursuance of this act, and the constitution of the United States.

SECTION 7. And be it further enacted, That if any ship or vessel shall be found, from and after the first day of January, one thousand eight hundred and eight, in any river, port, bay, or harbor, or on the high seas, within the jurisdictional limits of the United States, or hovering on the coast thereof, having on board any negro, mulatto, or person of colour, for the purpose of selling them as slaves, or with intent to land the same, in any port or place within the jurisdiction of the United States, contrary to the prohibition of this act, every such ship or vessel, together with her tackle, apparel, and furniture, and the goods or effects which shall be found on board the same, shall be forfeited to the use of the United States, and may be seized, prosecuted, and condemned, in any court of the United States, having jurisdiction thereof. And it shall be lawful for the President of the United States, and he is hereby authorized, should he deem it expedient, to cause any of the armed vessels of the United

States to be manned and employed to cruise on any part of the coast of the United States, or territories thereof, where he may judge attempts will be made to violate the provisions of this act, and to instruct and direct the commanders of armed vessels of the United States, to seize, take, and bring into any port of the United States all such ships or vessels, and moreover to seize, take, and bring into any port of the United States all ships or vessels of the United States, wheresoever found on the high seas, contravening the provisions of this act, to be proceeded against according to law, and the captain, master, or commander of every such ship or vessel, so found and seized as aforesaid, shall be deemed guilty of a high misdemeanor, and shall be liable to be prosecuted before any court of the United States, having jurisdiction thereof; and being thereof convicted, shall be fined not exceeding ten thousand dollars, and be imprisoned not less than two years, and not exceeding four years. And the proceeds of all ships and vessels, their tackle, apparel, and furniture, and the goods and effects on board of them, which shall be so seized, prosecuted and condemned, shall be divided equally between the United States and the officers and men who shall make such seizure, take, or bring the same into port for condemnation, whether such seizure be made by an armed vessel of the United States, or revenue cutters hereof, and the same shall be distributed in like manner, as is provided by law, for the distribution of prizes taken from an enemy: Provided, that the officers and men, to be entitled to one half of the proceeds aforesaid, shall safe keep every negro, mulatto, or person of colour, found on board of any ship or vessel so by them seized, taken, or brought into port for condemnation, and shall deliver every such negro, mulatto, or person of colour, to such person or persons as shall be appointed by the respective states, to receive the same, and if no such person or persons shall be appointed by the respective states, they shall deliver every such negro, mulatto, or person of colour, to the overseers of the poor of the port or place where such ship or vessel may be brought or found, and shall immediately transmit to the governor or chief magistrate of the state, an account of their proceedings, together with the number of such Negroes, mulattoes, or persons of colour, and a descriptive list of the same, that he may give directions respecting such Negroes, mulattoes, or persons of colour.

SECTION 8. And be it further enacted, That no captain, master or commander of any ship or vessel, of less burthen than forty tons, shall, from and after the first day of January, one thousand eight hundred and eight, take on board and transport any negro, mulatto, or person of colour, to any port or place whatsoever, for the purpose of selling or disposing of the same as a slave, or with intent that the same may be sold or disposed of to be held to service or labour, on penalty of forfeiting for every such negro, mulatto, or person of colour, so taken on board and transported, as aforesaid, the sum of eight hundred dollars; one moiety thereof to the use of the United States, and the other moiety to any person or persons who shall sue for, and prosecute the same to effect: Provided however, That nothing in this section shall extend to prohibit the taking on board or transporting on any river, or inland bay of the sea, within the jurisdiction of the United States, any negro, mulatto, or person of colour, (not imported contrary to the provisions of this act) in any vessel or species of craft whatever.

SECTION 9. And be it further enacted, That the captain, master, or commander of any ship or vessel of the burthen of forty tons or more, from and after the first day of January, one thousand eight hundred and eight, sailing coastwise, from any port in the United States, to any port or place within the jurisdiction of the same, having on board any negro, mulatto, or person of colour, for the purpose of transporting them to be sold or disposed of as slaves, or to be held to service or labour, shall, previous to the departure of such ship or vessel, make out and subscribe duplicate manifests of every such negro, mulatto, or person of colour, on board such ship or vessel, therein specifying the name and sex of each person, their age and stature, as near as may be, and the class to which they respectively belong, whether negro, mulatto, or person of colour, with the name and place of residence of every owner or shipper of the same, and shall deliver such manifests to the collector of the port, if there be one, otherwise to the surveyor, before whom the captain, master, or commander, together with the owner or shipper, shall severally swear or affirm to the best of their knowledge and belief, that the persons therein specified were not imported or brought into the United States, from and after the first day of January, one thousand eight hundred and eight, and that under the laws of the state, they are held to service or labour; whereupon the said collector or surveyor shall certify the same on the said manifests, one of which he shall return to the said captain, master, or commander, with a permit, specifying thereon the number, names, and general description of such persons, and authorizing him to proceed to the port of his destination. And if any ship or vessel, being laden and destined as aforesaid, shall depart from the port where she may then be, without the captain, master, or commander having first made out and subscribed duplicate manifests, of every negro, mulatto, and person of colour, on board such ship or vessel, as aforesaid, and without having previously delivered the same to the said collector or surveyor, and obtained a permit, in manner as herein required, or shall, previous to her arrival at the port of her destination, take on board any negro, mulatto, or person of colour, other than those specified in the manifests, as aforesaid, every such ship or vessel, together with her tackle, apparel and furniture, shall be forfeited to the use of the United States, and may be seized, prosecuted and condemned in any court of the United States having jurisdiction thereof; and the captain, master, or commander of every such ship or vessel, shall moreover forfeit, for every such negro, mulatto, or person of colour, so transported, or taken on board, contrary to the provisions of this act, the sum of one thousand dollars, one moiety thereof to the United States, and the other moiety to the use of any person or persons who shall sue for and prosecute the same to effect.

SECTION 10. And be it further enacted, That the captain, master, or commander of every ship or vessel, of the burthen of forty tons or more, from and after the first day of January, one thousand eight hundred and eight, sailing coastwise, and having on board any negro, mulatto, or person of colour, to sell or dispose of as slaves, or to be held to service or labour, and arriving in any port within the jurisdiction of the United States, from any other port within the same, shall, previous to the unlading or putting on shore any of the persons aforesaid, or suffering them to go on shore, deliver to the collector, if there be one, or if not, to the surveyor residing at the port of her arrival, the manifest certified by the collector or surveyor of the port from whence she sailed, as is herein before directed, to the truth of which, before such officer, he shall swear or affirm, and if the collector or surveyor shall be satisfied therewith, he shall thereupon grant a permit for unlading or suffering such negro, mulatto, or person of colour, to be put on shore, and if the captain, master, or commander of any such ship or vessel being laden as aforesaid, shall neglect or refuse to deliver the manifest at the time and in the manner herein directed, or shall land or put on shore any negro, mulatto, or person of colour, for the purpose aforesaid, before he shall have delivered his manifest as aforesaid, and obtained a permit for that purpose, every such captain, master, or commander, shall forfeit and pay ten thousand dollars, one moiety thereof to the United States, the other moiety to the use of any person or persons who shall sue for and prosecute the same to effect.

DOCUMENT 11:

The State v. John Mann, 1829. Thomas P. Devereaux [ed.], *Cases Argued and Determined in the Supreme Court of North Carolina from December Term, 1828, to December Term, 1830* (Raleigh: J. Gales and Sims, 1831), 2: 263–68.

This case involved Lydia, a slave whom John Mann had hired out from Elizabeth Jones. Jones takes Mann to court for assaulting Lydia, and Mann was convicted by the lower court. The decision is ultimately reversed by the Supreme Court, where Judge Thomas Ruffin, an opponent of slavery, wrote the majority decision, a victory for pro-slavery forces.

The State

v.

John Mann

From Chowan [County].

The Master is not liable to an indictment for a battery committed upon his slave.

One who has a right to the labor of a slave, has also a right to all the means of controlling his conduct which the owner has.

Hence one who has hired a slave is not liable to an indictment for a battery on him, committed during the hiring.

But this rule does not interfere with the owner's right to damages for an
injury affecting the value of the slave, which is regulated by the
law of bailment.

The Defendant was indicted for an assault and battery upon *Lydia*,
the slave of one *Elizabeth Jones.*

On the trial it appeared that the Defendant had hired the slave for a
year—that during the term, the slave had committed some small offence,
for which the Defendant undertook to chastise her—that while in the
act of so doing, the slave ran off, whereupon the Defendant called upon
her to stop, which being refused, he shot at and wounded her.

His honor Judge DANIEL charged the Jury, that if they believed the
punishment inflicted by the Defendant was cruel and unwarrantable,
and disproportionate to the offence committed by the slave, that in law
the Defendant was guilty, as he had only a special property in the slave.

A verdict was returned for the State, and the Defendant appealed.

No Counsel appeared for the Defendant.

The Attorney-General contended, that no difference existed between
this case and that of the *State v. Hall,* (2 *Hawks,* 582.) In this case the
weapon used was one calculated to produce death. He assimilated the
relation between a master and a slave, to those existing between parents
and children, masters and apprentices, and tutors and scholars, and upon
the limitations to the right of the superiors in these relations, he cited
Russell on Crimes, 866.

RUFFIN, Judge.—A Judge cannot but lament, when such cases as the
present are brought into judgment. It is impossible that the reasons on
which they go can be appreciated, but where institutions similar to our
own, exist and are thoroughly understood. The struggle, too, in the Judge's
own breast between the feelings of the man, and the duty of the magistrate is a severe one, presenting strong temptation to put aside such questions, if it be possible. It is useless however, to complain of things inherent
in our political state. And it is criminal in a Court to avoid any responsibility
which the laws impose. With whatever reluctance therefore it is done, the
Court is compelled to express an opinion upon the extent of the dominion
of the master over the slave in North-Carolina.

The indictment charges a battery on *Lydia,* a slave of *Elizabeth Jones.*

Upon the face of the indictment, the case is the same as the *State v. Hall.* (2 *Hawks* 582.)—No fault is found with the rule then adopted; nor would be, if it were now open. But it is not open; for the question, as it relates to the battery on a slave by a stranger, is considered as settled by that case. But the evidence makes this a different case. Here the slave had been *hired* by the Defendant, and was in his possession; and the battery was committed during the period of hiring. With the liabilities of the hirer to the general owner, for an injury permanently impairing the value of the slave, no rule now laid down is intended to interfere. That is left upon the general doctrine of bailment. The enquiry here is, whether a cruel and unreasonable battery on a slave, by the hirer, is indictable. The Judge below instructed the Jury, that it is. He seems to have put it on the ground, that the Defendant had but a special property. Our laws uniformly treat the master or other person having the posses- sion and command of the slave, as entitled to the same extent of author- ity. The object is the same—the services of the slave; and the same powers must be confided. In a criminal proceeding, and indeed in refer- ence to all other persons but the general owner, the hirer or possessor of a slave, in relation to both rights and duties, is, for the time being, the owner. This opinion would, perhaps dispose of this particular case; because the indictment, which charges a battery upon the slave of *Elizabeth Jones,* is not supported by proof of a battery upon Defendant's own slave; since different justifications may be applicable to the two cases. But upon the general questions, whether the owner is answerable *criminaliter,* for a battery upon his own slave, or other exercise of author- ity or force, not forbidden by statute, the Court entertains but little doubt—That he is so liable, has never yet been decided; nor, as far as is known, been hitherto contended. There have been no prosecutions of the sort. The established habits and uniform practice of the country in this respect, is the best evidence of the portion of power, deemed by the whole community, requisite to the preservation of the master's domin- ion. If we thought differently, we could not set our notions in array against the judgment of every body else, and say that this, or that author- ity, may be safely lopped off. This has indeed been assimilated at the bar to the other domestic relations; and arguments drawn from the well established principles, which confer and restrain the authority of the parent over the child, the tutor over the pupil, the master over the apprentice, have been pressed on us. The Court does not recognise their application. There is no likeness between the cases. They are in opposition to each other, and there is an impassable gulf between them.—The difference is that which exists between freedom and slavery—and a greater cannot be imagined. In the one, the end in view is the happiness of the youth, born equal rights with that governor, on whom the duty devolves of training the young to usefulness, in a station which he is afterwards to assume among freemen. To such an end, and with such a subject, moral and intellectual instruction seem the natural means; and for the most part, they are found to suffice. Moderate force is superadded, only to make the others effectual. If that fail, it is better to leave the party to his own headstrong passions, and the ultimate correction of the law, than to allow it to be immoderately inflicted by a private person. With slavery it is far otherwise. The end is profit of the master, his security and the public safety; the subject, one doomed in his own person, and his posterity, to live without knowledge, and without the capacity to make any thing on his own, and to toil that another may reap the fruits. What moral considerations shall be addressed to such a being, to convince him what, it is impossible but that the most stupid must feel and know can never be true—that he is thus to labour upon a principle of natural duty, or for the sake of his own personal happiness, such services can only be expected from one who has no will of his own; who surrenders his will in implicit obedience to that of another. Such obedience is the consequence only of uncontrolled authority over the body. There is nothing else which can operate to produce the effect. The power of the master must be absolute, to render the submission of the slave perfect. I most freely confess my sense of the harshness of this proposition, I feel it as deeply as any man can. And as a principle of moral right, every person in his retirement must repudiate it. But in the actual condition of things, it must be so. There is no remedy. This discipline belongs to the state of slavery. They cannot be disunited, without abrogating at once the rights of the master, and absolving the slave from his subjection. It constitutes the curse of slavery to both the bond and free portions of our population. But it is inherent in the relation of master and slave.

That there may be particular instances of cruelty and deliberate barbarity, where, in conscience the law might properly interfere, is most probable. The difficulty is to determine, where a *Court* may properly begin. Merely in the abstract it may well be asked, which power of the master accords with right. The answer will probably sweep away all of them. But we cannot look at the matter in that light. The truth is, that we are forbidden to enter upon a train of general reasoning on the subject. We cannot allow the right of the master to be brought into discussion in the Courts of Justice. The slave, to remain a slave, must be made sensible, that there is no appeal from his master; that his power is in no instance, usurped; but is conferred by the laws of man at least, if not by the law of God. The danger would be great indeed, if the tribunals of justice should be called on to graduate the punishment appropriate to every temper, and ever dereliction of menial duty. No man can anticipate the many and aggravated provocations of the master, which the slave would be constantly stimulated by his own passions, or the instigation of others to give; or the consequent wrath of the master, prompting him to bloody vengeance, upon the turbulent traitor—a vengeance generally practised with impunity, by reason of its privacy. The Court therefore disclaims the power of changing the relation, in which these parts or our people stand to each other.

We are happy to see, that there is daily less and less occasion for the interposition of the Courts. The protection already afforded by several statutes, that all-powerful motive, the private interest of the owner, the benevolences towards each other, seated in the hearts of those who have been born and bred together, the frowns and deep execrations o the community upon the barbarian, who is guilty of excessive and brutal cruelty to his unprotected slave, all combined, have produced a mildness of treatment, and attention to the comforts of the unfortunate class of slaves, greatly mitigating the rights of servitude, and ameliorating the condition of the slaves. The same causes are operating, and will continue to operate with increased action, until the disparity in numbers between the whites and blacks, shall have rendered the latter in no degree dangerous to the former, when the police now existing may be further relaxed. This result, greatly to be desired, may be much more rationally expected from the events above alluded to, and now in progress, than from any rash expositions of abstract truths, by a Judiciary tainted with a false and fanatical philanthropy, seeking to redress an acknowledged evil, by means still more wicked and appalling than even that evil.

I repeat, that I would gladly have avoided this ungrateful question. But being brought to it, the Court is compelled to declare, that while slavery exists amongst us in its present state, or until it shall seem fit to the Legislature to interpose express enactments to the contrary, it will be the imperative duty of the Judges to recognise the full dominion of the owner over the slave, except where the exercise of it is forbidden by statute. And this we do upon the ground, that this dominion is essential to the value of slaves as property, to the security of the master, and the public tranquillity, greatly dependent upon their subordination; and in fine, as most effectually securing the general protection and comfort of the slaves themselves.

PER CURIAM.—Let the judgment below be reversed, and judgment entered for the Defendant.

DOCUMENT 12:
Theodore Dwight Weld, *The Bible Against Slavery: An Inquiry into the Patriarchal and Mosaic Systems on the Subject of Human Rights,* 4th ed. (New York: American Anti-Slavery Society, 1838).

Weld was a minister, editor, writer, and well-known abolitionist in New York. This excerpt from *The Bible Against Slavery* denies the divine right to slavery and would have not found a wide audience in the American South. A year later, he published *American Slavery As It Is: Testimony of a Thousand Witnesses,* which influenced Harriet Beecher Stowe's famous novel, *Uncle Tom's Cabin,* that was published in 1852. Weld was married to Angelina Grimké, also a popular abolitionist and women's rights activist.

Evangelical Abolitionism

The spirit of slavery never seeks refuge in the Bible of its own accord. The horns of the altar are its last resort—seized only in desperation, as it rushes form the terror of the avenger's arm. Like other unclean spirits, it "hateth the light, neither cometh to the light, lest its deeds should be reproved." Goaded to phrenzy in its conflicts with conscience and common sense, denied all quarter, and hunted from every covert, it vaults over the sacred inclosure and courses up and down the Bible, "seeking rest, and finding none." THE LAW OF LOVE, glowing on every page, flashes around it an omnipresent anguish and despair. It shrinks from the hated light, and howls under the consuming touch, as demons quailed before the Son of God, and shrieked, "Torment us not." At last it slinks away under the types of the Mosaic system, and seeks to burrow out of sight among their shadows. Vain hope! Its asylum is its sepulchre; its city of refuge, the city of destruction. It flies from light into the sun; from heat, into devouring fire; and from the voice of God into the thickest of His thunders.

ENSLAVING MEN IS REDUCING THEM TO ARTICLES OF PROPERTY—making free agents, chattels—converting *persons* into *things*—sinking immortality into merchandize. A *slave* is one held in this condition. In law, "he owns nothing, and can acquire nothing." His right to himself is abrogated. If he says *my* hands, *my* body, *my* mind, MY*self,* they are figures of speech. To *use himself* for his own good, is a *crime.* To keep what he earns, is *stealing.* To take his body into his own keeping, is *insurrection.* In a word, the profit of his master is made the END of his being, and he, a *mere means* to that end—a mere means to an end into which his interests do not enter, of which they constitute no portion. MAN sunk to a *thing!* the intrinsic element, the *principle* of slavery; MEN, bartered, leased, mortgaged, bequeathed, invoiced, shipped on cargoes, stored as goods, taken on executions, and knocked off at a public outcry! Their *rights,* another's conveniences; their interests, wares on sale; their happiness, a household utensil; their personal inalienable ownership, a serviceable article or a plaything, as best suits the humour of the hour; their deathless nature, conscience, social affections, sympathies, hopes— marketable commodities! We repeat it, THE REDUCTION OF PERSONS TO THINGS! Not robbing a man of privileges, but of *himself;* not loading him with burdens, but making him a *beast of burden;* not restraining liberty, but his neighbour of a *cent,* yet commission him to rob his neighbour of *himself? . . .* Slaveholding is the highest possible violation of the eight[h] commandment. To take from a man his earnings, is theft. But to take the *earner,* is a compound, a life-long theft—supreme robbery that vaults up the climax at a leap—the dread, terrific, giant robbery, that towers among other robberies a solitary horror. The eight[h] commandment forbids the taking away, and the tenth adds, "Thou shalt not *covet* any thing that is thy neighbor's"; thus guarding every man's right to himself and property, by making not only the actual taking away a sin, but even that state of mind which would *tempt* to it. Who ever made human beings slaves, without *coveting* them? Why take from them their time, labor, liberty, right of self-preservation and improvement, their right to acquire property, to worship according to conscience, to search the Scriptures, to live with their families, and their right to their own bodies, if they do not *desire* them? They COVET them for purposes of gain, convenience, lust of dominion, of sensual gratification, of pride and ostentation. THEY BREAK THE TENTH COMMANDMENT, and pluck down upon their heads the plagues that are written in the book. *Ten* commandments constitute the brief compend of human duty. *Two* of these brand slavery as sin.

DOCUMENT 13:
Petition, *Ruthey Ann Hansley v. Samuel G. Hansley, 1845.
James Iredell [ed.], Reports of Cases at Law Argued and Determined in the Supreme Court of North Carolina from August Term, 1849, to December Term, 1849 . . .*
(Raleigh: Seaton Gales, 1850), 10: 506–16.

In this petition, Ruthey Ann Hansley, a white woman in Hanover County, North Carolina, sued for divorce because of her husband's sexual relations with one of his enslaved women. The Superior Court of Hanover County awarded her the decree, but in an appeal, the Supreme Court of North Carolina reversed the decision. The following excerpt is the decision by the Superior Court. The appeal, which is not included here, promotes reconciliation and denies Ruthey Hansley the opportunity to divorce.

Ruthey Ann Hansley vs. *Samuel G. Hansley.*

On the trial of issues directed by the Court, upon a petition for a divorce,
     the mere confession of the husband, and he was guilty of the adultery charged, is not admissible evidence.
A divorce *a vinculo matrimonii* will not be granted, unless it is alleged and
     shewn that the husband or wife lived in adultery, after the separation had taken place.

Appeal from the Superior Court of Law of New Hanover County, at the Spring Term 1848, his Honor Judge CALDWELL presiding.

This is a suit instituted by Ruth A. Hansley against her husband Samuel G. Hansley, for a divorce *a vinculo matrimonii,* and for alimony. The parties were married in 1836 and lived together until August 1844; when the wife left her husband and went to reside with her brother in the same neighborhood and has lived there ever since.

The petition was filed on the 25th day of March 1845. It states, that the "petitioner lived for many years the wife of the said Samuel, enjoying much happiness, and fondly hoped to do so for many years yet to come, as she cheerfully fulfilled all the duties of an affectionate wife, until the conduct of her husband became so intolerable that it could no longer be endured: that, without any cause known to her, her husband took to drink, and while in that state, would commit so many outrages against the modesty and decency of the petitioner, that she refrains from repeating them: that the influence of his intoxication would last sometimes for a month; all of which time the conduct of said Samuel G. towards the petitioner would be intolerable; and the petitioner was often cruelly beaten by him, and his whole course of conduct towards her would be so entirely different from what she might have reasonably anticipated, that he rendered her life burdensome and too intolerable to be borne, from a habit so well calculated to destroy the reason, the affections and all the social relations of life, and to which the petitioner must attribute this brutal conduct of her said husband: that for weeks the said Samuel G. would absent himself from the petitioner during the whole night, although during the day time residing on the same farm, while so absenting himself; that it has come to the knowledge of the petitioner, that her husband did habitually, while so absenting himself from the petitioner, bed and cohabit with a negro woman named Lucy, belonging to him: that for some time previous to this fact coming to her knowledge with that degree of certainty, upon which she could rely, her suspicions were aroused, that such must be the fact; but that, not being able to prove the charge, and not being satisfied to abandon her husband until the proof could be clearly satisfactory to her own mind, the petitioner tried to endure, as long as it was reasonable for any wife to endure, the conduct of her husband; and that, during all the said time, her husband not only abandoned her bed entirely, and bedded with the said negro Lucy, but he deprived the petitioner of the control of all those domestic duties and privileges connected with the house, which belong to a wife, and placed the said Lucy in the full possession and enjoyment of those privileges and duties, and insulted the petitioner by openly and repeatedly ordering her to give place to the said negro, and saying that the petitioner was an incumbrance, and encouraged the said Lucy to treat her also: that, when the petitioner would no longer endure these things, and became entirely satisfied of the cause of such treatment, and of the truth of her previous suspicions, the petitioner abandoned her said husband: that, besides all this, her said husband, not satisfied with the treatment as above set forth, would go from home and take with him the keys of the house, and deprive the petitioner of food for two or three days at a time, and of every comfort, to which, as a wife, she was entitled: that often he would, at night, compel the petitioner to sleep in bed with said negro Lucy, when he would treat the said Lucy as his wife, he occupying the same bed with the petitioner and the negro Lucy: that from the cruel and severe treatment of her husband towards the petitioner, she was afraid to resist or to decline so occupying the same bed with her husband and the said negro woman: that, when it was not agreeable to her husband to permit the petitioner to occupy the house, he would often lock her out of doors and there compel her to remain, during the whole night, unprotected and exposed to all the trials incident to such a situation: that she, at length, abandoned the residence of her husband in August 1844, and has made her home with one of her brothers ever since: and that, since her knowledge of the adulterous conduct of her said husband wit the said negro Lucy, the petitioner has not admitted him to conjugal embraces, and is resolved never again so to do."

The petition then sets out the husband's estate, with a view to alimony, and it prays for a divorce from the bonds of matrimony and for a suitable provision.

The answer admits, that, at one period the defendant was intemperate and in the habit of intoxication; but it states, that, for several years before his wife left him, he had been perfectly sober. The defendant also admits that he chastised his wife once: but he denies that he ever did so but at that time, or that that was a violent or severe beating: and he says, that he immediately regretted having done so, and acknowledged that he was wrong and made the most humble apologies to her therefor, which he thought reconciled her: but that on the same night she abandoned his house. The answer then denies all the other allegations of the libel specially.

Upon issues submitted to a jury, it was found, that the parties had been inhabitants of this State for three years immediately before the filing of the petition: that the defendant, by habits of adultery with his slave Lucy, by degrading his wife, the petitioner, by beating her, by insulting her, and by abandoning her bed for that of the slave Lucy, rendered the petitioner's life burthensome, and her condition intolerable, so as to compel her to leave his house, and seek an asylum elsewhere: that the defendant did separate himself from the petitioner and live in adultery with the salve Lucy: and that was known to the petitioner for six months previous to filing the petition: that the petitioner always conducted herself properly as a wife and a chaste woman: and that the petitioner had not admitted the defendant conjugal embraces since her knowledge of his adulterous intercourse with the said slave Lucy.

Upon the trial, in order to prove that the defendant was living in adultery with his own slave named Lucy, the plaintiff offered evidence, that the defendant had a female slave, named Lucy, and that she had a child; and also of acts of familiarity on the part of the defendant with the said Lucy, and that she acted as a sort of manager of his house: and furthermore, that, in conversations respecting this suit, the defendant said, that he would spend every thing he had in defending it, except the said Lucy and his child; and that, in a conversation between a brother of the petitioner and the defendant about a reconciliation between the parties, the former said to the latter, if he would sell Lucy he did not know what the petitioner might do as to living with him again, and that the defendant replied thereto, that he would part with all the property he had before he would with the said Lucy and his child, and that the petitioner might stay where she was. Objection was made to the admissibility of the defendant's declarations, but, as it was not suggested, that those declarations were made by collusion, the Court allowed them to go to the jury. There was a decree for a divorce *a vinculo matrimonii,* and for the costs against the defendant: and an enquiry was directed as to the settlement it would be proper to make on the petitioner; from all which the husband was allowed an appeal.

DOCUMENT 14:
Lithograph, Practical Illustration of the Fugitive Slave Law, 1851.

Courtesy Library of Congress, LC-USZ62–28755.

This satirical illustration focuses on the conflict between Northern abolitionists and supporters of the Fugitive Slave Law, notably Secretary of State Daniel Webster. In this illustration, the abolitionist William Lloyd Garrison points a gun at a slave catcher who is riding Webster. Edward Williams Clay is believed to be the artist, and the print was likely produced in Boston, a city that was widely opposed to the Fugitive Slave Act.

PRACTICAL ILLUSTRATION OF THE FUGITIVE SLAVE LAW.

Document 14

DOCUMENT 15:
Fugitive Slave Act, 1850.

The Fugitive Slave Law was part of the larger "Compromise of 1850" between pro- and antislavery forces on the eve of the Civil War. In exchange for allowing California to be admitted to the Union as a free state and ending slavery in Washington, D.C., Congress passed this law to help protect Southern slave owners' property. It was received negatively in the free states and frequently ignored and sometimes violently resisted.

Be it enacted by the Senate and House of Representatives of the United States of America in Congress assembled, That the persons who have been, or may hereafter be, appointed commissioners, in virtue of any act of Congress, by the Circuit Courts of the United States, and Who, in consequence of such appointment, are authorized to exercise the powers that any justice of the peace, or other magistrate of any of the United States, may exercise in respect to offenders for any crime or offense against the United States, by arresting, imprisoning, or bailing the same under and by the virtue of the thirty-third section of the act of the twenty-fourth of September seventeen hundred and eighty-nine, entitled "An Act to establish the judicial courts of the United States" shall be, and are hereby, authorized and required to exercise and discharge all the powers and duties conferred by this act.

SEC. 2. And be it further enacted, That the Superior Court of each organized Territory of the United States shall have the same power to appoint commissioners to take acknowledgments of bail and affidavits, and to take depositions of witnesses in civil causes, which is now possessed by the Circuit Court of the United States; and all commissioners who shall hereafter be appointed for such purposes by the Superior Court of any organized Territory of the United States, shall possess all the powers, and exercise all the duties, conferred by law upon the commissioners appointed by the Circuit Courts of the United States for similar purposes, and shall moreover exercise and discharge all the powers and duties conferred by this act.

SEC. 3. And be it further enacted, That the Circuit Courts of the United States shall from time to time enlarge the number of the commissioners, with a view to afford reasonable facilities to reclaim fugitives from labor, and to the prompt discharge of the duties imposed by this act.

SEC. 4. And be it further enacted, That the commissioners above named shall have concurrent jurisdiction with the judges of the Circuit and District Courts of the United States, in their respective circuits and districts within the several States, and the judges of the Superior Courts of the Territories, severally and collectively, in term-time and vacation; shall grant certificates to such claimants, upon satisfactory proof being made, with authority to make and remove such fugitives from service or labor, under the restrictions herein contained, to the State or Territory from which such persons may have escaped or fled.

SEC. 5. And be it further enacted, That it shall be the duty of all marshals and deputy marshals to obey and execute all warrants and precepts issued under the provisions of this act, when to them directed; and should any marshal or deputy marshal refuse to receive such warrant, or other process, when tendered, or to use all proper means diligently to execute the same, he shall, on conviction thereof, be fined in the sum of one thousand dollars, to the use of such claimant, on the motion of such claimant, by the Circuit or District Court for the district of such marshal; and after arrest of such fugitive, by such marshal or his deputy, or whilst at any time in his custody under the provisions of this act, should such fugitive escape, whether with or without the assent of such marshal or his deputy, such marshal shall be liable, on his official bond, to be prosecuted for the benefit of such claimant, for the full value of the service or labor of said fugitive in the State, Territory, or District whence he escaped: and the better to enable the said commissioners, when thus appointed, to execute their duties faithfully and efficiently, in conformity with the requirements of the Constitution of the United States and of this act, they are hereby authorized and empowered, within their counties respectively, to appoint, in writing under their hands, any one or more suitable persons, from time to time, to execute all such warrants and other process as may be issued by them in the lawful performance of their respective duties; with authority to such commissioners, or the persons to be appointed by them, to execute process as aforesaid, to summon and call to their aid the bystanders, or posse comitatus of the proper county, when necessary to ensure a faithful observance of the clause of the Constitution referred to, in conformity with the provisions of this act; and all good citizens are

hereby commanded to aid and assist in the prompt and efficient execution
of this law, whenever their services may be required, as aforesaid, for that
purpose; and said warrants shall run, and be executed by said officers, any
where in the State within which they are issued.

SEC. 6. And be it further enacted, That when a person held to service
or labor in any State or Territory of the United States, has heretofore or
shall hereafter escape into another State or Territory of the United
States, the person or persons to whom such service labor may be due,
or his, her, or their agent or attorney, duly authorized, by power of attorney, in writing, acknowledged and certified under the seal of some legal
officer or court of the State or Territory in which the same may be executed, may pursue and reclaim such fugitive person, either by procuring
a warrant from some one of the courts, judges, or commissioners aforesaid, of the proper circuit, district, or county, for the apprehension of
such fugitive from service or labor, or by seizing and arresting such fugitive, where the same can be done without process, and by taking, or
causing such person to be taken, forthwith before such court, judge, or
commissioner, whose duty it shall be to hear and determine the case of
such claimant in a summary manner; and upon satisfactory proof being
made, by deposition or affidavit, in writing, to be taken and certified by
such court, judge, or commissioner, or by other satisfactory testimony,
duly taken and certified by some court, magistrate, justice of the peace,
or other legal officer authorized to administer an oath and take depositions under the laws of the State or Territory from which such person
owing service or labor may have escaped, with a certificate of such mag-
istracy or other authority, as aforesaid, with the seal of the proper court
or officer thereto attached, which seal shall be sufficient to establish the
competency of the proof, and with proof, also by affidavit, of the identity of the person whose service or labor is claimed to be due as aforesaid, that the person so arrested does in fact owe service or labor to the
person or persons claiming him or her, in the State or Territory from
which such fugitive may have escaped as aforesaid, and that said person
escaped, to make out and deliver to such claimant, his or her agent or
attorney, a certificate setting forth the substantial facts as to the service
or labor due from such fugitive to the claimant, and of his or her escape
from the State or Territory in which he or she was arrested, with author-

ity to such claimant, or his or her agent or attorney, to use such reasonable force and restraint as may be necessary, under the circumstances of the case, to take and remove such fugitive person back to the State or Territory whence he or she may have escaped as aforesaid. In no trial or hearing under this act shall the testimony of such alleged fugitive be admitted in evidence; and the certificates in this and the first [fourth] section mentioned, shall be conclusive of the right of the person or persons in whose favor granted, to remove such fugitive to the State or Territory from which he escaped, and shall prevent all molestation of such person or persons by any process issued by any court, judge, magistrate, or other person whomsoever.

SEC. 7. And be it further enacted, That any person who shall knowingly and willingly obstruct, hinder, or prevent such claimant, his agent or attorney, or any person or persons lawfully assisting him, her, or them, from arresting such a fugitive from service or labor, either with or without process as aforesaid, or shall rescue, or attempt to rescue, such fugitive from service or labor, from the custody of such claimant, his or her agent or attorney, or other person or persons lawfully assisting as aforesaid, when so arrested, pursuant to the authority herein given and declared; or shall aid, abet, or assist such person so owing service or labor as aforesaid, directly or indirectly, to escape from such claimant, his agent or attorney, or other person or persons legally authorized as aforesaid; or shall harbor or conceal such fugitive, so as to prevent the discovery and arrest of such person, after notice or knowledge of the fact that such person was a fugitive from service or labor as aforesaid, shall, for either of said offences, be subject to a fine not exceeding one thousand dollars, and imprisonment not exceeding six months, by indictment and conviction before the District Court of the United States for the district in which such offence may have been committed, or before the proper court of criminal jurisdiction, if committed within any one of the organized Territories of the United States; and shall moreover forfeit and pay, by way of civil damages to the party injured by such illegal conduct, the sum of one thousand dollars for each fugitive so lost as aforesaid, to be recovered by action of debt, in any of the District or Territorial Courts aforesaid, within whose jurisdiction the said offence may have been committed.

SEC. 8. And be it further enacted, That the marshals, their deputies, and the clerks of the said District and Territorial Courts, shall be paid, for their services, the like fees as may be allowed for similar services in other cases; and where such services are rendered exclusively in the arrest, custody, and delivery of the fugitive to the claimant, his or her agent or attorney, or where such supposed fugitive may be discharged out of custody for the want of sufficient proof as aforesaid, then such fees are to be paid in whole by such claimant, his or her agent or attorney; and in all cases where the proceedings are before a commissioner, he shall be entitled to a fee of ten dollars in full for his services in each case, upon the delivery of the said certificate to the claimant, his agent or attorney; or a fee of five dollars in cases where the proof shall not, in the opinion of such commissioner, warrant such certificate and delivery, inclusive of all services incident to such arrest and examination, to be paid, in either case, by the claimant, his or her agent or attorney. The person or persons authorized to execute the process to be issued by such commissioner for the arrest and detention of fugitives from service or labor as aforesaid, shall also be entitled to a fee of five dollars each for each person he or they may arrest, and take before any commissioner as aforesaid, at the instance and request of such claimant, with such other fees as may be deemed reasonable by such commissioner for such other additional services as may be necessarily performed by him or them; such as attending at the examination, keeping the fugitive in custody, and providing him with food and lodging during his detention, and until the final determination of such commissioners; and, in general, for performing such other duties as may be required by such claimant, his or her attorney or agent, or commissioner in the premises, such fees to be made up in conformity with the fees usually charged by the officers of the courts of justice within the proper district or county, as near as may be practicable, and paid by such claimants, their agents or attorneys, whether such supposed fugitives from service or labor be ordered to be delivered to such claimant by the final determination of such commissioner or not.

SEC. 9. And be it further enacted, That, upon affidavit made by the claimant of such fugitive, his agent or attorney, after such certificate has been issued, that he has reason to apprehend that such fugitive will be rescued by force from his or their possession before he can be taken beyond the limits of the State in which the arrest is made, it shall be the duty of the officer making the arrest to retain such fugitive in his custody, and to remove him to the State whence he fled, and there to deliver him to said claimant, his agent, or attorney. And to this end, the officer aforesaid is hereby authorized and required to employ so many persons as he may deem necessary to overcome such force, and to retain them in his service so long as circumstances may require. The said officer and his assistants, while so employed, to receive the same compensation, and to be allowed the same expenses, as are now allowed by law for transportation of criminals, to be certified by the judge of the district within which the arrest is made, and paid out of the treasury of the United States.

SEC. 10. And be it further enacted, That when any person held to service or labor in any State or Territory, or in the District of Columbia, shall escape there from, the party to whom such service or labor shall be due, his, her, or their agent or attorney, may apply to any court of record therein, or judge thereof in vacation, and make satisfactory proof to such court, or judge in vacation, of the escape aforesaid, and that the person escaping owed service or labor to such party. Whereupon the court shall cause a record to be made of the matters so proved, and also a general description of the person so escaping, with such convenient certainty as may be; and a transcript of such record, authenticated by the attestation of the clerk and of the seal of the said court, being produced in any other State, Territory, or district in which the person so escaping may be found, and being exhibited to any judge, commissioner, or other officer authorized by the law of the United States to cause persons escaping from service or labor to be delivered up, shall be held and taken to be full and conclusive evidence of the fact of escape, and that the service or labor of the person escaping is due to the party in such record mentioned. And upon the production by the said party of other and further evidence if necessary, either oral or by affidavit, in addition to what is contained in the said record of the identity of the person escaping, he or she shall be delivered up to the claimant. And the said court, commissioner, judge, or other person authorized by this act to grant certificates to claimants or fugitives, shall, upon the production of the record and other evidences aforesaid, grant to such claimant a certificate of his right to take any such person identified and proved to be owing service or labor as aforesaid, which certificate shall authorize such claimant to seize or arrest and transport such person to the State or Territory from which he escaped: Provided, That nothing herein contained shall be construed as requiring the production of a transcript of such record as evidence as aforesaid. But in its absence the claim shall be heard and determined upon other satisfactory proofs, competent in law.

Approved, September 18, 1850

DOCUMENT 16:
Dr. J. H. Van Evrie, *Negroes and Negro Slavery: The First, an Inferior Race—The Latter, Its Normal Condition* (Baltimore, 1853).

This excerpt from his article, "A Scientific Proof of the Biological Inferiority of the Negro," claims that slavery is a natural condition, resulting from the inherent inferiority of blacks, a common supposition of this period. Evrie was a well-respected physician in Washington, D.C., who later published *White Supremacy and Negro Subordination* in 1868.

The human creation like the animal creation, like all the families or forms of being, is composed of a certain number of races, all generally resembling each other, yet each specifically different from all others.

This simple, though mighty truth, hitherto obscured by ignorance and covered by a monstrous falsehood, underlies all our sectional troubles and needs only to be recognized by our people to end them forever.

The Negro is a man, but an inferior *species* of man, who could no more originate from the same parentage with us than could the owl from the eagle, or the shad from the salmon, or the cat from the tiger, and can no more be *forced* by human power, to manifest the qualities or fulfil the duties imposed by the Almighty on the Caucasian man than can either of these forms of life be forced to manifest qualities other than those eternally impressed upon them by the hand of God.

The Caucasian brain measures 92 cubic inches—with the cerebrum, the centre of the intellectual functions, relatively predominating over the cerebellum, the centre of the animal instincts; thus, it is capable of indefinite progression, and transmits the knowledge or experience acquired by one generation to subsequent generations—the record of which is history.

The Negro brain measures form 65 to 75 cubic inches—with the cerebellum, the centre of the animal instincts relatively predominating over the cerebrum, the centre of the intellectual powers; thus, its acquisition of knowledge is limited to a single generation, and incapable of transmitting this to subsequent ones, *it can have no history.* A single glance at eternal and immutable *facts,* which perpetually separate these forms of human existence will be sufficient to cover the whole ground—thus, could the deluded people who propose to improve on the works of the Creator, and *elevate* the Negro to the standard of the white, actually perform an act of omnipotence, and, add 20 or 30 percent to the totality of the Negro brain, they would still be at as great a distance as ever from their final object, while the relations of the anterior and posterior portions of the brain remained as at present. . . .

The notion that so-called slavery is an "evil" is equally a fallacy as that which supposes it a wrong. It arises to a great extent from confounding two very different things—the presence of a Negro population with the *peculiar* institutions necessary for its governance; thus, while it might be desirable in certain localities to get rid of the former, to destroy the latter would be as absurd and indeed as *wrong* as it would be to tear all boys of a certain age from their parents and guardians and to turn them loose upon the world.

Instead of an "evil" in any sense whatever it is an unmixed good to the Negro, to the master, to the North, to civilization, to the world; it is "the best relation between capital and labor ever known," the "corner stone of our Republican edifice," and the presence of the inferior race on this continent, the most fortunate conjuncture that has ever happened in human affairs.

DOCUMENT 17:
Illustration, Dred Scott and His Family, 1857.

Courtesy Library of Congress. LCUSZ62–79305.

This sympathetic illustration of the Dred Scott case was printed in *Frank Leslie's Illustrated Newspaper,* a news and literary magazine founded in 1852. It shows Dred Scott and his wife, Hariett, and their two children, Eliza and Lizzie. The article details their struggle for freedom, which Scott first sued for in 1847.

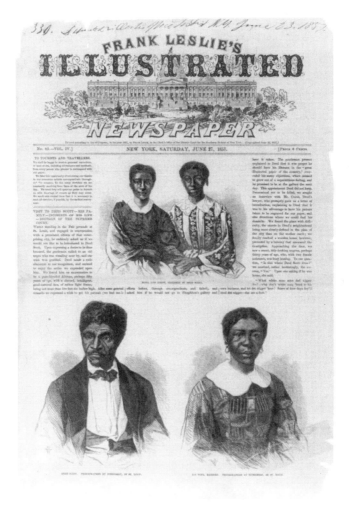

Document 17

DOCUMENT 18:
Dred Scott v. Sardford, 1857.

Dred Scott sued for his freedom in 1847, and ten years later the case was heard by the U.S. Supreme Court. The court ruled that men and women of African ancestry could never become United States citizens and were thus denied the right to sue in federal court. The decision also noted that the federal government could not prohibit slavery in its territories, which left Scott, who lived in the Wisconsin Territory, a slave. As seven of the Supreme Court justices were appointed by pro-slavery presidents, the decision was not surprising. However, no judicial ruling of the nineteenth century provoked a stormier response. It also spurred the nomination of Abraham Lincoln as president by the Republican Party. After the decision, the sons of Scott's former master purchased him and set Scott and his wife free. Sadly, Scott died shortly thereafter. The following is an excerpt from the majority decision (7 to 2) that was delivered to the court by Chief Justice Roger B. Taney.

. . . Can a negro, whose ancestors were imported into this country, and sold as slaves, become a member of the political community formed and brought into existence by the Constitution of the United States, and as such become entitled to all the rights, and privileges, and immunities, guarantied by that instrument to the citizen? One of which rights is the privilege of suing in a court of the United States in the cases specified in the Constitution.

We think they [people of African ancestry] are not [citizens], and that they are not included, and were not intended to be included, under the word "citizens" in the Constitution, and can therefore claim none of the rights and privileges which that instrument provides for and secures to citizens of the United States.

. . . [T]he legislation and histories of the times, and the language used in the Declaration of Independence, show, that neither the class of persons who had been imported as slaves, nor their descendants, whether they had become free or not, were then acknowledged as a part of the people, nor intended to be included in the general words used in that memorable instrument.

For if they were so received, and entitled to the privileges and immunities of citizens, it would exempt them from the operation of the special laws and from the police regulations which they considered to be necessary for their own safety. It would give to persons of the negro race, who were recognized as citizens in any one State of the Union, the right to enter every other State whenever they pleased . . . to go where they pleased at every hour of the day or night without molestation, unless they committed some violation of law for which a white man would be punished; and it would give them the full liberty of speech in public and in private upon all subjects upon which its own citizens might speak; to hold public meetings upon political affairs, and to keep and carry arms wherever they went. And all of this would be done in the face of the subject race of the same color, both free and slaves, and inevitably producing discontent and insubordination among them, and endangering the peace and safety of the State.

The act of Congress, upon which the plaintiff relies, declares that slavery and involuntary servitude, except as a punishment for crime, shall be forever prohibited in all that part of the territory ceded by France, under the name of Louisiana, which lies north of thirty-six degrees thirty minutes north latitude, and not included within the limits of Missouri. And the difficulty which meets us at the threshold of this part of the inquiry is, whether Congress was authorized to pass this law under any of the powers granted to it by the Constitution; for if the authority is not given by that instrument, it is the duty of this court to declare it void and inoperative, and incapable of conferring freedom upon any one who is held as a slave under the laws of any one of the States.

There is certainly no power given by the Constitution to the Federal Government to establish or maintain colonies bordering on the United States or at a distance, to be ruled and governed at its own pleasure; nor to enlarge its territorial limits in any way, except by the admission of new States. That power is plainly given; and if a new State is admitted, it needs no further legislation by Congress, because the Constitution itself defines the relative rights and powers, and duties of the State, and the citizens of the State, and the Federal Government. But no power is given to acquire a Territory to be held and governed permanently in that character.

. . . [I]t may be safely assumed that citizens of the United States who migrate to a Territory belonging to the people of the United States, cannot be ruled as mere colonists, dependent upon the will of the General Government, and to be governed by any laws it may think proper to impose. The principle upon which our Governments rests is the union of States, sovereign and independent within their own limits in . . . their internal and domestic concerns, and bound together as one people by a General Government, possessing certain enumerated and restricted powers, delegated to it by the people of the several States. . . .

But the power of Congress over the person or property of a citizen can never be a mere discretionary power under our Constitution and form of Government. The powers of the Government and the rights and privileges of the citizen are regulated and plainly defined by the Constitution

itself. And when the Territory becomes a part of the United States, the
Federal Government enters into possession in the character impressed
upon it by those who created it. It enters upon it with its powers over the
citizen strictly defined, and limited by the Constitution, from which it
derives its own existence, and by virtue of which alone it continues to exist
and act as a Government and sovereignty. It has no power of any kind
beyond it; and it cannot, when it enters a Territory of the United States,
put off its character, and assume discretionary or despotic powers which
the Constitution has denied to it.

. . . [T]he rights of private property have been guarded with . . . care.
Thus the rights of property are united with the rights of person, and
placed on the same ground by the fifth amendment to the Constitution,
which provides that no person shall be deprived of life, liberty, and property, without due process of law. And an act of Congress which deprives
a citizen of the United States of his liberty or property, merely because
he came himself or brought his property into a particular Territory of
the United States, and who had committed no offence against the laws,
could hardly be dignified with the name of due process of law.

Upon these considerations, it is the opinion of the court that the act
of Congress which prohibited a citizen from holding and owning property
of this kind in the territory of the United States north of the line therein
mentioned, is not warranted by the Constitution, and is therefore void;
and that neither Dred Scott himself, nor any of his family, were made free
by being carried into this territory; even if they had been carried there by
the owner, with the intention of becoming a permanent resident.

But there is another point in the case which depends on State power
and State law. And it is contended, on the part of the plaintiff, that he is
made free by being taken to Rock Island, in the State of Illinois, independ-
ently of his residence in the territory of the United States; and being so
made free, he was not again reduced to a state of slavery by being brought
back to Missouri.

. . . [I]n the case of *Strader et al. v. Graham* . . . the slaves had been
taken from Kentucky to Ohio, with the consent of the owner, and afterwards brought back to Kentucky. And this court held that their status or
condition, as free or slave, depended upon the laws of Kentucky, when
they were brought back into that State, and not of Ohio. . . .

So in this case. As Scott was a slave when taken into the State of
Illinois by his owner, and was there held as such, and brought back in

that character, his status, as free or slave, depended on the laws of Missouri, and not of Illinois.

Upon the whole, therefore, it is the judgment of this court, that it appears by the record before us that the plaintiff in error is not a citizen of Missouri, in the sense in which that word is used in the Constitution; and that the Circuit Court of the United States, for that reason, had no jurisdiction in the case, and could give no judgment in it. Its judgment for the defendant must, consequently, be reversed, and a mandate issued, directing the suit to be dismissed for want of jurisdiction.

DOCUMENT 19:
Petition of Lucy Andrews, 1859 and response.

In this unusual document, sixteen-year-old Andrews who is a "free Person of color" in South Carolina asks to become a slave. She is unable to find work to support herself as a free woman and, in her own words, argues that slaves are "far more happy, and enjoy themselves far better, than she does in her present and isolated condition of freedom." The response, written by citizens of Lancaster District, offers fifty signatures in support for Andrew's petition.

Petition of Lucy Andrews, 1859

To the Honorable, the Senate, and House of Representatives, of the Legislature, of the State of South Carolina. The humble Petition of Lucy Andrews, a free Person of color, would respectful[l]y represent unto your Honorable Body that she is now sixteen years of age (and the Mother of an Infant Child) being a Descendant, of a White Woman, and her Father a Slave; That she is dissatisfied with her present condition being compelled to go about from place to place, to seek employment for her support, and not permitted to stay at any place, more than a week or two at a time, no one caring about employing her. That she expects to raise a family, and will not be able to support them. That she sees, and knows, to her own sorrow, and regret, that Slaves are far more happy, and enjoy themselves far better, than she does, in her present isolated condition of freedom; and are well treated, and cared for by their Masters, whilst she is going about, from place, to place, hunting employment for her support. That she cannot enjoy herself, situated as She now is, and prefers Slavery, to freedom, in her present condition. Your Petitioner therefore prays, that your Honorable Body, would enact a law, authorizing, and permitting her, to go voluntarily, into Slavery, and select her own Master; and your Petitioner will, as in duty bound, ever pray &C—In the presence of—

her
Lucy X Andrews
mark

J. R. Trusdel
H. H. Duncan
Jas. Vinson

We the undersigned Citizens, of Lancaster District, are well acquainted with the Petitioner, Lucy Andrews, and believe the facts stated in the Petition to be true, and we are well satisfied in our own minds, that the Petitioner would be in a far better condition in a State of Slavery, than in a State of freedom—and that her Petition ought to be granted— [Fifty signatures follow.]

The Committee on Coloured Population to whom was referred the Petition of Lucy Andrews praying the passage of an Act making herself and her two children slaves beg leave to

Report

That they have considered the same and recommend [sic] that the prayer of the Petition be granted and for this purpose they recommend the passage of the accompanying Bill

Respectfully Submitted
Randall Croft for The Committee

DOCUMENT 20:
Excerpt, Rebecca Latimer Felton, *Country Life in Georgia in the Days of My Youth* (Atlanta: Index Publishing, 1919), 77–80.

Courtesy Documenting the American South, University Library, The University of North Carolina at Chapel Hill.

Born in Cartersville, Georgia, north of Atlanta, Rebecca married
Dr. William H. Felton and helped guide his political career. In 1922,
she assisted the populist candidate Thomas E. Watson win the U.S.
Senate seat, and upon his death later that year served for one day
in his place at the age of eighty-seven, making her the first woman
appointed to the U.S. Senate in history. Her memoir reveals her
complex history, both rabidly racist and anti-Catholic, but also supportive of women's suffrage and expanded educational opportunities. This excerpt details her perspective on slavery, referencing
"Pitchfork Ben" Tillman, the combative and racist senator from
South Carolina.

SLAVERY IN THE SOUTH

When I received the Congressional Record, bearing date July 16, 1917,
I found Hon. Ben Tillman of South Carolina recorded therein and dis-
cussing slavery in the nation. He uses the following words: "Slavery was
a curse and the Civil War was necessary to destroy it. Nothing else could
have done it because of the profit there was in it. The same struggle for
freedom and the rights of the laboring classes in Europe is going on right
now." He reprinted also a part of an address he made at Arlington
Cemetery some years ago. "I never believed it possible I could do it, but
slowly and by degrees I have come to think it was best that the South
should be defeated and for me to say that is a marvel to myself. Slavery
was a curse that had to be destroyed ere the South and the world could
advance. It was a curse for which the South was no more responsible
than the North. Both sections were responsible and both paid as penance
four long bloody years for their joint sin."

This discussion grew out of the late riots in East St. Louis, where
negroes were mobbed and killed and ordered to vacate. I think this confession of Hon. "Pitchfork Ben" was perhaps good for himself, lately
returned from a sanitarium and not a candidate for reselection to the
U. S. Senate, but it will not be enthusiastically received in the State of South
Carolina by the "fire-eating" politicians of the Palmetto State. It is only
human nature to defend the actions and opinions of our forbears, and
South Carolina's record on "nullification" and "secession" make it
absolutely impossible that Mr. Tillman's confession will be echoed by
those who will hereafter vote in Senator Tillman's successor. But this

belated confession gives me a text for my present writing, and I propose to set down the very words employed by Georgia's political leaders, when Georgia followed South Carolina out of the Federal Union in the winter of 1860–61. I own a complete copy of the proceedings of the Secession convention. There are very few in perfect preservation, and this book hoary with age presents the official statement of Georgia's grievances against those who opposed the institution of domestic slavery.

What Mr. Tillman thinks or what I think is a very small matter, but the results of the Georgia Secession convention are sufficiently important to be carefully remembered by succeeding generations. As a preamble I will also say that Georgia, in General Oglethorpe's time, discounted and discredited African slavery, but the "profit in it" overcame these prudential considerations. After the Yazoo Fraud was finally settled, the inrush of slaveholders to the Carolinas and Georgia became very great, and the new comers brought along their slaves that they owned in Maryland and Virginia under the laws prevailing in the early colonies.

I will not attempt to record in this connection the opposition that northern states early evinced towards the abolition agitators. The "profit in it" and the sale of negroes to Southern owners made business lively. The abolitionists were frequently rotten-egged in the state of Massachusetts in their attempts to secure a hearing. Perhaps I am justified in saying that abolition oratory continued to be distasteful to the public so long as there were slaves to sell to southern planters and until the "profit" in them became nil. These abolition agitators did not become popular until the politicians enlisted the northern churches in this work of reform. When the preachers and the politicians joined forces the row began in dead earnest, and grew apace.

I was a small girl when I became acquainted with Bishop James O. Andrew and I was only nine years old when the Methodist church split over a negro girl owned by Bishop Andrew's second wife in 1844. The story of the split has been so often discussed—abused and defended—that I am not inclined to say any more on that line, at this time. From the hour when the Methodist brethren separated at a General Conference, until Georgia seceded in January, 1861, this slavery question was kept to the front. The preachers of the Southern church quoted the Bible, when they took slavery for a pulpit discourse. Our Southern bishops owned slaves and vigorously defended the institution by voice and pen.

Slave property increased rapidly. Child bearing sometimes began at twelve years and frequent births made a heavy per cent of "profit." According to Hon. Thos. R. R. Cobb, who was killed at the battle of Fredericksburg, "the greatest evidence of wealth in the planter was the number of his slaves. They gave the most remunerative income. It was considered the very best property to give to children and children parted from their slaves with greatest reluctance." These are plain and accurate statements.

Therefore, these Southern planters clung to their slave property and continued to invest money in slave property in Georgia after Sherman marched to the sea. It was nothing out of the common for a planter to pay twelve hundred dollars for a young, stalwart negro man, and a girl who brought easily eight hundred or a thousand dollars on the court house block might be relied upon to bear a healthy slave child once in two years. Anybody who could raise sufficient money invested in slaves.

As I look back on that time of eager slave buying, I am amazed at the lack of foresight in a business way. Every nation that was civilized had abandoned domestic slavery except Brazil, when our people were apparently confident that it was a permanent thing, commanded by the Bible and ordained of God.

There were abuses, many of them. I do not pretend to defend these abuses. There were kind masters and cruel masters. There were violations of the moral law that made mulattoes as common as blackberries. In this one particular slavery doomed itself. When white men were willing to put their own offspring in the kitchen and corn field and allowed them to be sold into bondage as slaves and degraded them as another man's slave, the retribution of wrath was hanging over this country and the South paid penance in four years of bloody war.

The Southern slaveholders looked on the "profit" side so long that they believed what they said. They proved their sincerity by buying and herding together large slave families. The abolitionists were the best hated people ever known within my knowledge and the slave owner had no mercy when the abolitionists in the pulpit discussed him. It was a time of madness, the sort of mad-hysteria that always presages war. There seems to be nothing left but war—when any population in any sort of a nation gets violently angry, civilization falls down and religion forsakes its hold on the consciences of human kind in such times of public madness. "Whom the gods would destroy they first make mad."

CHAPTER 2

Work and Daily Life

Documents in this section examine the diversity of labor in which female slaves engaged, from working on rice plantations in South Carolina to hiring out as seamstresses in Atlanta. It also examines the labor of white women—involved in slavery as owners or members of slave owning families—that was often inextricably linked to the labor of enslaved women.

DOCUMENT 21:

Excerpt, Hunter Dickinson Farish, ed., *Journal and Letters of Philip Vickers Fithian: A Plantation Tutor of the Old Dominion, 1773–1774* (Princeton, NJ: The University Library, 1900).

Philip Fithian was born in New Jersey in 1747 and, while on hiatus during ministerial training, traveled to Virginia as tutor to the children of Robert Carter III, where he kept a diary that was critical of plantation life and slavery. This excerpt explores the sexual relationship between a young white man and an enslaved teenager named Sukey. This is an important, but often overlooked, aspect of slavery that raises complex issues of violence, coercion, and consent. Fithian served as chaplain in the New Jersey state militia, and died October 8, 1776.

Fryday 24 [December 1773]. In the Evening I read the two first Books of *popes* Homer. Dr. Jones supped with us, & is to stay the Night. The conversation at supper was on Nursing Children; I find it is common here for people of Fortune to have their young Children suckled by the

Negroes! Dr Jones told us his first and only Child is now with such a Nurse; & Mrs Carter said that Wenches have suckled several of hers— Mrs Carter has had thirteen Children She told us to night and she has nine now living; of which seven are with me. Guns are fired this Evening in the Neighbourhood [a Christmas season custom], and the Negroes seem to be inspired with a new Life. The Day has been serene and mild, but the Evening is hazy.

Supp'd on Oysters.

Sunday 27 [March 1774]. An odd Jumble of affairs happened this morning— *Bob* drest himself & came into our Room & in his usual way began to be pretty free in telling us *News.* Amongst a vast quantity of other stuff he informed *Ben* & I that he heard Mr *Randolph* has the P . . . we both join'd severely reprimanding for attempting to propagate so unlikely a tale— Why, Brother Ben, said the mischievous Wretch, I heard in this Neighbourhood, yesterday a Report concerning you not much to your— but I will conceal it. This enraged Ben; he at first however persuaded him but soon began to threaten loudly unless he told the whole—why then, Brother, said Bob, it is reported that two Sundays ago you took Sukey (a young likely Negro Girl maid to Mrs Carters youngest Son) into your stable, & there for a considerable time lock'd yourselves together!—Before Bob had done, the Bell rung for Breakfast & we parted.

Monday 5 [September 1774]. There is wonderful *To do,* this morning among the Housekeeper & children, at the great house. They assert that a Man or a Spirit came into the Nursery about one o-Clock this morning—That if it was indeed a Spirit the Cause of his appearance is wholly unknown; but if it was Flesh & blood they are pretty confident that the design was either to rob the House, or commit fornication with *Sukey* (a plump, sleek, likely Negro Girl about sixteen)—That the doors & windows were well secured, but that by some secret manner, unknown to all, the *Thing* opened the Cellar door, went through the Cellar, & up the narrow dark Stairs (Which are used only on necessary occasions, as when the great Stair way is washing or on some such account)—That it left the said Cellar door. . . . That it had previously put a small wedge in the Lock of the Nursery Door, where several of the young Ladies, & the said *Sukey* sleep, so that when they were going to bed they could not Lock nor bolt the

door, but this they all believed was done in mischief by the children, &
went thereupon to bed, without suspicion of harm, with the door open—
that Sukey some time in the Night discovered Something lying on her Side
which she knew to be a Man by his having Breeches—That She was greatly
surprised, & cry'd out suddenly to the others that a Man was among them,
& that the Man *tickled* her, & said *whish, whish*—That on this She left the
Bed & squeased herself in by the side of Miss Sally the Housekeeper, but
that by this time the Whole Room was awake & alarmed—That when
the thing knew there was a discovery it stamped several times on the floor,
shook the Bedstead by the side of which it lay, rattled the Door several
Times & went down stairs walking very heavy for one barefoot. That on
its leaving the Room the Hous[e] Keeper went to Ben Carter's Chamber,
& that he rose & they all went down & found the Doors & windows as I
have mentioned. . . . All this with many other material accidents is circulating through the family to Day; some conclude it was a Ghost because
it would not speak—But, more probably it was one of the warm-blooded,
well fed young Negroes, trying for the company of buxom *Sukey*—The
Colonel however, at Breakfast gave out that if any one be caught in the
House, after the family are at Rest, on any Pretence what ever, that Person
he will cause to be hanged!

Fryday 9 [September 1774]. Ben with great Humour either out of a *Bravado*
or for Revenge gave out in the Family to day that it is the opinion of a
certain *Female,* of considerable Note in the family, that all the male
Children which shall be born in this unlucky year, tho' they may be fair
to the Sight, will be yet unable, from a Debility of Constitution, to do
their Duty, with respect to Women, either married or single—That She
has two reasons for this opinion,

　　1. Because the Air appears to her extremely *barren, weak, &
ungenerative*—2. Because the Peaches & other Fruit, are observed this
year to have in them very few Kernels, at the same time that the Peaches
are sweet & fair—I think that *Ben,* by this strategem, whether it be real
or otherwise, is evil with the invidious Vixen which suspected him of
entering the Nursery to visit black-faced Sukey—

DOCUMENT 22:
Advertisement, *Charleston Courier,* October 11, 1813.

Courtesy Library of Congress.

This advertisement does not detail whether the African American woman to be hired is enslaved or free or whether it was placed by her master or herself, but it does illustrate the various trades in which women became skilled in urban settings. Charleston, South Carolina, played a significant role in the slave trade, as nearly three fourths of all enslaved Africans came through that port city. By 1790, it had a black majority.

To be hired immediately, a very complete Seamstress; a complete worker of muslin, sober, and no runaway; she is a young colored Woman in her eighteenth year; she is very fond of children, can make their clothes and dress them with taste.

DOCUMENT 23:
Letter from Matilda, *Freedom's Journal,* August 10, 1827.

Courtesy Library of Congress.

This letter urges readers to support the liberal education of African American women. The author, who does not give her full name, makes an argument often used by women's rights advocates, as early as the American Revolution—that their education helped educate the next generation. *Freedom's Journal* was the first newspaper owned and operated by African American publishers (Samuel Cornish and John B. Russwurm) in the United States. A weekly published in New York from 1827 to 1829, it was renamed *The Rights of All* in 1829 and published for one more year. The periodical focused on regional, national, and international events and widely criticized slavery and lynching. It was available in eleven states, Europe, Canada, and Haiti.

Messrs. Editors,

Will you allow a female to offer a few remarks upon a subject that you must allow to be all important? I don't know that in any of your papers, you have said sufficient upon the education of females. I hope you are not to be classed with those, who think that our mathematical knowledge should be limited to "fathoming the dish-kettle," and that we have acquired enough of history, if we know that our grandfather's father lived and died. 'Tis true the time has been, when to darn a stocking, and cook a pudding well, was considered the end and aim of a woman's being. But those were days when ignorance blinded men's eyes. The diffusion of knowledge has destroyed those degraded opinions, and men of the present age, allow, that we have minds that are capable and deserving of culture. There are difficulties, and great difficulties in the way of our advancement; but that should only stir us to greater efforts. We possess not the advantages with those of our sex, whose skins are not coloured like our own, but we can improve what little we have, and make our one talent produce two-fold. The influence that we have over the male sex demands, that our minds should be instructed and improved with the principles of education and religion, in order that this influence should be properly directed. Ignorant ourselves, how can we be expected to form the minds of our youth, and conduct them in the paths of knowledge? There is a great responsibility resting somewhere, and it is time for us to be up and doing. I would address myself to all mothers, and say to them, that while it is necessary to possess a knowledge of cookery, and the various mysteries of pudding-making, something more is requisite. It is their bounden duty to store their daughters' minds with useful learning. They should be made to devote their leisure time to reading books, then whence they would derive valuable information, which could never be taken from them. I will no longer trespass on your time and patience. I merely throw out these hints, in order that some more able pen will take up the subject.

MATILDA

DOCUMENT 24:

"Attending a Quadroon Ball" from Karl Bernhard, Duke of Saxe-Wiemar Eisenach, *Travels through North America* (Philadelphia: Carey, Lea and Carey, 1828), 2:61–63.

Courtesy Library of Congress.

New Orleans crafted a complex relationship to slavery and women's roles within it. French Creoles and enslaved and free blacks occasionally entered into common-law marriages. Quadroon balls, first introduced in 1805, became social events in the Crescent City that sanctioned interracial sex. The children from these marriages faced difficult lives, not quite enslaved, yet not completely free.

. . . At the masked balls, each paid a dollar for admission. As I visited it for the second time, I observed, however, many present by free tickets, and I was told that the company was very much mixed. The unmasked ladies belonging to good society, sat in the recesses of the windows, which were higher than the saloon, and furnished with galleries. There were some masks in character, but none worthty of remark. Two quarrels took place, which commenced in the ball-room with blows, and terminated in the vestibule, with pocket-pistols and kicking, without any interruption from the police.

On the same evening, what was called a quadroon ball took place. A quadroon is the child of a mestize mother and a white father, as a mestize is the child of a mulatto mother and a white father. The quadroons are almost entirely white: from their skin no one would detect their origin; nay many of them have as fair a complexion as many of the haughty creole females. Such of them as frequent these balls are free. Formerly they were known by their black hair and eyes, but at present they are completely fair quadroon males and females. Still, however, the strongest prejudice reigns against them on account of their black blood, and the white ladies maintain, or affect to maintain, the most violent aversion towards them. Marriage between the white and coloured population is forbidden by the law of the state. As the quadroons on their part regard the negros and mulattoes with contempt, and will not mix with them, so nothing remains for them but to be the friends, as it is termed, of the white men. The female quadroon looks upon such an engagement as a matrimonial contract, though it goes no farther than a formal contract by which the "friend" engages to pay the father or mother of the quadroon a specified sum. The quadroons both assume the name of their friends, and as I am assured preserve this engagement with as much fidelity as ladies espoused at the altar. Several of these girls have inherited property from their fathers or friends, and possess handsome fortunes. Notwithstanding this, their situation is always very humiliating. They cannot drive through the streets in a carriage, and their "friends" are forced to bring them in their own conveyences after dark to the ball: they dare not sit in the presence of white ladies, and cannot enter their apartments without especial premission. The whites have the privlege to procure these unfortunate creatures a whipping like that inflicted on slaves, upon an accusation, proved by two witnesses. Several of these females have enjoyed the benefits of as careful an education as most of the whites; the conduct themselves ordinarily with more propriety and decorum, and confer more happiness on their "friends," then many of the white ladies to their married lords. Still, the white ladies constantly speak with the greatest contempt, and even with animosity, of these unhappy and oppressed beings. The strongest language of high nobility in the monarchies of the old world, cannot be more haughty, overweening or contemptuous towards their fellow creature, than the expressions of the creole females with regard to the quadroons, in one of the much vaunted states of the free Union. In fact, such comparison strikes the mind of a thinking being very singularly! Many wealthy fathers, on account of the existing prejudices send daughters of this description to France, where these girls with a good education and property, find no difficulty in forming a legitimate establishment. At the quadroon ball, only coloured ladies are admitted, the men of that caste, be it understood, are shut out by the white gentlemen. To take away all semblance of vulgarity, the price of admission is fixed at two dollars, so that only persons of the better class can appear there.

As a stranger in my sitiation should see every thing, to aquire a knowledge of the habits, customs, opinions and prejudices of the people he is among, therefore I accepted the offer of some gentlemen who proposed to carry me to this quadroon ball. And I must avow I found it much more decent than the masked ball. The coloured ladies were under the eyes of their mothers, they were well and gracefully dressed, and conducted themselves with much propriety and modesty. Cotillions and waltzes were danced, and several of the ladies performed elegantly. I did not remain long there that I might not utterly destroy my standing in New Orleans, but returned to the masked ball and took grat care not to disclose to the white ladies where I had been. I could not however refrain from making comparisons, which is no wise redounded to the advantage of the white assembly.

DOCUMENT 25:

Mary Prince, *The History of Mary Prince, a West Indian Slave. Related by Herself. With a Supplement by the Editor. To Which is Added, the Narrative of Asa-Asa, a Captured African* (London: F. Westley and A. H. Davis, 1831).

Courtesy Documenting the American South, University Library, The University of North Carolina at Chapel Hill.

Born in Bermuda in 1788, Mary was a slave there and in Antigua, where she endured harsh working conditions and brutal beatings. She was taken to England in 1828, where she escaped and was technically free, and the Anti-Slavery Society petitioned Parliament on her behalf. Her purpose in writing this memoir is clear on the first page; to make certain that "the good people in England might hear from a slave what a slave had felt and suffered." Her story, a dictated narrative written by the editor Thomas Pringle, is included here to offer a comparison between North American and Caribbean slavery. This excerpt focuses on the affection she had for some of the people who owned her.

. . . I had scarcely reached my twelfth year when my mistress became too poor to keep so many of us at home; and she hired me out to Mrs. Pruden, a lady who lived about five miles off, in the adjoining parish, in a large house near the sea. I cried bitterly at parting with my dear mistress and Miss Betsey, and when I kissed my mother and brothers and sisters, I thought my young heart would break, it pained me so. But there was no help; I was forced to go. Good Mrs. Williams comforted me by saying that

I should still be near the home I was about to quit, and might come over and see her and my kindred whenever I could obtain leave of absence from Mrs. Pruden. A few hours after this I was taken to a strange house, and found myself among strange people. This separation seemed a sore trial to me then; but oh! 'twas light, light to the trials I have since endured!— 'twas nothing—nothing to be mentioned with them; but I was a child then, and it was according to my strength.

I knew that Mrs. Williams could no longer maintain me; that she was fain to part with me for my food and clothing; and I tried to submit myself to the change. My new mistress was a passionate woman; but yet she did not treat me very unkindly. I do not remember her striking me but once, and that was for going to see Mrs. Williams when I heard she was sick, and staying longer than she had given me leave to do. All my employment at this time was nursing a sweet baby, little Master Daniel; and I grew so fond of my nursling that it was my greatest delight to walk out with him by the sea-shore, accompanied by his brother and sister, Miss Fanny and Master James.—Dear Miss Fanny! She was a sweet, kind young lady, and so fond of me that she wished me to learn all that she knew herself; and her method of teaching me was as follows:—Directly she had said her lessons to her grandmamma, she used to come running to me, and make me repeat them one by one after her; and in a few months I was able not only to say my letters but to spell many small words. But this happy state was not to last long. Those days were too pleasant to last. My heart always softens when I think of them.

At this time Mrs. Williams died. I was told suddenly of her death, and my grief was so great that, forgetting I had the baby in my arms, I ran away directly to my poor mistress's house; but reached it only in time to see the corpse carried out. Oh, that was a day of sorrow,—a heavy day! All the slaves cried. My mother cried and lamented her sore; and I (foolish creature!) vainly entreated them to bring my dear mistress back to life. I knew nothing rightly about death then, and it seemed a hard thing to bear. When I thought about my mistress I felt as if the world was all gone wrong; and for many days and weeks I could think of nothing else. I returned to Mrs. Pruden's; but my sorrow was too great to be comforted, for my own dear mistress was always in my mind. Whether in the house or abroad, my thoughts were always talking to me about her.

I staid at Mrs. Pruden's about three months after this; I was then sent back to Mr. Williams to be sold. Oh, that was a sad sad time! I recollect the day well. Mrs. Pruden came to me and said, "Mary, you will have to go home directly; your master is going to be married, and he means to sell you and two of your sisters to raise money for the wedding." Hearing this I burst out a crying,—though I was then far from being sensible of the full weight of my misfortune, or of the misery that waited for me. Besides, I did not like to leave Mrs. Pruden, and the dear baby, who had grown very fond of me. For some time I could scarcely believe that Mrs. Pruden was in earnest, till I received orders for my immediate return.— Dear Miss Fanny! how she cried at parting with me, whilst I kissed and hugged the baby, thinking I should never see him again. I left Mrs. Pruden's, and walked home with a heart full of sorrow. The idea of being sold away from my mother and Miss Betsey was so frightful, that I dared not trust myself to think about it. We had been bought of Mr. Myners, as I have mentioned, by Miss Betsey's grandfather, and given to her, so that we were by right *her* property, and I never thought we should be separated or sold away from her.

When I reached the house, I went in directly to Miss Betsey. I found her in great distress; and she cried out as soon as she saw me, "Oh, Mary! my father is going to sell you all to raise money to marry that wicked woman. You are *my* slaves, and he has no right to sell you; but it is all to please her." She then told me that my mother was living with her father's sister at a house close by, and I went there to see her. It was a sorrowful meeting; and we lamented with a great and sore crying our unfortunate situation. "Here comes one of my poor picaninnies!" she said, the moment I came in, "one of the poor slave-brood who are to be sold to-morrow."

Oh dear! I cannot bear to think of that day,—it is too much.—It recalls the great grief that filled my heart, and the woeful thoughts that passed to and fro through my mind, whilst listening to the pitiful words of my poor mother, weeping for the loss of her children. I wish I could find words to tell you all I then felt and suffered. The great God above alone knows the thoughts of the poor slave's heart, and the bitter pains which follow such separations as these. All that we love taken away from us—Oh, it is sad, sad! and sore to be borne!—I got no sleep that night for thinking of the morrow; and dear Miss Betsey was scarcely less distressed. She could not bear to part with her old playmates, and she cried sore and would not be pacified.

The black morning at length came; it came too soon for my poor mother and us. Whilst she was putting on us the new osnaburgs in which we were to be sold, she said, in a sorrowful voice, (I shall never forget it!) "See, I am *shrouding* my poor children; what a task for a mother!"—She then called Miss Betsey to take leave of us. "I am going to carry my little chickens to market," (these were her very words.) "take your last look of them: may be you will see them no more." "Oh, my poor slaves! my own slaves!" said dear Miss Betsey, "you belong to me: and it grieves my heart to part with you."—Miss Betsey kissed us all, and, when she left us, my mother called the rest of the slaves to bid us good bye. One of them, a woman named Moll, came with her infant in her arms. "Ay!" said my mother, seeing her turn away and look at her child with the tears in her eyes, "your turn will come next." The slaves could say nothing to comfort us; they could only weep and lament with us. When I left my dear little brothers and the house in which I had been brought up, I thought my heart would burst.

Our mother, weeping as she went, called me away with the children Hannah and Dinah, and we took the road that led to Hamble Town, which we reached about four o'clock in the afternoon. We followed my mother to the market-place, where she placed us in a row against a large house, with our backs to the wall and our arms folded across our breasts. I, as the eldest, stood first, Hannah next to me, then Dinah; and our mother stood beside, crying over us. My heart throbbed with grief and terror so violently, that I pressed my hands quite tightly across my breast, but I could not keep it still, and it continued to leap as though it would burst out of my body. But who cared for that? Did one of the many bystanders, who were looking at us so carelessly, think of the pain that wrung the hearts of the negro woman and her young ones? No, no! They were not all bad, I dare say, but slavery hardens white people's hearts towards the blacks; and many of them were not slow to make their remarks upon us aloud, without regard to our grief—though their light words fell like cayenne on the fresh wounds of our hearts. Oh those white people have small hearts who can only feel for themselves.

At length the vendue master, who was to offer us for sale like sheep or cattle, arrived, and asked my mother which was the eldest. She said nothing, but pointed to me. He took me by the hand, and led me out into the middle of the street, and, turning me slowly round, exposed me to the view of those who attended the vendue. I was soon surrounded by strange men, who examined and handled me in the same manner that a butcher would a calf or a lamb he was about to purchase, and who talked about my shape and size in like words—as if I could no more understand their meaning than the dumb beasts. I was then put up to sale. The bidding commenced at a few pounds, and gradually rose to fifty-seven,* when I was knocked down to the highest bidder; and the people who stood by said that I had fetched a great sum for so young a slave.

I then saw my sisters led forth, and sold to different owners: so that we had not the sad satisfaction of being partners in bondage. When the sale was over, my mother hugged and kissed us, and mourned over us, begging of us to keep up a good heart, and do our duty to our new masters. It was a sad parting; one went one way, one another, and our poor mammy went home with nothing.*

DOCUMENT 26:

Excerpt, [Rebecca Warren Brown?], *Memoir of Mrs. Chloe Spear, a Native of Africa, Who was Enslaved in Childhood, and Died in Boston, January 3, 1815 . . . Aged 65 years. By a Lady of Boston* (Boston: James Loring, 1832), 9–13.

Courtesy Documenting the American South, University Library, The University of North Carolina at Chapel Hill.

Chloe Spear was a young teenager when she and her family were captured in Africa and enslaved in the North, which is the topic of this excerpt. After slavery was outlawed in Massachusetts, she and her husband operated a boardinghouse in Boston. The author of the memoir is unknown, though scholars note that it could be either Rebecca Warren Brown or Mary Webb.

CHAPTER I.

The time and manner of her Capture—Arrival in America—
Separation from those who were taken with her—She is sold,
and brought to Boston—Recollection of her native country—
Desire to learn to read—Partial success in the undertaking,
and subsequent grievous disappointment.

About seventy years ago, on the coast of Afriac, the subject of the following memoir, in company with four neighbouring children, herself the youngest, according, to the statements from her own lips to the writer, resorted to the shore for amusement, either by bathing in the cooling stream, or other playful sports to which they were accustomed, with the full expectation of returning to their several homes, as usual, after such seasons of childish diversion.

While engaged in these innocent and healthful recreations, they were suddenly surprised by the appearance of several persons, who had secreted themselves behind the bushes: they knew not what to imagine they were, having never seen a white man; from whose frightful presence they attempted to shrink away, but from whose cruel grasp they found it impossible to escape. Not withstanding the piteous cries and tears of these poor defenceless children, they were arrested by cruel hands, put in to a boat, and carried to the dismal Slave Ship, which lay off a few miles in the river, the horrid receptacle of a living cargo, stolen from its rightful soil, by barbarous hunters of human prey for the purposes of traffic. Terror and amazement, as may be supposed, took full possession of their minds. Every thing around them was as novel as it was dreadful. A ship, they had never before seen; the language of these strange intruders was perfectly unintelligible to them and their intentions they were unable to comprehend: and no tender *mother,* no avenging *father* near, to know or to alleviate their wretchedness. Ah! little did these hapless children realize, when they quitted their native huts and frolicked, away to the woody beach, that they had left, for the last time, the places of their birth, and the fond embraces of their parents and brothers and sisters—that the last parting kiss of maternal affection had rested on their lips, and that they were about to participate *once for all,* in those much-loved plays which had hitherto been undisturbed and joyous. Little! nay, not at all did they realize, that their hostile invaders lay there in ambush, "like the lion that is greedy of his prey," with ferocious intent forever to deprive them of all their domestic felicities, as dear to them as to the rosy children of America. But, alas! such was the fact. We can better conceive than express the feelings of their parents and friends when night came on, and the looked for children returned not. Silence— silence has ensued, from that to the present hour. From their injured children, they heard *no more.* The bitter wailings of a bereft mother, the deep anxiety of an afflicted father, the tender lamentations and suffused eyes of brothers and sisters, were utterly disregarded by those inhuman wretches, who had plundered them of what they held so dear.

DOCUMENT 27:
Woodcut, White woman whipping a slave girl, 1834.

Courtesy, Library of Congress, LC-USZ62–30825.

Physical violence was common in slavery, and white women sometimes played a critical role in punishing both male and female slaves. Whipping was particularly brutal. One former slave explained that this kind of violence was one reason why enslaved men and women attempted to live on different plantations. Moses Grandy argued: "No colored man wishes to live at the house where his wife lives, for he has to endure the continual misery of seeing her flogged and abused without daring to say a word in her defence." This illustration was published in Middleton, Connecticut.

DOCUMENT 28:
Letter to Miss Virginia Campbell from Lethe Jackson, April 18, 1838. Hannah Valentine and Lethe Jackson, Slave Letters in the Campbell Family Papers.

Courtesy Rare Book, Manuscript, and Special Collections Library, Duke University.

Hannah Valentine and Lethe Jackson were house slaves at Montcalm in Abingdon, Virginia, owned by David and Mary Campbell, who taught them to read and write. When Campbell served as governor of the state, Hannah and Lethe remained to care for the home. Their letters reveal a great deal about daily life for slaves as well as their relationship with whites. In this letter, Lethe Jackson writes her mistress and focuses on issues related to growing old and her belief in God.

Ladies Whipping Girls.   Page 109.

Document 27

Montcalm April 18th 1838

My dear and much respected Miss Virginia

I was much pleased at receiving your letter and was very highly flattered to think that you in the gay metropolis so much admired and caressed should still condescend to remember old Aunt Lethe on the retired hill of Montcalm and be assured my sweet young mistress that old Aunt Lethe still remembers you with feelings of the utmost respect and esteem—And my Mistress too I am glad to hear she is getting better and that she has not forgotten lowly *me*—I hope she will still live to be a blessing to all of us—

Everything is going on finely and prosper in my hands—The flowers in the garden are putting out and it begins to look like a little paradise and the Calves and the Chickens and the children are all fine and lively—just waiting your return to complete their happiness—I am sorry that Masters cow has so little manners as to eat Onions—in the City of Richmond too—well what a disgrace! I wish you to tell her that our Mountain Cows are better trained than that—and that if she will come up here we will learn her to be more genteel and not spoil the Governers milk—Tell My Master I think all the world of him and long once more to see his dignified steps up our hill—Tell Mistress I hope I shall soon hear of her recovery and that we long for the time when she will be again here to give her directions and have every thing as it ought to be and as she wants it—We have all done the best we could since she went away but still there is nothing like having a person of sense to dictate—and then if we are obedient every thing goes on smoothly and happy—I try Miss Virginia to be contented at all times and am determined not to let anything make me unhappy, we are taught to resemble our Maker and He is always happy, therefore it is our duty to be happy too—knowing that his divine Providence is over all our changes and that the very hairs of our head are numbered—I feel very happy and my mind if continually aspiring to that heavenly place where all our sorrows will terminate—You say in your letter "that we have a very good lot if we will improve it" I think so too and when we know that our good Lord is Divine Love & Wisdom in its utmost perfection and that, *that* Love & Wisdom is continually exerted for our welfare how grateful, how active, and how obedient, ought we to be and how confident, in all his mercies—Miss Virginia I feel extremely happy when I think what a good Lord & Savior we have and I feel determined to serve him to the best of my knowledge. You say that "the spring is a bright season and that the hours flit so lightly away we scarcely notice them" And so it is with the spring time of Life—When one is young the days and weeks pass rapidly by and we are surprised when we find them gone. and how pat we are in the buoyant days of youth to forget   that the Autumn of age, and Winter of death, is coming. But I am persuaded it is not so with you—I know that you *do* reflect on *these things*—I know there are a few young persons who are pious as you are and I have a well grounded hope that in all the relations of life you will sustain yourself like a Christian I wish I could hear some of the good preaching you speak of but the good being is every where. he is at Montcalm in the still breath of evening as much as in the "City full" yes he is evry where present—and even condescends to visit old Aunt Lethe's heart—Oh Miss Virginia my heart is so full I know not what to say—Tell Eliza I thank her for her letter and she must take part of this to herself as I think one letter is enough for such a poor creature as me for I can tell you all I am setting very frail—to what I used to be. Oh Master! Oh Mistress! Oh Miss Virginia I want to see you al and Michael and Eliza and Richard and David and all; my heart is large enough to hold you all—I pray that the Lord will take care of you and keep you from all evil—I hope I have not made to free in any thing I said—I wanted to write as if I was talking to you—With every sentiment of veneration and esteem I remain You faithful servant

Lethe Jackson

I have a keg of butter which will be too old to use when you come—if you are willing Mr Lathem thinks it best to sell it—please to write by the next mail and say if you wish us to sell it or not. I think it would be best to sell it—L J

[Addressed in center of page:]
Miss Virginia T. T. Campbell
Richmond Virginia

DOCUMENT 29:
Excerpt, Frances Ann Kemble, *Journal of a Residence on a Georgian Plantation in 1838–1839* (New York: Harper & Brothers, 1863).

Courtesy Library of Congress.

Frances Kemble was a British actress who marred a Georgia planter. They eventually divorced, and she published the journal in England in May 1863, hoping to persuade readers to support President Abraham Lincoln's Emancipation Proclamation. A version of this memoir was published two months later in the United States. In this excerpt, Kemble supports the plea from the enslaved women on the plantation to have four weeks of rest after giving birth.

. . . In considering the whole condition of the people on this plantation, it appears to me that the principal hardships fall to the lot of the women. . . .

[These were one day's petitioners:] Fanny has had six children; all dead but one. She came to beg to have her work in the field lightened. Nanny has had three children; two of them are dead. . . . Leah has had six children; three are dead. Sophy . . . came to beg for some old linen. She is suffering fearfully; she had had ten children; five of them are dead. Sally. . . . has had two miscarriages and three children born, one of whom is dead. She came complaining of incessant pain and weakness in her back. Sarah . . . She had had four miscarriages, had brought seven children into the world, five of whom were dead, and was again with child. She complained of dreadful pains in the back, and an internal tumor which swells with the exertion of working in the fields; probably, I think, she is ruptured. . . . Molly . . . Hers was the best account I have yet received; she had had nine children, and six of them were still alive. . . . There was hardly one of these women . . . who might not have been a candidate for a bed in a hospital, and they had come to me after working all day in the fields. . . .

[One woman has a particularly dismal story to tell.] She had had sixteen children, fourteen of whom were dead; she had had four miscarriages: one had been caused with falling down with a very heavy burden on her head, and one from having her arms strained up to be lashed. . . . She said their hands were first tied together . . . and they were then drawn up to a tree or post . . . and then their clothes rolled round their waist, and a man with a cowhide stands and stripes them. I give you the woman's words. She did not speak of this as of anything strange, unusual, or especially horrid and abominable; and when I said: "Did they do that to you when you were with child?" she simply replied: "Yes, missis." And to all this I listen—I an Englishwoman, the wife of the man who owns these wretches, and I cannot say: "That thing should not be done again . . ." I remained choking with indignation and grief long after they had all left me to my most bitter thoughts.

DOCUMENT 30:
Excerpts, Sir Charles Lyell, *A Second Visit to the United States of North America*, 2 vols. (New York: Harper & Bros., 1849), 1:271–73.

Courtesy Library of Congress.

In this excerpt, Sir Charles Lyell, an English geologist who made
four trips to the United States, examines the issues of interracial
sex by putting it in comparative perspective with working women
in England. He shows little sympathy for the enslaved women who
suffer under this system. Lyell's observations were made at a plantation in Glynn County, Georgia.

. . . Some of the planters in Glynn County have of late permitted the
distribution of Bibles among their slaves, and it was curious to remark
that they who were unable to read were as anxious to possess them as
those who could. Besides Christianizing the blacks, the clergy of all sects
are doing them incalculable service, by preaching continually to both
races that the matrimonial tie should be held sacred, without repsect to
color. To the dominant race one of the most serious evils of slavery is
its tendency to blight domestic happiness; and the anxiety of parents for
their sons, and a constant fear of their licentious intercourse with slaves,
is painfully great. We know but too much of this evil in free countries,
wherever there is a vast distance between the rich and poor, giving a
power to wealth which insures a frighful amount of prostitution. Here
it is accompianied with a publicity which is keenly felt as a disgrace by
the more refined of the white women. The female slave is proud of her
connection with a white man, and thinks it an honor to have a mulatto
child, hoping that it will be better provided for than a black child. Yet
the mixed offspring is not very numerous. The mulattoes alone represent
nearly all the illicit intercourse between the white man and negro of the
living generation. I am told that they do not constitute more than two
and a half per cent. of the whole population. If the statisitcs of the ille-
gitimate children of the whites born here could be compared with those
in Great Britain, it might lead to conclusions by no means favorable to
the free country. Here there is no possibility of concealment, the color
of the child stamps upon him the mark of bastardy, and transmits it to
great-grand-children born in wedlock; whereas if, in Europe, there was
some mark or indelible stain betraying all the delinquencies and frailties,
not only of parents, but of ancestors for three or four generations back,
what unexpected disclosures should we not witness!

There are scarcely any instances of mulattoes born of a black father
and a white mother. The colored women who become the mistresses of

the white men are neither rendered miserable nor degraded, as are the white women who are seduced in Europe, and who are usually abandoned in the end, and left to be the victims of want and disease. In the northern states of America there is so little profligacy of this kind, that their philanthropists may perhaps be usefully occupied in considering how the mischief may be alleviated south of the Potomac; but in Great Britain there is so much need of reform at home, that the whole thoughts and energies of the rich ought to be concentrated in such schemes of improvement as may enable us to set an example of a higher moral standard to the slaveowning aristocracy of the Union.

On one of the estates in this part of Georgia, there is a mulatto mother who has nine children by a full black, and the difference of shade between them and herself is scarcely perceptible. If the white blood usually predominates in this way in the second generation, as I am told is the case, amalgamation would proceed very rapidly, if marriages between the races were once legalized; for we see in England that black men can persuade very respectful white women to marry them, when all idea of the illegality and degredation of such unions is foreign to their thoughts.

Among the obstacles which the Christian missionaries encounter here when they teach the virtue of chastity, I must not omit to mention the loose code of morality which the Africans have inherited from their parents. My wife made the acquaintance of a lady in Alabama, who had brought up with great care a colored girl, who grew up modest and well-behaved, till at length she became the mother of a mulatto child. The mistress reproached her very severely for her misconduct, and the girl at first took the rebuke much to heart; but having gone home one day to visit her mother, a native African, she returned, saying, that her parent had assured her she had done nothing wrong, and had no reason to feel ashamed. When we are estimating, therefore, the amount of progress made by the American negroes since they left their native country, we ought always to bear in mind from how low a condition, both morally and intellectually considered, they have had to mount up.

DOCUMENT 31:
Receipt, 1849.

Courtesy Library of Congress LC-USZ62–125134.

The caption accompanying this photograph reads: "Ownership of children that might be born in the future is defined in this photograph of a receipt for six hundred dollars paid by Judge S. Williams of Eufala, December 20, 1849 for Jane, a Negro woman aged 18 and her son Henry, one year old. This paper is owned by Judge Williams' grandson, Richard Malcolm McEachern, Eufala, Ala." This receipt illustrates how slavery disrupted families.

Document 31

DOCUMENT 32:
Excerpt, Emily P. Burke, *Reminiscences of Georgia* (n.p.:
James M. Fitch, 1850), 111–13, 115–17, 120–24.

Courtesy Library of Congress.

Emily Burke, a schoolteacher from the North who moved to
Georgia in the 1830s, provides a sensitive account of the status of
slave women and their daily work in the fields as well as in the
kitchen.

Letter XVI.

Agreeable to my promise in my last letter, I will now go on with my
description of the buildings belonging to a Southern Plantation.

In the first place there was a paling enclosing all the buildings belonging to the family and all the house servants. In the centre of this enclosure
stood the principal house, the same I have already in a previous letter
described. In this the father of the family and all the females lodged. The
next house of importance was the one occupied by the steward of the
plantation, and where all the white boys belonging to the family had their
sleeping apartments. The next after this was a school house consisting of
two rooms, one for a study, the other the master's dormitory. Then the
cook, the washer-woman, and the milkmaid, had each their several houses,
the children's nurses always sleeping upon the floor of their mistress'
apartment. Then again there was the kitchen, the store-house, corn-house,
stable, hen-coop, the hound's kennel, the shed for the corn mill, all these
were separate little buildings within the same enclosure. Even the milk-
safe stood out under one great tree, while under another the old washer
woman had all her apparatus arranged; even her kettle was there suspended from a cross-pole. Then to increase the beauty of the scene, the
whole establishment was completely shaded by ornamental trees, which
grew at convenient distances among the buildings, and towering far above
them all. The huts of the field servants formed another little cluster of
dwellings at considerable distance from the master's residence, yet not
beyond the sight of his watchful and jealous eye. These latter huts were
arranged with a good deal of order and here each slave had his small patch
of ground adjacent to his own dwelling, which he assiduously cultivated

after completing his daily task. I have known the poor creatures, notwith-standing "tired nature" longed for repose, to spend the greater part of a moonlight night on these grounds. In this way they often raise consider-able crops of corn, tobacco, and potatoes, besides various kinds of garden vegetables. Their object in doing this is to have something with which to purchase tea, coffee, sugar, flour, and all such articles of diet as are not provided by their masters, also such clothing as is necessary to make them appear decent in church, but which they can not have unless they procure it by extra efforts.

From this you see the slave is obliged to work the greater part of his time, for one coarse torn garment a year, and hardly food enough of the coarsest kind to support nature, without the least luxury that can be named. Neither can they after the fatigues of the day repose their toil worn bodies upon a comfortable bed unless they have earned it by laboring many a long, weary hour after even the beasts and the birds have retired to rest. It is a common rule to furnish every slave with one coarse blanket each, and these they always carry with them, so when night overtakes them, let it be where it may, they are not obliged to hasten home to go to rest. Poor creatures! all the home they have is where their blanket is, and this is all the slave pretends to call his own besides his dog. . . .

I found after I had been in the country a few months that the season when I first went there was the most gloomy part of the year. At this time there were but few slaves upon the plantation, many of them being let out to boatmen who at this season of the year are busily engaged in the transportation of goods and produce of all kinds up and down the rivers. The sweet singing birds, too, were all gone to their winter quar-ters still farther South, but when they had all returned, and the trees began to assume the freshness of summer, and the plants to put forth their blossoms, I found it was far from being a dull and gloomy place. During the greater part of the winter season the negro women are busy in picking, ginning, and packing the cotton for market.

In packing the cotton, the sack is suspended from strong spikes, and while one colored person stands in it to tread the cotton down, others throw it into the sack. I have often wondered how the cotton could be sold so cheap when it required so much labor to get it ready for the mar-ket, and certainly it could not be if all their help was hired at the rate of northern labor.

The last of January the servants began to return to the plantation to repair the fences and make ready for planting and sowing. The fences are built of poles arranged in a zigzag manner, so that the ends of one tier of poles rests upon the ends of another. In this work the women are engaged as well as the men. They all go into the woods and each woman as well as man cuts down her own pine sapling, and brings it upon her head. It certainly was a most revolting sight to see the female form scarcely covered with one old miserable garment, with no covering for the head, arms, or neck, nor shoes to protect her feet from briers and thorns, employed in conveying trees upon her head from one place to another to build fences. When I beheld such scenes I felt culpable in living in ease and enjoying the luxuries of life, while so many of my own sex were obliged to drag out such miserable existences merely to procure these luxuries enjoyed by their masters. When the fences were completed, they proceeded to prepare the ground for planting. This is done by throwing the earth up in ridges from one side of the field to the other. This work is usually executed by hand labor, the soil is so light, though sometimes to facilitate the process a light plough, drawn by a mule, is used. The ground there is reckoned by tasks instead of acres. If a person is asked the extent of a certain piece of land, he is told it contains so many tasks, accordingly so many tasks are assigned for a day's work. In hoeing corn, three tasks are considered a good day's work for a man, two for a woman and one and a half for a boy or girl fourteen or fifteen years old. . . .

I have, in a previous letter, spoken of the slaves grinding corn; this is done by hand-mills constructed of two round flat stones, the upper one being turned around upon the other by hand labor. One person can, though, with a good deal of difficulty, grind corn alone, but it is customary for two at a time to engage in this labor. This mill is probably the same in kind with those used in Oriental countries, respecting which our Savior said, "Two women shall be grinding at the mill, the one shall be taken the other left." The time for the grinding of corn was always in the evening after the daily tasks were done.

About seven o'clock, in the summer season, the colored people would generally begin to assemble in the yard belonging to the planter's residence. Here they would kindle little bonfires, not only to ward off the musquitoes, but because they are considered essential in the hot season to purify the air when it is filled with feverish vapors that arise from decayed vegetable matter. Then while two of their number are engaged at the mill, all the rest join in a dance around the burning fagots. In this manner were spent the greater part of the summer evenings, and it was usual for the white members of the family to assemble on the piazza to witness their pastimes, and sometimes at the request of a favorite slave, I have seen the white children engage in the waltz, or take their places in the quadrille. Slaves from adjoining plantations would often come to spend an evening with their acquaintances, and bring their corn with them to grind. The grinding generally commences at about six in the evening, and the hoarse sound of the mill seldom ceased much before midnight.

Though the slaves in general, notwithstanding all their hard toils and sorrows, had their happy hours, there was one old woman on the plantation who always looked cast down and sorrowful, and never appeared to take any interest in what caused the joy and mirth of those around her. She was one of Afric's own home born daughters, and she had never forgotten those who nursed her in infancy, nor the playmates of her childhood's happy hours. She told me she was stolen one day while gathering shells into a little basket on the sea shore, when she was about ten years old, and crowded into a vessel with a good many of her own race, who had also been stolen and sold for slaves, and from that hour when she left her mother's hut to go out to play she had never seen one of her own kindred, though she had always hoped that Providence might bring some of them in her way; "but now," she replied, "I begin to despair of ever seeing those faces which are still fresh in my memory, for now I am an old woman, and shall soon get through all my troubles and sorrows, and I only think now of meeting them in heaven." When requested she would favor us with a song in her own language, learned before she was stolen, but when she came to sing of her native hills and sparkling streams, the tears would trickle down her sunburnt and furrowed cheeks, and my heart could but ache for this poor creature, stolen away in the innocence of youth, from parents, kindred, home, and country, which were as dear to her as mine to me.

Of all the house-servants, I thought the task of the cook was the most laborious. Though she did no other housework she was obliged to do everything belonging to the kitchen department, and that, too, with none of those conveniences without which a Northern woman would think it was impossible for her to prepare a meal of victuals. After having cooked the supper and washed the dishes she goes about making preparations for the next morning's meal. In the first place she goes into the woods to gather sticks and dried limbs of trees, which she ties in bundles and brings to the kitchen on her head, with which to kindle the morning fire; to get as much fuel as she will want to use in preparing the breakfast she is often obliged to go into the woods several times. When this is done she has all the corn to grind for the hommony and bread, then the evening's preparations are completed. In the morning she is obliged to rise very early, for she has every article of food that comes on to the table to cook, nothing ever being prepared till the hour it is needed. When she has gone through with all the duties connected with the morning's repast, then she goes about the dinner, bringing fuel from the woods, grinding corn, etc. In this manner the cook spends her days, for in whatever department the slaves are educated, they are generally obliged to wear out their lives.

DOCUMENT 33:
Notice of Sale, February 14, 1851.

Courtesy Mississippi Department of Archives and History, Z/1405.001/S: Slavery Collection, Accretion.

This notice, posted by the Probate Court of Hinds County, Mississippi, announces a public auction of "five Negroes," including Nelly and Frances on the occasion of the death of their owner Hez. Walker. This document shows how tenuous the concept of family is under slavery and how quickly it could be dismantled.

Exhibit B
Notice

By virtue of an Order of the Probate Court of Hinds County Miss made at the Feby Term 1851. Thereof the Undersigned Executor of the last Will and Testament of Hez Walker deceased will on Saturday the 15th day of March Next between the Hours prescribed by laws In the Town of Brownsville in said County Expose for Sale at Public Auction to the Highest bidders On a Credit of Nine Months from the day of Sale Five Negroes, Viz., Nelly, a woman Frances a girl Thomas and Peter Boys and Jim an Infant child the purchasers of said Negroes will be required to give bonds with good and ample Security for the purchase Money

Allen W. Walker, Esq

Of Hez. Walker, Deceased

February 14th 1851

DOCUMENT 34:

Title Page, Aunt Phillis's Cabin, 1852.

Courtesy Library of Congress, LC-USZ62–107753.

This title page from *Aunt Phillis's Cabin; or Southern Life as It Is,* by Mrs. Mary H. Eastman depicts the substandard conditions in which slaves were often expected to live. It is not, however, consistent with the theme of the novel, which was largely seen as a response to Harriet Beecher Stowe's *Uncle Tom's Cabin* (1852). Eastman focused on the happiness of slaves in the South, in stark contrast to free blacks who were living in the North. Eastman was born in 1818 in Virginia; she wrote this novel when living in Washington, D.C.

DOCUMENT 35:

Letter, Stancil Barwick to Colonel John B. Lamar, July 15, 1855, from Ulrich B. Phillips, ed., *Plantation and Frontier* (Cleveland: A. H. Clark, 1909), 1:312-13.

Courtesy Library of Congress.

This letter from overseer in Americus, Georgia, denies cruelty "as regards the wimin loosing children." Lamar was an absentee owner and had no firsthand knowledge of how enslaved women reacted when their children were taken from them.

Georgia Overseer to a Georgia Absentee Planter [near Americus, Georgia, 15 July 1855]

Dear Sir:

AUNT PHILLIS'S CABIN;

OR,

SOUTHERN LIFE AS IT IS.

BY MRS. MARY H. EASTMAN.

Philadelphia:
Lippincott, Grambo & Co.
1852.

I received your letter yesterday ev'ng was vary sorry to hear that you had heard that I was treating your Negroes so cruely. Now sir I do say to you in truth that the report is false thear is no truth in it. No man nor set of men has ever seen me mistreat one of the Negroes on the Place. Now as regards the wimin loosing children, treaty lost one it is true. I never heard of her being in that way until she lost it. She was at the house all the time, I never made her do any work at all. She said to me in the last month that she did not know she was in that way her self untill she lost the child. As regards Louisine she was in the field it is true but she was workt as she please. I never said a word to her in any way at all untill she com to me in the field and said she was sick. I told her to go home. She started an on the way she miscarried. She was about five months gone. This is the true statement of case. Now sir a pon my word an honnor I have tride to carry out your wishes as near as I possibly could doo. Ever since I have been on the place I have not been to three neighbours houses since I have been hear I com hear to attend to my Businiss I have done it faithfully the reports that have been sent must have been carried from this Place by Negroes the fact is I have made the Negro men work an made them go strait that is what is the matter an is the reason why that my Place is talk of the settlement. I have found among the Negro men two or three hard cases an I have had to deal rite Ruff but not cruly at all. Among them Abram has been as triflin as any man on the place. Now sir what I have wrote you is truth an it cant be disputed by no man on earth.

N.B. As regards my crop of corn I think I will make a plenty to doo the Place next year my cotton is injured by the wate weather an lice the weed is large enough but nothing on it. I will [be] done working it a week or ten days from this time.

DOCUMENT 36:
Wood Engraving, Slave Auction at Richmond, Virginia, 1856.

Courtesy Library of Congress, LC-USZ62–15398.

The British author William Makepeace Thackeray toured the United States in the 1850s and recounted his experience visiting a slave auction in Richmond: "After these sales we saw the usual exodus of negro slaves, marched under escort of their new owners across the town to the railway station, where they took places, and 'went South.' They held scanty bundles of clothing, their only possession."

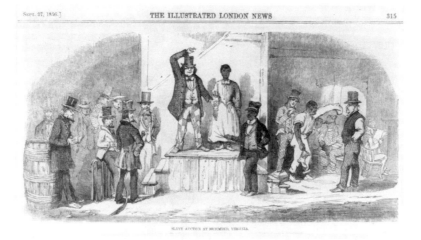

SEPT. 27, 1856.]   THE ILLUSTRATED LONDON NEWS   315

SLAVE AUCTION AT RICHMOND, VIRGINIA.

Document 36

DOCUMENT 37:
Martha Griffith Browne, *Autobiography of a Female Slave* (New York: Redfield, 1857), 212–20.

Courtesy Documenting the American South, University Library, The University of North Carolina at Chapel Hill.

This novel is written by a white woman, a former slaveowner turned abolitionist in Kentucky. Browne regularly wrote for the *National Anti-Slavery Standard* and published another novel entitled *Madge Vertner*, also about slavery. This excerpt focuses on the murder of a female slave.

. . . There is no telling how long the garrulous Nace would have continued the narration of what he saw in L—, had he not been suddenly interrupted by the entrance of Miss Tildy, inquiring for Amy.

Instantly all of them assumed that cheerful, smiling, sycophantic manner, which is well known to all who have ever looked in at the kitchen of a slaveholder. Amy stood out from the group to answer Miss Tildy's summons. I shall never forget the expression of subdued misery that was limned upon her face.

"Come in the house and account for the loss of those forks," said Miss Tildy, in the most peremptory manner.

Amy made no reply to this; but followed the lady into the house. There she was court-marshalled, and of course, found guilty of a high misdemeanor.

"Wal," said Mr. Peterkin, "we'll see if the 'post' can't draw from you whar you've put 'em. Come with me."

With a face the picture of despair, she followed.

Upon reaching the post, she was fastened to it by the wrist and ankle fetters; and Mr. Peterkin, foaming with rage, dipped his cowhide in the strongest brine that could be made, and drawing it up with a flourish, let it descend upon her uncovered back with a lacerating stroke. Heavens! what a shriek she gave! Another blow, another and a deeper stripe, and cry after cry came from the hapless victim!

"Whar is the forks?" thundered Mr. Peterkin, "tell me, or I'll have the worth out of yer cussed hide."

"Indeed, indeed, Masser, I doesn't know."

"You are a liar," and another and a severer blow.

"Whar is they?"

"I give 'em to Miss Jane, Masser, indeed I did."

"Take that, you liar," and again he struck her, and thus he continued until he had to stop from exhaustion. There she stood, partially naked, bleeding at every wound, yet none of us dared go near and offer her even a glass of cold water.

"Has she told where they are?" asked Miss Tildy.

"No, she says she give 'em to you."

"Well, she tells an infamous lie; and I hope you will beat her until pain forces her to acknowledge what she has done with them."

"Oh, I'll git it out of her yet, and by blood, too."

"Yes, father, Amy needs a good whipping," said Miss Jane, for she has been sulky ever since we took her in the house. Two or three times I've thought of asking you to have her taken to the post."

"Yes, I've noticed that she's give herself a good many ars. It does me rale good to take 'em out of her."

"Yes, father, you are a real negro-breaker. They don't dare behave badly where you are."

This, Mr. Peterkin regarded as high praise; for, whenever he related the good qualities of a favorite friend, he invariably mentioned that he was a "tight master;" so he smiled at his daughter's compliment.

"Yes," said Miss Tildy, "whenever father approaches, the darkies should set up the tune, 'See the conquering hero comes.' "

"Good, first-rate, Tildy," replied Miss Jane.

"'Till is a wit."

"Yes, you are both high-larn't gals, a-head of yer pappy."

"Oh, father, please don't speak in that way."

"It was the fashion when I was edicated."

"Just listen," they both exclaimed.

"Jake," called out Mr. Peterkin, whose wrath was getting excited by the criticisms of his daughters, "go and bring Amy here."

In a few moments Jake returned, accompanied by Amy. The blood was oozing through the body and sleeves of the frock that she had hastily thrown on.

"Whar's the spoons?" thundered out Mr. Peterkin.

"I give 'em to Miss Tildy."

"You are a liar," said Miss Tildy, as she dashed up to her, and struck her a severe blow on the temple with a heated poker. Amy dared not parry the blow; but, as she received it, she fell fainting to the floor. Mr. Peterkin ordered Jake to take her out of their presence.

She was taken to the cabin and left lying on the floor. When I went in to see her, a horrid spectacle met my view! There she lay stretched upon the floor, blood oozing from her whole body. I washed it off nicely and greased her wounds, as poor Aunt Polly had once done for me; but these attentions had to be rendered in a very secret manner. It would have been called treason, and punished as such, if I had been discovered.

I had scarcely got her cleansed, and her wounds dressed, before she was sent for again.

"Now," said Miss Tildy, "if you will tell me what you did with the forks, I will excuse you; but, if you dare to say you don't know, I'll beat you to death with this," and she held up a bunch of briery switches, that she had tied together. Now only imagine briars digging and scraping that already lacerated flesh, and you will not blame the equivocation to which the poor wretch was driven.

"Where are they?" asked Miss Jane, and her face was frightful as the Medusa's.

"I hid 'em under a barrel out in the back yard."

"Well, go and get them."

"Stay," said Miss Jane, "I'll go with you, and see if they are there." Accordingly she went off with her, but they were not there.

"Now, where are they, *liar?*" she asked.

"Oh, Miss Jane, I put 'em here; but I 'spect somebody's done stole 'em."

"No, you never put them there," said Miss Tildy. "Now tell me where they are, or I'll give you this with a vengeance," and she shook the briers.

"I put 'em in my box in the cabin."

And thither they went to look for them. Not finding them there, the tortured girl then named some other place, but with as little success they looked elsewhere.

"Now," said Miss Tildy, "I have done all that the most humane or just could demand; and I find that nothing but a touch of this can get the truth from you, so come with me." She took her to the "lock-up," and secured the door within. Such screams as issued thence, I pray heaven may never hear again. It seemed as if a fury's strength endowed Miss Tildy's arm.

When she came out she was pale from fatigue.

"I've beaten that girl till I've no strength in me, and she has less life in her; yet she will not say what she did with the forks."

"I'll go in and see if I can't get it out of her," said Miss Jane.

"Wait awhile, Jane, maybe she will, after a little reflection, agree to tell the truth about it.

"Never," said Miss Jane, "a nigger will never tell the truth till it is beat out of her." So saying she took the key from Miss Tildy, and bade me follow her. I had rather she had told me to hang myself.

When she unlocked the door, I dared not look in. My eyes were riveted to the ground until I heard Miss Jane say:

"Get up, you hussy."

There, lying on the ground, more like a heap of clotted gore than a human being, I beheld the miserable Amy.

"Why don't she get up?" inquired Miss Jane. I did not reply. Taking the cowhide, she gave her a severe lick, and the wretch cried out, "Oh, Lord!"

"The Lord won't hear a liar," said Miss Jane.

"Oh , what will 'come of me?"

"*Death,* if you don't confess what you did with the forks."

"Oh God, hab mercy! Miss Jane, please don't beat me any more. My poor back is so sore. It aches and smarts dreadful," and she lifted up her face, which was one mass of raw flesh; and wiping or trying to wipe the blood away from her eyes with a piece of her sleeve that had been cut from her body, she besought Miss Jane to have mercy on her; but the spirit of her father was too strongly inherited for Jane Peterkin to know aught of human pity.

"Where are the forks?"

"Oh, law! oh, law!" Amy cried out, "I swar I doesn't know anything 'bout 'em."

Such blows as followed I have not the heart to describe; for they descended upon flesh already horribly mangled.

The poor girl looked up to me, crying out:

"Oh, Ann, beg for me."

"Miss Jane," I ventured to say; but the tigress turned and struck me such a blow across the face, that I was blinded for full five minutes.

"There, take that! you impudent hussy. Do you dare to ask me not to punish a thief?"

I made no reply, but withdrew from her presence to cleanse my face from the blood that was flowing from the wound.

As I bathed my face and bound it up, I wondered if acts such as these had ever been reported to those clergymen, who so stoutly maintain that slavery is just, right, *and almost* available unto salvation. I cannot think that they do understand it in all its direful wrongs. They look upon the institution, doubtless, as one of domestic servitude, where a strong attachment exists between the slave and his owner; but, alas! all that is generally fabulous, worse than fictitious. I can fearlessly assert that I never knew a single case, where this sort of feeling was cherished. The very nature of slavery precludes the existence of such a feeling. Read the legal definition of it as contained in the statute books of Kentucky and Virginia, and how, I ask you, can there be, on the slave's part, a love for his owner? Oh, no, that is the strangest resort, the fag-end of argument; that most transparent fiction. Love, indeed! The slave-master love his slave! Did Cain love Abel? Did Herod love those innocents, whom, by a bloody edict, he consigned to death? In the same category of lovers will we place the slave-owner.

When Miss Jane had beaten Amy until *she* was satisfied, she came, with a face blazing, like Mars, from the "lock-up."

"Well, she confesses now, that she put the forks under the corner of a log, near the poultry coop."

"Its only another one of her lies," replied Miss Tildy.

"Well, if it is, I'll beat her until she tells the truth, or I'll kill her."

So saying, she started off to examine the spot. I felt that this was but another subterfuge, devised by the poor wretch to gain a few moments' respite.

The examination proved, as I had anticipated, a failure.

"What's to be done?" inquired Miss Tildy.

"Leave her a few moments longer to herself, and then if the truth is not obtained from her, kill her." These words came hissing though her clenched teeth.

"It won't do to kill her," said Miss Tildy.

"I don't care much if I do."

"We would be tried for murder."

"Who would be our accusers? Who the witnesses? You forget that Jones is not here to testify."

"Ah, and so we are safe."

"Oh, I never premeditate anything without, counting the cost."

"But then the loss of property!"

"I'd rather gratify my revenge than have five hundred dollars, which would be her highest market value."

Tell me, honest reader, was not she, at heart, a murderess? Did she not plan and premeditate the deed? Who were her accusers? That God whose first law she had outraged; that same God who asked Cain for his slain brother.

"Now," said Miss Jane, after she had given the poor creature only a few moments relief, "now let me go and see what that wretch has to say about the forks."

"More lies," added Miss Tildy.

"Then her fate is sealed," said the human hyena.

Turning to me, she added, in the most authoritative manner, "Come with me, and mind that you obey me; none of your impertinent tears, or I'll give you this."

And she struck me a lick across the shoulders. I can assure you I felt but little inclination to do anything whereby such a penalty might be incurred. Taking the key of the "lock up" from her pocket, she ordered me to open the door. With a trembling hand I obeyed. Slowly the old, rusty-hinged door swung open, and oh, heavens! what a sight it revealed! There, in the centre of the dismal room, suspended from a spoke, about three feet from the ground, was the body of Amy! Driven by desperation, goaded to frenzy, she had actually hung herself! Oh, God! that fearful sight is burnt in on my brain, with a power that no wave of Lethe can ever wash out! There, covered with clotted blood, bruised and mangled, hung the wretched girl! There, a bleeding, broken monument of the white man's and white woman's cruelty! God of my sires! is there for us no redress? And Miss Jane—what did she do? Why, she screamed, and almost swooned with fright! Ay, too late it was to rend the welkin with her cries of distress. She had done the deed! Upon her head rested the sin of that freshly-shed blood! She was the real murderess. Oh, frightful shall be her nights! Peopled with racks, execution-blocks, and ghastly gallows-poles, shall be her dreams! At the lone hour of midnight, a wan and bloody corse shall glide around her bed-side, and shriek into her trembling ear the horrid word "murderess!" Let me still remain in bondage, call me still by the ignoble title of slave, but leave me the unbought and priceless inheritance of a stainless conscience. I am free of murder before God and man. Still riot in your wealth; still batten on inhumanity, women of the white complexion, but of the black hearts! I envy you not. Still let me rejoice in a darker face, but a snowy, self-approving conscience.

Miss Jane's screams brought Mr. Peterkin, Miss Tildy and the servants to her side. There, in front of the open door of the lock-up, they stood, gazing upon that revolting spectacle! No word was spoken. Each regarded the others in awe. At length, Mr. Peterkin, whose heartlessness was equal to any emergency, spoke to Jake:

"Cut down that body, and bury it instantly."

With this, they all turned away from the tragical spot; but I, though physically weak of nerve, still remained. That poor, bereaved girl had been an object of interest to me; and I could not now leave her distorted and lifeless body. Cold-hearted ones were around her; no friendly eye looked upon her mangled corse, and I shuddered when I saw Jake and Dan rudely handle the body upon which death had set its sacred seal.

DOCUMENT 38:
Photograph, Plantation manual, 1857–1858.

Courtesy Library of Congress, LC-DIG-ppmsca-02942.

This page is from the manual of James Henry Hammond, author of the infamous "Mudsill Speech" to the Senate on March 4, 1858, where he compares slaves and free blacks to the mud-sill of the foundation of a house. This manual provides instructions for breastfeeding infants, as well as work arrangements for the elderly and for pregnant slaves. Hammond (1807–1864) was a politician from South Carolina who was an avid supporter of slavery and state's rights. He served as a congressman, a senator, and a governor from his home state and was the brother-in-law of Wade Hampton II and uncle of Wade Hampton III.

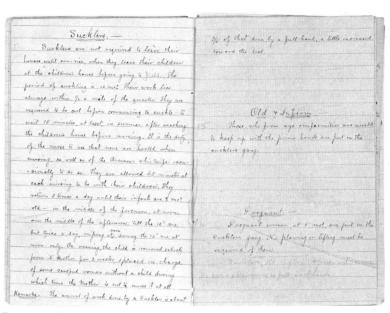

Document 38

DOCUMENT: 39:
Plantation manual, 1857–1858. MS Manual of Rules
[ca. 1840–1850], James Henry Hammond Papers.

Courtesy Library of Congress.

CLOTHING.—

7 Each woman gets in the fall 6 yds. of woolen cloth, 6 yds. of cotton drilling & a needle, skein of thread & ½ doz buttons. In the Spring 6 yds. of cotton shirting & 6 yds. of cotton cloth similar to that for men's pants, needle, thread & buttons.

CHILDREN.—

9 There is a separate building [in] the charge of a trusty nurse, where the children are kept during the day. Weaned children are brought to it at the last horn-blow in the morning—about good day light. The unweaned are brought to it at sun rise, after suckling, & left in cradles in charge of the nurse.

10 Allowance is given out daily to the children, at the rates for each child, of ⅓ of meal & meat that [is] given to work-hands. An abundant supply of vegetables should be always at hand, in a garden cultivated for the especial purpose, to be cooked with their meat. Each child must have daily at laest [least] 1 pint of skimmed milk. Their food should be cooked by the nurse, & consist, for breakfast & supper, of hominy & milk and cold corn bread: their dinner of vegetable soup—& dumplings or bread. Cold bread or potatos should be kept on hand for occasional demands between meals. Their meat may be the same as that given to work hands, except that the only fresh meat allowed them is the beef bones for soup. They should have a little molasses once or twice a week, & well roasted sweet potato every day. Each child is provided with a pan & spoon, placed in charge of a nurse.

11 Each child gets 2 shirts of drilling every fall, & 2 of shirting in the spring, made very long. The girls get 2 frocks, & the boys 2 pr of pants reaching the neck & with sleeves, in the fall, & 1 each in the spring—of lighter woolens in the fall than that given to the work hands.

12 Each child gets a blanket every 3rd year. Children born in the interval

can have a blanket at the time, or the fall following, according to the necessities of the Mother. Mothers are required to put entirely clean clothes on their children twice a week, & it is the duty of the nurse to report any omission to do so.

SUCKLERS.—

13 Sucklers are not required to leave their houses until sun-rise, when they leave their children at the children's house before going to field. The period of suckling in 12 mos. Their work lies always within ½ mile of the quarter. They are required to be cool before commencing to suckle—to wait 15 minutes, at laest, in summer, after reaching the children's house before nursing. It is the duty of the nurse to see that none are heated when nursing, as well as of the Overseer & his wife occasionally to do so. They are allowed 45 minutes at each morning to be with their children. They return 3 times a day until their infants are 8 mos. old—in the middle of the forenoon, at noon, & in the middle of the afternoon: till the 12th mo. but twice a day, missing at noon: during the 12th mo. at noon only. On weaning, the child is removed entirely from its Mother for 2 weeks, & placed in charge of some careful woman without a child, during which time the Mother is not to nurse it at all.
Remarks.—The amount of work done by a Suckler is about ⅔ of that done by a full-hand, a little increased toward the last.

OLD & INFIRM.—

15 Those, who from age & infirmities are unable to keep up with the prime hands, are put in the suckler's gang.

PREGNANT.—

16 Pregnant women, at 5 mos. are put in the suckler's gang. No plowing or lifting must be required of them.

Sucklers, old, infirm, & pregnant, receive the same allowances as full-work hands.

CONFINEMENT.—

17 The regular plantation midwife shall attend all women in confinement. Some other woman learning the art is usually with her during delivery. The confined woman lies up one month, & the midwife remains in constant attendance for 7 days. Each woman on confinement has a bundle given to her containing articles of clothing for the infant, pieces of cloth

& rag, & some extra nourishment, as sugar, coffee, rice & flour for the Mother.

MARRIAGE.—

21 Marriage is to be encouraged as it adds to the comfort, happiness & health of those who enter upon it, besides insuring a greater increase. Permission must always be obtained from the master before marriage, but no marriage will be allowed with negroes not belonging to the master. When sufficient cause can be shewn on either side, a marriage may be annulled, but the offending party must be severely punished. Where both are in wrong both must be punished, & if they insist on separating must have 100 lashes apiece. After such a separation neither can marry again for 3 years. For first marriage a bounty of $5.00 to be invested in household articles, shall be given. If either has been married before, the bounty shall be $3.50. A third marriage shall not be allowed but in extreme cases, & in such cases, or where both have been married before, no bounty will be given.

TOWN.—

Each work-hand is allowed to go to Town once a year (the women always selecting some of the men to go for them) on a Sunday between crop gathering & Christmas. Not more than 10 shall be allowed to go the same day. The head driver may have a cart some Saturday after Christmas that it is convenient for him to go to Town.

This rule is objectionable & must be altered.[1]

REWARDS.—

The head driver receives on Christmas day $5.00 from the master; the plow driver $3.00; the midwife $2.00 & the nurse $1.00 for every actual increase of two on the place; the ditch driver $1.00 & the Stock Minder $1.00. Any of these rewards may be with-held where any negligence or misbehavior has occurred in the various departments, attributable to, or not promptly reported or corrected by the recipients. For every infant 13 months & in sound health, that has been properly attended to the Mother shall receive a muslin or calico frock.

[1]Governor Hammond added this line at some later period that that of the original composition of his manual. (*Editor's note*)

DOCUMENT 40:
Letter, T. D. Jones to Eliza, September 7, 1860.

Courtesy Thomas Butler Papers, Louisiana State University.

In this letter from Maryland, a slave owner writes to the mother of a child, Jenny, who is his property. It shows the attachment between the two, which was not uncommon, but also the master's interest in maximizing his own self-interest.

T. D. Jones to Eliza.

Princess Anne Somerset Co. Md
Septr 7th. 1860.

Eliza.

About two months ago Sandy handed me a letter directed to Mr. Levin Waters from you, requesting me to let you hear from your daughter, Jenny, and expressing hope that I will let her go to live with you. I read your letter to her. She seemed glad to hear from you, & her countenance lightened up with smile at the names of Aunt Liza & Tillie Anne (as she calls you and her sister.) But she says she does not want to go away from her master. She is a sprightly lively active girl: & has enjoyed good health, except that she has suffered for some time from three very severe boils— one on the top of her head, one over her left ear & one on the side of her neck, the last just ruptured. She is very fond of me & is a considerable annoyance to me for I cannot keep her off my heels in the street. & viewing her in the light of a little orphan I cannot spurn her caresses. Sandy & Sally are as well as usual: Charlotte has a severe and dangerous attack of brain fever, but is now able to perform her duties. Her child Sarah is well. As to letting Jennie go to live with you I can hardly make up my mind what to say. I would be reluctant to part with her. She is petted as you used to be. She is a watchful little spy as you used to be. She has a good disposition, is neither cross obstinate nor mischievous: She is very useful for her services in the house, for going on errands, and for nursing: & I should miss her very much. Nevertheless I know how to estimate the claims of a Mother and to appreciate the affection of a Mother for her child. A request has been made of me thro' Mr. Henry Morris to let Jennie go with you, but I have not yet come to a decision.

However I profess to be a christian & have the happy and comforting assurance that I am, by the grace of God, what I profess to be. I am governed by christian principles which impose upon me the obligation of love mercy deal justly and walk humbly. Mercy will open a listening ear to your request. Justice will prompt me to do what is right and humility constrains me to condescend to answer the communication of her who, although formerly my servant, is not, on that account, excluded from the consideration of human sympathy, altho' you make no inquiry after my welfare, were you restrained by indignation or malice because I parted with you? I think you will acknowledge that I was to you a kind & forbearing master & that you were an ungrateful servant, & I think you feel assured that if you had conducted yourself faithfully, no offer would have tempted me to part with you. Your tender & affectionate services to your afflicted former mistress, created in me an attachment for you, that nothing but your ingratitude & faithlessness could have broken. But situated as I was after the death of [my] dear beloved and still lamented wife, the only alternative presented to me was to quit housekeeping or part with you—a painful one. Up to the period of this bad event you were as fine a servant as I ever knew. I wish you well. I am glad you have got a good home & hope you will try to deserve it. Let me advise you as your former Master—as one who takes an interest in your welbeing in this world, and still greater interest for welbeing in the eternal world & above as the one who stood sponsor for your baptism, to repent of your misdeeds—to cease to do evil & learn to do well, to live up to the precepts of the gospel, & by the faith once delivered to the saints, & daily pray to God, thro' Jesus Christ, for his good spirit to help your infirmities & to lead you in the way everlasting. Serve your heavenly Master & present owner faithfully, and be assured that I greatly regret the occasion that resulted in the separation of you from your child. Those to whom you sent your love return their's to you. With unfeigned benevolence & charity

I am

Your former owner

T. D. Jones

DOCUMENT 41:
Wood Engraving, "A Slave Auction at the South" by Theodore R. Davis, 1861.

Courtesy Library of Congress, LC-USZ62–2582.

This illustration shows African American men, women, and children being auctioned off in front of crowd of men. It was published in *Harper's Weekly* in the first year of the Civil War, presumably to generate support for the Union cause.

Document 41

DOCUMENT 42:
Elizabeth Keckley, *Behind the Scenes, or, Thirty years a Slave, and Four Years in the White House* (New York: G. W. Carlton and Company, 1868).

Courtesy Documenting the American South, University Library, The University of North Carolina at Chapel Hill.

Elizabeth Keckley (1818–1907) was born a slave in Virginia and became a dressmaker while living in St. Louis, which helped her purchase her freedom. In 1860, she moved to Washington, D.C., and set up shop to become the dressmaker to many wealthy whites in the city, including First Lady Mary Todd Lincoln. This memoir, somewhat controversial for revealing private information about the first family, was edited by James Redpath, whose involvement in the text is unknown. Keckley's memoir angered Mrs. Lincoln and compromised their relationship. This excerpt focuses on Keckley's introduction to Mrs. Lincoln.

CHAPTER V.
MY INTRODUCTION TO MRS. LINCOLN.

EVER since arriving in Washington I had a great desire to work for the ladies of the White House, and to accomplish this end I was ready to make almost any sacrifice consistent with propriety. Work came in slowly, and I was beginning to feel very much embarrassed, for I did not know how I was to meet the bills staring me in the face. It is true, the bills were small, but then they were formidable to me, who had little or nothing to pay them with. While in this situation I called at the Ringolds, where I met Mrs. Captain Lee. Mrs. L. was in a state bordering on excitement, as the great event of the season, the dinner-party given in honor of the Prince of Wales, was soon to come off, and she must have a dress suitable for the occasion. The silk had been purchased, but a dress-maker had not yet been found. Miss Ringold recommended me, and I received the order to make the dress. When I called on Mrs. Lee the next day, her husband was in the room, and handing me a roll of bank bills, amounting to one hundred dollars, he requested me to purchase the trimmings, and to spare no expense in making a selection. With the money in my pocket I went out in the street, entered the store of Harper & Mitchell, and asked to look at their laces. Mr. Harper waited on me himself, and was polite and kind. When I asked permission to carry the laces to Mrs. Lee, in order to learn whether she could approve my selection or not, he gave a ready assent. When I reminded him that I was a stranger, and that the goods were valuable, he remarked that he was not afraid to trust me—that he believed my face was the index to an honest heart. It was pleasant to be spoken to thus, and I shall never forget the kind words of Mr. Harper. I often recall them, for they are associated with the dawn of a brighter period in my dark life. I purchased the trimmings, and Mr. Harper allowed me a commission of twenty-five dollars on the purchase. The dress was done in time, and it gave complete satisfaction. Mrs. Lee attracted great attention at the dinner-party, and her elegant dress proved a good card for me. I received numerous orders, and was relieved from all pecuniary embarrassments. One of my patrons was Mrs. Gen. McClean, a daughter of Gen. Sumner. One day when I was very busy, Mrs. McC. drove up to my apartments, came in where I was engaged with my needle, and in her emphatic way said:

"Lizzie, I am invited to dine at Willard's on next Sunday, and positively I have not a dress fit to wear on the occasion. I have just purchased material, and you must commence work on it right away."

"But Mrs. McClean," I replied, "I have more work now promised than I can do. It is impossible for me to make a dress for you to wear on Sunday next."

"Pshaw! Nothing is impossible. I must have the dress made by Sunday;" and she spoke with some impatience.

"I am sorry," I began, but she interrupted me.

"Now don't say no again. I tell you that you must make the dress. I have often heard you say that you would like to work for the ladies of the White House. Well, I have it in my power to obtain you this privilege. I know Mrs. Lincoln well, and you shall make a dress for her provided you finish mine in time to wear at dinner on Sunday."

The inducement was the best that could have been offered. I would undertake the dress if I should have to sit up all night—every night, to make my pledge good. I sent out and employed assistants, and, after much worry and trouble, the dress was completed to the satisfaction of Mrs. McClean. It appears that Mrs. Lincoln had upset a cup of coffee on the dress she designed wearing on the evening of the reception after the inauguration of Abraham Lincoln as President of the United States, which rendered it necessary that she should have a new one for the occasion. On asking Mrs. McClean who her dress-maker was, that lady promptly informed her,

"Lizzie Keckley."

"Lizzie Keckley? The name is familiar to me. She used to work for some of my lady friends in St. Louis, and they spoke well of her. Can you recommend her to me?"

"With confidence. Shall I send her to you?"

"If you please. I shall feel under many obligations for your kindness."

The next Sunday Mrs. McClean sent me a message to call at her house at four o'clock P.M., that day. As she did not state why I was to call, I determined to wait till Monday morning. Monday morning came, and nine o'clock found me at Mrs. McC.'s house. The streets of the capital were thronged with people, for this was Inauguration day. A new President, a man of the people from the broad prairies of the West, was to accept the solemn oath of office, was to assume the responsibilities attached to the high position of Chief Magistrate of the United States. Never was such deep interest felt in the inauguration proceedings as was felt to-day; for threats of assassination had been made, and every breeze from the South came heavily laden with the rumors of war. Around Willard's hotel swayed an excited crowd, and it was with the utmost difficulty that I worked my way to the house on the opposite side of the street, occupied by the McCleans. Mrs. McClean was out, but presently an aide on General McClean's staff called, and informed me that I was wanted at Willard's. I crossed the street, and on entering the hotel was met by Mrs. McClean, who greeted me:

"Lizzie, why did you not come yesterday, as I requested? Mrs. Lincoln wanted to see you, but I fear that now you are too late."

"I am sorry, Mrs. McClean. You did not say what you wanted with me yesterday, so I judged that this morning would do as well."

"You should have come yesterday," she insisted. "Go up to Mrs. Lincoln's room"—giving me the number—"she may find use for you yet."

With a nervous step I passed on, and knocked at Mrs. Lincoln's door. A cheery voice bade me come in, and a lady, inclined to stoutness, about forty years of age, stood before me.

"You are Lizzie Keckley, I believe."

I bowed assent.

"The dress-maker that Mrs. McClean recommended?"

"Yes, madam."

"Very well; I have not time to talk to you now, but would like to have you call at the White House, at eight o'clock to-morrow morning, where I shall then be."

I bowed myself out of the room, and returned to my apartments. The day passed slowly, for I could not help but speculate in relation to the appointed interview for the morrow. My long-cherished hope was about to be realized, and I could not rest.

Tuesday morning, at eight o'clock, I crossed the threshold of the White House for the first time. I was shown into a waiting-room, and informed that Mrs. Lincoln was at breakfast. In the waiting-room I found no less than three mantua-makers waiting for an interview with the wife of the new President. It seems that Mrs. Lincoln had told several of her lady friends that she had urgent need for a dress-maker, and that each of these friends had sent her mantua-maker to the White House. Hope fell at once. With so many rivals for the position sought after, I regarded my chances for success as extremely doubtful. I was the last one summoned to Mrs. Lincoln's presence. All the others had a hearing, and were dismissed. I went up-stairs timidly, and entering the room with nervous step, discovered the wife of the President standing by a window, looking out, and engaged in lively conversation with a lady, Mrs. Grimsly, as I afterwards learned. Mrs. L. came forward, and greeted me warmly.

"You have come at last. Mrs. Keckley, who have you worked for in the city?"

"Among others, Mrs. Senator Davis has been one of my best patrons," was my reply.

"Mrs. Davis! So you have worked for her, have you? Of course you gave satisfaction; so far, good. Can you do my work?"

"Yes, Mrs. Lincoln. Will you have much work for me to do?"

"That, Mrs. Keckley, will depend altogether upon your prices. I trust that your terms are reasonable. I cannot afford to be extravagant. We are just from the West, and are poor. If you do not charge too much, I shall be able to give you all my work."

"I do not think there will be any difficulty about charges, Mrs. Lincoln; my terms are reasonable."

"Well, if you will work cheap, you shall have plenty to do. I can't afford to pay big prices, so I frankly tell you so in the beginning."

The terms were satisfactorily arranged, and I measured Mrs. Lincoln, took the dress with me, a bright rose-colored moire-antique, and returned the next day to fit it on her. A number of ladies were in the room, all making preparations for the levee to come off on Friday night. These ladies, I learned, were relatives of Mrs. L.'s,—Mrs. Edwards and Mrs. Kellogg, her own sisters, and Elizabeth Edwards and Julia Baker, her nieces. Mrs.

Lincoln this morning was dressed in a cashmere wrapper, quilted down the front; and she wore a simple head-dress. The other ladies wore morning robes.

I was hard at work on the dress, when I was informed that the levee had been postponed from Friday night till Tuesday night. This, of course, gave me more time to complete my task. Mrs. Lincoln sent for me, and suggested some alteration in style, which was made. She also requested that I make a waist of blue watered silk for Mrs. Grimsly, as work on the dress would not require all my time.

Tuesday evening came, and I had taken the last stitches on the dress. I folded it and carried it to the White House, with the waist for Mrs. Grimsly. When I went up-stairs, I found the ladies in a terrible state of excitement. Mrs. Lincoln was protesting that she could not go down, for the reason that she had nothing to wear.

"Mrs. Keckley, you have disappointed me—deceived me. Why do you bring my dress at this late hour?"

"Because I have just finished it, and I thought I should be in time."

"But you are not in time, Mrs. Keckley; you have bitterly disappointed me. I have no time now to dress, and, what is more, I will not dress, and go down-stairs."

"I am sorry if I have disappointed you, Mrs. Lincoln, for I intended to be in time. Will you let me dress you? I can have you ready in a few minutes."

"No, I won't be dressed. I will stay in my room. Mr. Lincoln can go down with the other ladies."

"But there is plenty of time for you to dress, Mary," joined in Mrs. Grimsly and Mrs. Edwards. "Let Mrs. Keckley assist you, and she will soon have you ready."

Thus urged, she consented. I dressed her hair, and arranged the dress on her. It fitted nicely, and she was pleased. Mr. Lincoln came in, threw himself on the sofa, laughed with Willie and little Tad, and then commenced pulling on his gloves, quoting poetry all the while.

"You seem to be in a poetical mood to-night," said his wife.

"Yes, mother, these are poetical times," was his pleasant reply. "I declare, you look charming in that dress. Mrs. Keckley has met with great success." And then he proceeded to compliment the other ladies.

Mrs. Lincoln looked elegant in her rose-colored moire-antique. She wore a pearl necklace, pearl ear-rings, pearl bracelets, and red roses in her hair. Mrs. Baker was dressed in lemon-colored silk; Mrs. Kellogg in a drab silk, ashes of rose; Mrs. Edwards in a brown and black silk; Miss Edwards in crimson, and Mrs. Grimsly in blue watered silk. Just before starting down-stairs, Mrs. Lincoln's lace handkerchief was the object of search. It had been displaced by Tad, who was mischievous, and hard to restrain. The handkerchief found, all became serene. Mrs. Lincoln took the President's arm, and with smiling face led the train below. I was surprised at her grace and composure. I had heard so much, in current and malicious report, of her low life, of her ignorance and vulgarity, that I expected to see her embarrassed on this occasion. Report, I soon saw, was wrong. No queen, accustomed to the usages of royalty all her life, could have comported herself with more calmness and dignity than did the wife of the President. She was confident and self-possessed, and confidence always gives grace.

This levee was a brilliant one, and the only one of the season. I became the regular modiste of Mrs. Lincoln. I made fifteen or sixteen dresses for her during the spring and early part of the summer, when she left Washington; spending the hot weather at Saratoga, Long Branch, and other places. In the mean time I was employed by Mrs. Senator Douglas, one of the loveliest ladies that I ever met, Mrs. Secretary Wells, Mrs. Secretary Stanton, and others. Mrs. Douglas always dressed in deep mourning, with excellent taste, and several of the leading ladies of Washington society were extremely jealous of her superior attractions.

DOCUMENT 43:
Excerpt, Sarah H. Bradford, *Scenes in the Life of Harriet Tubman* (Auburn: W. J. Moses, Printer, 1869), 117–29.

Courtesy Documenting the American South, University Library, The University of North Carolina at Chapel Hill.

Harriet Tubman (1821–1913) was known as the "Moses of Her People" for her heroic work rescuing nearly two hundred slaves via the Underground Railroad. She escaped slavery in 1849, and she worked as a nurse and cook during the Civil War. This biography begins with the following words from Sarah H. Bradford, a teacher from Auburn, "It is proposed in this little book to give a plain and unvarnished account of some scenes and adventures in the life of a woman who, thought one of earth's lowly ones, and of dark-hued skin, has shown the amount of heroism and character rarely possessed by those of any station in life." This excerpt focuses on the cruelty of white women, and the violence in which they engaged.

ESSAY ON WOMAN-WHIPPING.

THE subject of the preceding memoir appears to have retained all her life a feeling recollection of the effects of the whip in the hands of her youthful mistress. Considering the vigor and frequency of the application, this is not strange. Infinite cuffs and thwacks, more or less, pass into oblivion; but a flogging with a raw-hide is not easily forgotten. A slave's experience of the whip, however, was not confined to his or to *her* early days. A slave race must be controlled by fear and pain: and the discipline, it was naturally thought, could not begin too early. From childhood to old age they were liable to stripes, for any reason or for no reason. If the slave was guilty of no fault, he might be whipped, as appears from the preceding narrative, merely to impress him with a salutary sense of the master's right and disposition to whip.

A Northern man, born and bred under the influences of freedom and the protection of law, and made acquainted with slavery in its old palmy days, can never forget his sensations at his first sight of a slave-whipping. The utmost he has ever seen in the way of corporal punishment has been the switching of some obstreperous child by competent authority; a discipline administered with prudence and moderation; drawing no blood and leaving no scar. He now sees an adult person stripped to the skin, his arms tied at their utmost stretch above his head, or across some object which binds him into a posture the best adapted to feel the full force of each blow. The instrument of suffering is not a birch twig or a ferule, but a twisted raw-hide, or heavy "black snake;" either of them highly effective weapons in the hands of a stout executioner. Our Northern novice stands horror-stricken and paralyzed for a moment; but at the second or third blow, and the piteous scream of *Oh Lord! Massa!* which follows, he digs his fingers into his ears, and rushes to the furthest corner of his tent or dwelling, to escape the scene. Even if he *could* have endured the sight and sound a while longer, he dared not. The horror in his face, and perhaps the irrepressible word or act of interference was too sure to bring upon himself the vengeance due to a "d—d Abolitionist." The little knot of Southern *habitués* look on with critical inspection, squirting tobacco-juice, with their hands in their pockets.

If the subject is a woman, the interest rises higher, and the crowd would be greater. There is a refinement of cruelty in the whipping of a woman which used to stimulate agreeably the dull sensibilities of a Southern mob. A dish of torture had to be peppered very high to please the palates of those epicures in brutality. The helplessness and terror of the victim, the exposure of her person, the opportunity for coarse jests at her expense, all combined to make it a scene of rare enjoyment. How the "chivalric" mind can endure the loss of such gratifications it is difficult to conceive. The Romans were weaned from crucifixions and gladiatorial combats very gradually. The process of ameliorating criminal law and humanizing public sentiment went on for more than two centuries. It was full four hundred years after the epoch of our redemption when the monk Telemachus threw himself between the hired swordsmen, whom a Christian audience was applauding, and laid down his own life to wind up the spectacle. But the bloody morsel has been snatched from the mouths of the "chivalry" at one clutch. No wonder their mortification vents itself in weeping and wailing, and knashing of teeth, and in such miscellaneous atrocities as their "Ku-Klux-Klans" can venture to inflict on helpless freedmen and radicals.*

A recent Southern paper (the *Virginia Advertiser*) finds a providential provision for the enslavement of the negro race in the thickness of their skulls, enabling them to bear without injury the blows inflicted in sudden rage by their masters; a suggestive confession, by the way, of the influence of slavery on the tempers of the slaveholders. The whole race must be prepared, it seems, for blows on the head with whatever weapon came to hand! But admitting the thickness of the skulls, it appears from an incident in the preceding pages, as well as from other known instances, that the

* It is curiously illustrative of the mixed childishness and ferocity which characterizes the Southern civilization, that this secret association of ruffians, organized to terrorize the loyal South, styles itself by an absurd, misspelled name, and goes about on its nightly work of murder in harlequin costume, with one of its leaders acting the part of ghost, to frighten the superstitious blacks. Some more courageous freedman occasionally makes a *bona fide* ghost of this masquerade.

inventive genius of the slave-whipping chivalry contrived to baffle the humane designs of Providence—a negro skull well padded with wool might bear without injury the blow of a boot-jack or a hammer, and yet prove insufficient to resist the impact or a musket-ball or a ten-pound weight.

It is of no avail to plate a vessel with six inches of iron, if she is to be pounded with bolts that can mash an eight-inch armor. Apparently, Divine Providence stopped short of the necessary security for the predestined slave race. It should have arranged for a progressive thickening of the negro cranium to meet the increase of violence on the part of the master; until at length slavery might be encountered with a difficulty like that which besets naval gunnery, viz., what would be the result if an infrangible African skull should be beaten by an *irresistable* Caucasian club?

But even this Virginia *laudator temporis acti,* this melancholy mourner at the tomb of defunct slavery, does not allege any such Providential thickening of the negro cuticle as to amount to a satisfactory anæsthesis against whipping. It has never been proven that a Virginia paddle or a Georgia raw-hide well applied did not make the blood spin as freely through a black skin as through a white one; nor has any Southern savant of the Nott and Gliddon school shown that there was not the same *relative* delicacy of organization in the slave woman as in the free. A black woman was, relatively to the black man, the more delicate subject for the whip; something more sensitive to the shame of stripping, more liable to terror, and of rather softer fiber; so that the lash went deeper both into soul and sense than in the case of her sable brother.

And this fact made the black woman a very suitable subject for the whip in the hands of the Southern lady. To succeed in slave-whipping as in any other fine art, the Horatian canon must be regarded, which requires us to take a subject suited to our strength. It would have been unreasonable, in ordinary cases, to expect a "dark-eyed daughter of the South" to flog handsomely a stalwart negro man; she sometimes did it, after he had been well tied up. But the slave girl was exactly suited to her flagellating capacities. A good many women, North as well as South, manifest a tendency to become tyrants in their own households, and love to bully their servants. But this is an evil of a mitigated nature in Northern society. The stupidest "help" in the kitchen knows she is safe from any other lash than her mistress' tongue, and is commonly an adept at the business of answering back again.

But the Southern mistress was a domestic devil with horns and claws; selfish, insolent, accustomed to be waited on for everything. She grew up with the instinct of tyranny—to punish violently the least neglect or disobedience in her servants. The variable temper of girlhood, not ugly unless thwarted, became in the "Southern matron" a chronic fury. She was her own "overseer," and, like that out-door functionary, had her own scepter, which she did not bear in vain. The raw-hide lay upon the shelf within easy reach, and her arm was vigorous with exercise. The breaking of a plate, the spilling of a cup, the misplacing of a pin in her dress, or any other misadventure in the chapter of accidents, was promptly illustrated with numerous cuts. The lash well laid on the shoulders of a black *femme-de-chambre,* or screaming child, was an agreeable titillation of the nervous sensibilities of the languid creole; a headache, or a heartache, transferred itself through the medium of the rawhide to the back of Phillis or Araminta. They no doubt whipped sometimes, like Mr. Squeers, for the mere fun of the thing. It is an exquisite pleasure to a cowardly nature to have some creature to torment; and there is this nemesis about cruelty that it engenders an appetite which, like that for alcoholic stimulents, for ever demands increased indulgence. It was the vindictive woman's nature in the South that protracted and gave added ferocity to the rebellion. These woman-whipping wives and mothers it was who hounded on the masculine chivalry to the work of exterminating the "accursed Yankees," and thus made their own punishment so much sorer than it need have been.

The mention of these amiable Southern characteristics cannot fail to recall that highly suggestive scene of the Malebolge, with the illustration of Gustave Doré, in which the tempters and destroyers of women are seen scourged with whips, in the hands of demons; especially when we remember that the whipping of slave women to make them consent to their own dishonor, was one of the usages of the patriarchal chivalry. There is not a scene in which the imaginings of Dante have been better seconded by the pencil of the great French artist: the flying wretches hurrying in opposite directions, as the crowds in the Jubilee year trampled each other, going and returning across the St. Angelo Bridge; among them the bat-winged fiends with whips, lashing right and left! In the throng are female figures: women who in life tortured and corrupted other women. What terror in face an attitude! How desperately they grapple with the rocks to lift themselves out of reach of the scourge! And these two demons in the foreground! What an absolute idealization of muscular ferocity! Every sinewy line in their cantour displays the force of a fallen demi-god; their very tails curl with delight in their ministry of vengeance.

> Ah! come facen levar le berze,
>
> Alle prime percosse, e gia nessuno,
>
> Le second aspettava ne le terze!

Ah! how they make them skip! There is Legree and Tom Gordon, and Madame de Schlangenbad, from Louisiana, and Mrs. Crawley (*née* Sharp) from South Carolina, squirming under the torture! A very instructive, if not agreeable exhibition!

But this fury in celestial Southern bosoms was merely institutional. Dip the gentlest nature into the element of irresponsible power, and it becomes in time covered over with a foul incrustation of cruelty. Those beastly Roman ladies of Juvenal's time, who could order a slave woman to be whipped to death without condeseending to give any other reason than their *sic volo, sic jubeo,* were not naturally worse than others. Take any Roman or Southern girl of ten years of age, put a whip in her hands, and a helpless slave child at her mercy; let her see nothing but brutality to inferiors all around her, and by the time she is ready to be married, she can hold up her thumb to the standing gladiator in the arena, or beg her lover to bring her back from Bull Run a ring from the bones of some Yankee soldier. It is a publicly known private fact, illustrative of the influence of slavery on the female character, that when a certain Northern clergyman applied to her father for the hand of a celebrated Maryland heiress, the reply was, "You are quite welcome to her! but I think it only fair to tell you that if I were going to storm hell, I should put her in the advance."

There is every reason to hope, therefore, that the Southern character, both male and female, will become gradually ameliorated by the changed condition under which it will hereafter be formed. It is a common error, one in which the Southern people themselves share, that there is something in their climate to nurse and to justify their "high spirit," *anqlicé* their quarrelsomeness and brutality of temper. It is very pleasant to lay off upon Nature or Providence what belongs only to will or institutions. A man indulges in violent passions with little restraint or remorse, so long as he can persuade himself he is merely what certain positive natural laws make him. What an opiate for a conscience defiled with lust and blood, to think that this is only natural to the "sunny South." But in fact, the people of warm, temperate, and tropical regions are most commonly gentle of mood; the climate acts as an anodyne, and soothes them into a peaceful equilibrium of the passions. The negroes of the Southern States are not passionate or vindictive—well for their late masters and present persecutors that they are not! What they may become from the treatment they are experiencing from those preternatural and predestinated fools, is another question.

The only reason the "chivalry" are bad-tempered and quarrelsome, is found in that despotism in which they have been nursed, and which associates the idea of personal dignity with an instant resort to violence at any contradiction. But for slavery, the people of Mississippi would have been no more addicted to street fights, dueling, midnight assassinations, etc., than the people of Massachusetts. That the former have any advantage in respect to courage, has been sufficiently disproved by the rebellion. Whether the ex-Confederate ladies may or may not be able to "fire the Southern heart" for another attempt to overthrow the Government, it will at least never be done under the persuasion that one Southerner is equal to five or any other number above unity, of Yankees.

The traditions of slavery, indeed, will remain to keep alive among the late slaveholding caste, the insolent and unchristian temper on which they have prided themselves. But having no more helpless pendants to storm at and abuse, their valor will needs submit to gradual modifications. Some degree of self-government will become a necessity. It may require several generations; but *institutions* ceasing to corrupt them, the loss of wealth, the necessity of work and a new Gospel of peace, better than their old slaveholding Christianity, will gradually educate them into a law-abiding, orderly, and virtuous people.

The Southern woman will of course share early in this beneficent change—no longer perverted into a she-devil by the possession of unrestrained power, and paying just wages to servants, who, if not suited with their work, can leave without having to run off; her gentler virtues will have a chance to assert themselves. Her striking qualities will subside into a charming vivacity of temper. She will become a gracious and pious mater-familias; she will perhaps in time learn to apply to her own children a portion of that discipline of which her slaves enjoyed a monopoly. In short, there neither is nor ever was any reason, slavery excepted, why the Southern whites should not possess a character for industry, peacefulness, and religion, equal to that of the rural districts of New York and New England.

Thank God that we have lived to see such awful barbarisms extinct! In fifty years the last woman-whipper at the South will be as dead as Cleopatra; as dead as the pre-Adamite brute organizations. History will be ashamed to record their doings. The fictions in which they are enbalmed will be lost in the better coming era of morals and letters. By the time the South has been overflowed and regenerated by a beneficent inundation of Northern "carpet-baggers," with Yankee capital and enterprise, it will be forgotten that a race capable of the crimes referred to in the preceding story, ever existed.

DOCUMENT 44:

Excerpt, Interview with Rose, Federal Writers' Project. Manuscript Slave Narrative Collection, Federal Writers' Project (Washington, D.C.: Library of Congress, 1930), Texas Narratives, pt. 4, 174–78.

Courtesy Library of Congress.

In this interview, collected in 1930 by the Federal Writers' Project, an enslaved woman from Texas is expected to have children with Rufus. As an incentive, her master gave her additional food and clothing, as well as time off. Rose was ninety years old when she gave this testimony.

Rose Describes Being Forced To Live with Rufus

"What I say am de facts. If I's one day old, I's way over 90, and I's born in Bell County, right here in Texas, and am owned by Massa William Black. He owns mammy and pappy, too. Massa Black has a big plantation but he has more niggers dan he need for work on dat place, 'cause he am a nigger trader. He trade and buy and sell all de time.

"Massa Black am awful cruel and he whip de cullud folks and works 'em hard and feed dem poorly. We'uns have for rations de cornmeal and milk and 'lasses and some beans and peas and meat once a week. We'uns have to work in de field every day from daylight till dark and on Sunday we'uns do us washin'. Church? Shucks, we'uns don't know what dat mean.

"I has de correct mem'randum of when de war start. Massa Black sold we'uns right den. Mammy and pappy powerful glad to git sold, and dey and I is put on de block with 'bout ten other niggers. When we'uns gits te de tradin' block, dere lots of white folks dere what come to look us over. One man shows de intres' in pappy. Him named Hawkins. He talk to pappy and pappy talk to him and say, 'Dem my woman and chiles. Please buy all of us and have mercy on we'uns.' Massa Hawkins say, 'Dat gal am a likely lookin' nigger, she am portly and strong, but three am more dan I wants, I guesses.'

"De sale starts and 'fore long pappy a put on de block. Massa Hawkins wins de bid for pappy and when mammy am put on de block, he wins de bid for her. Den dere am three or four other niggers sold befo' my time comes. Den massa Black calls me to de block and de auction man say, 'What am I offer for dis portly, strong young wench. She's never been 'bused and will make de good breeder.'

"I wants to hear Massa Hawkins bid, but him say nothin'. Two other men am biddin' 'gainst each other and I sho' has de worryment. Dere am tears comin' down my cheeks 'cause I's bein' sold to some man dat would make sep'ration from my mammy. One man bids $500 and de auction man ask, 'Do I hear more? She am gwine at $500.00.' Den someone say, $525.00 and de auction man say, 'She am sold for $525.00 to Massa Hawkins.' Am I glad and 'cited! Why, I's quiverin' all over.

"Massa Hawkins takes we'uns to his place and it am a nice plantation. Lots better am dat place dan Massa Black's. Dere is 'bout 50 niggers what is growed and lots of chillen. De first thing massa de when we'uns gits home am give we'uns rations and a cabin. You mus' believe dis nigger when I says dem rations a feast for us. Dere plently meat and tea and coffee and white flour. I's never tasted white flour and coffee and mammy fix some biscuits and coffee. Well, de biscuits was yum, yum, yum to me, but de coffee I doesn't like.

"De quarters am purty good. Dere am twelve cabins all made from logs and a table and some benches and bunks for sleepin' and a fireplace for cookin' and de heat. Dere am no floor, jus' de ground.

"Massa Hawkins am good to he niggers and not force 'em work too hard. Dere am as much diff'ence 'tween him and old Massa Black in de way of treatment as 'twixt de Lawd and de devil. Massa Hawkins 'lows he niggers have reason'ble parties and go fishin', but we'uns am never tooken to church and has no books for larnin'. Dere am no edumcation for de niggers.

"Dere am one thing Massa Hawkins does to me what I can't shunt from my mind. I knows he don't do it for meanness, but I allus holds it 'gainst him. What he done am force me to live with dat nigger, Rufus, 'gainst my wants.

"After I been at he place 'bout a year, de massa come to me and say, 'You gwine live with Rufus in dat cabin over yonder. Go fix it for livin'.' I's 'bout sixteen year old and has no larnin', and I's jus' igno'mus chile. I's thought dat him mean for me to tend de cabin for Rufus and some other niggers. Well, dat am start de pestigation for me.

"I's took charge of de cabin after work am done and fixes supper. Now, I don't like that Rufus, 'cause he a bully. He am big and 'cause he so, he think everybody do what him say. We'uns has supper, den I goes here and dere talkin', till I's ready for sleep and den I's gits in de bunk. After I's in, dat nigger come and crawl in de bunk with me 'fore I knows it. I says, 'What you means, you fool nigger?' He say for me to hush de mouth. 'Dis am my bunk, too,' he say.

"'You's teched in de head. Git out,' I's told him, and I puts de feet 'gainst him and give him a shove and out he go on de floor 'fore he know what I's doin'. Dat nigger jump up and he mad. He look like de wild bear. He starts for de bunk and I jumps quick for de poker. It am 'bout three feet long and when he comes at me I lets him have it over de head. Did dat nigger stop in he tracks? I's say he did. He looks at me steady for a minute and you's could tell he thinkin' hard. Den he go and set on de bench and say, 'Jus wait. You thinks it am smart, but you's am foolish in de head. Dey's gwine larn you somethin'.'

"'Hush yous big mouth and stay 'way from dis nigger, dat all I wants,' I say, and jus' sets and hold dat poker in de hand. He jus' sets, lookin' like de bull. Dere we'uns sets and sets for 'bout an hour and den he go out and I bars de door.

"De nex' day I goes to de missy and tells her what Rufus wants and missy say dat am de massa's wishes. She say, 'Yous am de portly gal and Rufus am de portly man. De massa wants you'uns fer to bring forth portly chillen.'

"I's thinkin' 'bout what de missy say, but say to myse'f, 'I's not gwine live with dat Rufus.' Dat night when him come in de cabin, I grabs de poker and sits on de bench and says, 'Git 'way from me, nigger, 'fore I busts yous brains out and stomp on dem.' He say nothin' and git out.

"De nex' day de massa call me and tell me, 'Woman, I's pay big money for you and I's done dat for de cause I wants yous to raise me chillens. I's put yous to live with Rufus for dat purpose. Now, if you doesn't want whippin' at de stake, yous do what I wants.'

"I thinks 'bout massa buyin' me offen de block and savin' me from bein' sep'rated from my folks and 'bout bein' whipped at de stake. Dere it am. What am I's to do? So I 'cides to do as de massa wish and so I yields.

"When we'uns am given freedom, Massa Hawkins tells us we can stay and work for wages or share crop de land. Some stays and some goes. My folks and me stays. We works de land on shares for three years, den moved to other land near by. I stays with my folks till they dies.

"If my mem'randum am correct, it am 'bout thirty year since I come to Fort Worth. Here I cooks for white folks till I goes blind 'bout ten year ago.

"I never marries, 'cause one 'sperience am 'nough for dis nigger. After what I does for de massa, I's never want no truck with any man. De Lawd forgive dis cullud woman, but he have to 'scuse me and look for some others for to 'plenish de earth.

CHAPTER 3

Building Community

Despite harsh conditions and little opportunity for escape or hope for freedom, slave women were the backbone of many slave societies. The documents in this section examine the role they played in helping to develop vibrant communities that were always under the threat of being torn apart.

DOCUMENT 45:
Petition for Freedom, New Netherlands, 1661. Series A1809 Dutch Colonial Council Minutes, 1638–1665, Volume 9, page 557 (box 9).

Courtesy New York State Archives.

During the Revolutionary period, inspired by arguments for justice and freedom, enslaved men and women sometimes petitioned the government for freedom. In this case, dating from 1661, the petition is written in Dutch to the Director-General and Lords Councillors of New Netherlands (which later became the state of New York) and was later granted.

To the Noble Right Honorable Director-General and Lords Councillors of New Netherlands

Herewith very respectfully declare Emanuel Pieterson, a free Negro, and Reytory, otherwise Dorothy, Angola, free Negro woman, together husband and wife, the very humble petitioners of your noble honors, that she, Reytory, in the year 1643, on the third of August, stood as god-parent or witness at the Christian baptism of a little son of one Anthony van Angola, begotten with his own wife named Louise, the which aforementioned Anthony and Louise were both free Negroes; and about four weeks thereafter the aforementioned Louise came to depart this world, leaving behind the aforementioned little son named Anthony, the which child your petitioner out of Christian affection took to herself, and with the fruits of her hands' bitter toil she reared him as her own child, and up to the present supported him, taking all motherly solicitude and care for him, without aid of anyone in the world, not even his father (who likewise died about five years thereafter), to solicit his nourishment; and also your petitioner [i.e., Emanuel] since he was married to Reytory, has done his duty and his very best for the rearing . . . to assist . . . your petitioners . . . very respectfully address themselves to you, noble and right honorable lords, humbly begging that your noble honors consent to grant a stamp in this margin of this [document], or otherwise a document containing the consent and approval of the above-mentioned adoption and nurturing, on the part of your petitioner, in behalf of the aforementioned Anthony with the intent [of declaring] that he himself, being of free parents, reared and brought up without burden or expense of the [West Indian] Company, or of anyone else than your petitioner, in accordance therewith he may be declared by your noble honors to be a free person: this being done, [the document] was signed with the mark of Anthony Pieterson.

DOCUMENT 46:
Letter, Thomas Basye to William H. Cabell, December 14, 1806.

Courtesy Executive Department, Executive Papers, Box 142, Library of Virginia, Richmond.

This letter describes the complex status of free blacks in Virginia, often isolated from slave communities and resented by whites. Basye requests that Governor William H. Cabell introduce legislation to curb the freedom of free blacks, including Robert Williams, who seems to have protected eight slaves owned by Basye's mother, Martha Turberville.

Thomas Basye to William H. Cabell.

Peckatone (Westmoreland county) 14th December 1806
Wm. H. Cabell, Esquire,
   Sir,
   Although I have not the pleasure of a personal acquaintance with you, 'tis hoped the subject which superinduces this address will sufficiently apologize for the liberty used in making a communication thereon;—Your well-known patriotism will, no doubt, lead to a proper investigation of the points in question. It is deemed unnecessary however to give you a complete detail—having advised my friend General John Minor, by letter, under date hereof—the contents of which fully explains what should be represented in the *[illegible]*; and I have requested this Gentleman to exhibit the same to you—and have also written to my friend Ellison Currie Esq. (of the Senate) to the purpose. It may however be necessary to give the outlines, in order to *[make?]* a more immediate explanation. The subject relates in the first instance to the malconduct of some Magistrates of this county, to wit a John Murphy (Scotch fugitive) and a Mr. Stephen Baily, (an American:)—The partiality shown by these *pseudo majestrates* to a runaway negroe *harbourer* residing near this place—a mulatto man supposed to be *free,* but who actually is not, the Debts of his former master (Lewis *[illegible]*) having not been discharged, previous to the date of the Record of the emancipation of the said mulatto should be seriously noticed:—he the said mulatto, named Robert Williams harboured eight runaway negroes the property of Mrs. Martha Turberville, nearly six months in the year 1804 & 1805—and publicly *boasted of the act*—added to this consideration he had been previously apprehended as a leader of the *negroe* Conspiracy of 1802:—*& arms & ammunition were found in his possession.*—Various other nefarious acts this mulatto has been guilty of, which it may not for the present be necessary to mention—Acting as a friend to my mother-in-law Mrs. Martha Turberville, I instructed the overseer at Peckatone, to chastise this mulatto, for *supporting the negroes* above mentioned, during the term of their elopement, which the said overseer, named Isaac Hutcheson did, by given the said mulatto, the punishment which the laws of our State justly inflict on negroe slaves—An Indictment upon this account, was preferred against me at the county court of Westmoreland in July 1805:—an *Ignoramus* was found:—but John Campbell, the Commonwealth Atty,

notorious for his deeprooted malignity against the Turberville family, carried this Indictment to the Northumberland District Court where by the false testimony of a Hog-thief (by the name of William Williams, whom a man by the name of Parker is well acquainted with) the grand jury were so far imposed upon; that a true Bill was found—after which a decision was made by a *packed* Jury at the last *[illegible]* Court for said District, and a Fine assessed against myself, to the amount of $250 as also against the overseer (Isaac Hutcheson) of $50.

The Executive I well know, have not the power of remitting fines—but 'tis hoped, your solicitude for the *public good,* will suggest the propriety of admonishing the legislature of our state, now in session, of the expedience of framing some legal correctives, as barriers against the daily increasing encroachments of negroes & mulattoes, upon the *Rights of White Persons.*

> I have the honor to be
> with the highest respect,
> Your most obedient
>
> Thomas Pope Basye

ENCLOSURE FROM MARTHA TURBERVILLE.
William H. Cabell, Esq.

Sir, I beg leave to annex a postscript to this letter & trust it will not be deemed a breach of decorum to state an opinion relative to the deportment of one of the members constituting the Court alluded to— The conduct of Judge Parker in my estimation was singular, if unprecedented I believe in the annals of the jurisprudence of our country:—he admitted the testimony of this mulatto villain Robert Williams, alias Robin the Taylor to give evidence against my son in law Thomas Pope Basye, in open court—his corpororal*[sic]* oath was insisted on by Judge Parker, and opposed by Judge Holmes—but notwithstanding the result had the intended effect—this mulatto fellow was allowed to address the Court & Jury, giving testimony the falsity of which 'twas hoped the most depraved character in the Commonwealth would blush at—Judge Parker had the impertinence to enquire of one of the witnesses (who is a Gentleman) whether my daughter was married to Mr. Basye or not— I appeal to the world to say with what propriety Judge Parker could have made this interrogation—the question, in my mind was highly unbecoming the dignity of a Gentleman, and was calculated to add insult to injury—

I have, Sir, the honour to be
    with our respects
    Your most obedient
    Martha Turberville

DOCUMENT 47:
The Afric-American Female Intelligence Society of Boston, *The Genius of Universal Emancipation*, Vol. 2, No. 10, 3rd. Ser. (March 1832): 162–63.

Courtesy Library of Congress.

Like so many organizations founded by free African American women of this period, this society in Boston was established to provide instruction for Christian women, to help uplift the community, and to foster intellectual discussion. The mission of the organization is stated in the preamble to their constitution below. Benjamin Lundy was editor of the antislavery newspaper in Baltimore, Maryland, *The Genius of Universal Emancipation,* in which this document that includes the organization's constitution appeared.

We are glad to find that Associations, benevolent and literary appear to be multiplying among our colored sisters. We learn by the *Liberator* that one has recently been established at Boston, under the name of The Afrc-American Female Intelligence Society. A literary association was also some months since organized by some of the colored females of Philadelphia. We wish them both success and a long career of usefulness.—We hail with delight every intimation that our Afric American sisters are becoming more sensible of the value of mental cultivation, and are exerting themselves to procure it. We have copied the Preamble and such articles of the Constitution of the Boston Society as will best explain their objects and be most useful to those who may wish to imitate them.

CONSTITUTION

Of the Afric-American Female Intelligence Society of Boston

PREAMBLE

Whereas the subscribers, women of color of the Commonwealth of Massachusetts, actuated by a natural feeling for the welfare of our friends, have thought fit to associate for the diffusion of knowledge, the suppression of vice and immorality, and for cherishing such virtues as will render us happy and useful to society, sensible to the gross ignorance under which we have too long labored, but trusting, by the blessing of God, we shall be able to accomplish the object of our union—we have therefore associated ourselves under the name of the Afric-American Female Intelligence Society, and have adopted the following Constitution.

Art. 1st. The officers of this society shall be a President, Vice-President, Treasurer, Secretary, and a Board of Directors of five—all of whom shall be annually elected.

Art. 2d. Regular meetings of the Society shall be held on the first Thursday of every month, at which each member shall pay twenty-five cents, and pay twelve and a half cents at every monthly meeting thenceforth.

Art 3d. The money thus collected shall be appropriated for the purchasing of books, the hiring of a room and other contingencies . . .

Art. 11th. All candidates for membership shall be of a good moral character, and shall be elected by a majority of the votes of the Society.

Art. 12th. All members who shall be absent at the regular monthly meetings, shall be fined six and a quarter cents, unless a satisfactory apology can be offered to the Society.

Art. 15th. Any member of the Society, of one year's standing, having regularly paid up her dues, who may be taken sick, shall receive one dollar per week out of the funds of the Society as long as consistent with the means of the institution.

Art. 18th. In case of any unforeseen and afflictive event should happen to any of the members, it shall be the duty of the Society to aid them as far as in their power. . . .

BY-LAWS

Art. 1st. Each member who wishes to speak shall rise and address the chair.

Art. 2d. While any member addresses the chair there shall be no interruption.

Art. 3d. If any member becomes sick, it shall be made known to the President, who will instruct the Directors to visit the sick person, and devise means for her relief.

Art. 4th. Twelve members shall constitute a quorum to transact business.

Art. 5th. Any person or persons who shall rashly sacrifice their own health, shall not be entitled to any aid or sympathy from the Society.

Art. 6th. Each meeting of the Society shall begin and end with prayer.

Art. 7th. The Treasurer shall make quarterly reports of the state of the funds.

Art. 8th. The Secretary shall read the proceedings of the last meeting at each succeeding one.

DOCUMENT 48:
Excerpt, [Rebecca Warren Brown?], *Memoir of Mrs. Chloe Spear, a Native of Africa, Who was Enslaved in Childhood, and Died in Boston, January 3, 1815 . . . Aged 65 years. By a Lady in Boston* (Boston: James Loring, 1832), 19–27.

Courtesy Documenting the American South, University Library, The University of North Carolina at Chapel Hill.

Chloe Spear was captured with her family as a young teenager in Africa and enslaved in the North. After slavery was outlawed in Massachusetts, she and her husband operated a boardinghouse in Boston. The memoir focused primarily on her religious life, and this excerpt notes the importance of her learning to read, which was an activity forbidden to slaves. Document 26 tells of Chloe Spear's capture and enslavement. The author of the memoir is unknown, though scholars note that it could either be Rebecca Warren Brown or Mary Webb.

CHAPTER XXXVII.
THE RE-UNION.

Although enlightened and good people must always have known, that it was a barbarous and wicked thing to take their fellow-beings from their native land, and bring them to ours, to sell or buy them for *slaves;* yet it is well known that then there was less knowledge of its wickedness than there now is. Hence we are willing to believe, that if the master and mistress of this poor, oppressed girl, whose story is here related, and whom they named *Chloe,* had lived in our day, they would have dealt very differently by her from what they then did. But at that time, here, as now in many parts of the world, slaves were considered *property,* and their owners thought themselves under no more obligations to *instruct* them, otherwise than to do their work in such a manner as best to subserve their own interests, than farmers do, to take, their horses and oxen into their houses, instead of the pasture or the barn. With such views, it is not singular that Chloe was taught nothing, comparatively, of her duty to God, nor to read the blessed Bible. She was, it is true, sent to meeting half the day on the Sabbath; but the seat assigned to herself and her associates was remote from the view of the congregation; and she confessed, that as they did not understand the preaching, they took no interest in it, and spent the time in playing, eating nuts, &c. and derived no benefit whatever, though the preaching probably was evangelical.

It was close personal instruction that she needed, to discover to her the beauty of religion, and her condition as a sinner. This she did not receive. But, being favoured by the munificent Author of her existence, with superior intellectual powers, which, if cultivated, would have raised her above many of a different complexion; when, (as she was accustomed to do,) she went to conduct the children of the family to, and from *school,* she discovered that the were obtaining something of which she remained ignorant. This excited an inclination to learn to read, and after becoming a little acquainted with the school-mistress, who, it would seem, manifested some sympathy for the enslaved youth, she ventured to express her desire.

How to accomplish her object, was a question which required consideration. She was aware that it would not do to make known her wishes at home, and she could not attend at the regular school hours, both for want of time, and because the children would expose the fact to their parents. But after some reflection, an expedient was devised that promised success. "So," said Chloe, "I ask de Mistress how much she hab week to teach me such time I get when school out, and my work done? She say, *'five copper,'** so she would chalk down mark, how many day I go, till make a week. She say too, I mus bring book."

To these conditions she agreed, as she occasionally received small presents of money from visiters at the house of her master.

Delighted with the prospect, she hastened to a bookseller's shop, and desired him to sell her a book. He asked, what book? She answered that she did not know; she wanted a *book.* He asked what money she had brought? She did not know this neither, but showing him her piece of silver, he found it to be a twenty-cent piece. Whether the bookseller willingly took advantage of her ignorance, or whether he supposed she was sent to purchase a book of that value, we cannot decide; but he gave her a *Psalter,* which contained the Psalms, Proverbs, and our Lord's Sermon on the mount. An unsuitable book indeed, on which to teach an untutored African her alphabet! but this event Chloe afterwards had occasion to review as a peculiar providence.

By diligence in her domestic avocations, and so much application to, study as circumstances would permit, she learned her letters, and became quite interested in attempting to spell. She kept the book secreted in her pocket, and whenever she had a few moments leisure, she would take it out and try to spell a word. While thus engaged one day, her master discovered the book in her hand, and inquired what she was doing. She told the truth,** and this led to a full disclosure of the case. He angrily forbade

*This was previous to the coinage of *cents.*
**She told the truth! What an example is this to all children and youth. Had Chloe done as have many who were better taught than she, no doubt she might for a time, have escaped the reproofs of her master, and possibly have continued to attend her school. But her *conscience* must all her life long have been accusing her of *lying,* and this would have been far worse than what she endured in consequence of the deprivation she suffered; for it is better to suffer wrong, than to do wrong. Besides, she would in all probability have been detected at some future period, and then the *mortification,* in addition to the guilt, would have been a severe aggravation of her punishment. But what is greater than all, she would have *sinned against God,* and thus have exposed herself to his holy displeasure.

her going again to the schoolmistress for instruction, even under penalty
of being suspended by her two thumbs, and severely whipped; he said it
made negroes saucy to know how to read, &c.

This was truly an afflictive stroke to poor Chloe, but she was obliged
to submit as well as she could, and altogether to desist from going to
school. She however hid her book under her pillow, and when not likely
to be detected, she used to labour over it, and strive to remember what
she had learned, and to find out as much as she could herself;* and years
afterward, even late in life, she frequently spoke of it as a striking providence, that the first verse she was able to spell out, so as to understand
it, was Psalm xxxv. 1. "Plead my cause, O Lord, with them that strive
with me: fight against them that fight against me."

DOCUMENT 49:
Excerpt, *Religious Experience and Journal of Mrs. Jarena
Lee Giving an Account of her Call to Preach the Gospel.
Revised and Corrected from the Original Manuscript,
written by herself* (Philadelphia: Printed and Published
for the Author, 1836).

Courtesy Library of Congress.

Jarena Lee became the first woman to be authorized to preach by
Richard Allen, founder of the African Methodist Episcopal Church
in 1819. She continued to face discrimination, but became a traveling minister. In 1840, she joined the American Antislavery Society,
a year after she published this pamphlet.

. . . I now began to think seriously of breaking up housekeeping,
and forsaking all to preach the everlasting Gospel. I felt a strong desire

---

*Such patient diligence, and persevering effort, under these trying and discouraging
circumstances, discover traits of a strong and penetrating genius, which would be
highly creditable to an enlightened student, and most powerfully reprove those children of kind and attentive parents, who are constantly prompting them to the
improvement of their minds by personal instruction, and by affording them superior
advantages of a literary character; but who are still negligent and remiss in their
attention to study.

to return to the place of my nativity, at Cape May, after an absence of
about fourteen years. To this place, where the heaviest cross was to be
met with, the Lord sent me, as Saul of Tarsus was sent to Jerusalem, to
preach the same gospel which he had neglected and despised before his
conversion. I went by water, and on my passage was much distressed by
sea sickness, so much so that I expected to have died, but such was not
the will of the Lord respecting me. After I had disembarked, I proceeded
on as opportunities offered, toward where my mother lived. When
within ten miles of that place, I appointed an evening meeting. There
were a goodly number came out to hear. The Lord was pleased to give
me light and liberty among the people. After meeting, there came an
elderly lady to me and said, she believed the Lord had sent me among
them: she then appointed me another meeting there two weeks from
that night. The next day I hastened forward to the place of my mother,
who was happy to see me, and the happiness was mutual between us.
With her I left my poor sickly boy, while I departed to do my Master's
will. In this neighborhood I had an uncle, who was a Methodist, and
who gladly threw open his door for meetings to be held there. At the
first meeting which I held at my uncle's house, there was, with others
who had come from curiosity to hear the coloured woman preacher, an
old man, who was a deist, and who said he did not believe the coloured
people had any souls—he was sure they had none. He took a seat very
near where I was standing, and boldly tried to look me out of countenance. But as I laboured on in the best manner I was able, looking to
God all the while, though it seemed to me I had but little liberty, yet
there went an arrow from the bent bow of the gospel, and fastened in
his till then obdurate heart. After I had done speaking, he went out, and
called the people around him, said that my preaching might seem a small
thing, yet he believed I had the worth of souls at heart. This language
was different from what it was a little time before, as he now seemed to
admit that coloured people had souls, *as it was to these I was chiefly speaking; and unless they had souls,* whose good I had in view, his remark must
have been without meaning. He now came into the house, and in the
most friendly manner shook hands with me, saying, he hoped God had
spared him to some good purpose. This man was a great slave holder,
and had been very cruel; thinking nothing of knocking down a slave
with a fence stake, or whatever might come to hand. From this time it

was said of him that he became greatly altered in his ways for the better. At that time he was about seventy years old, his head as white as snow; but whether he became a converted man or not, I never heard.

The week following, I had an invitation to hold a meeting at the Court House of the County, when I spoke from the 53d chap. of Isaiah, 3d verse. It was a solemn time, and the Lord attended the word; I had life and liberty, though there were people there of various denominations. Here again I saw the aged slaveholder, who notwithstanding his age, walked about three miles to hear me. This day I spoke twice, and walked six miles to the place appointed. There was a magistrate present, who showed his friendship, by saying in a friendly manner, that he had heard of me: he handed me a hymn-book, pointing to a hymn which he had selected. When the meeting was over, he invited me to preach in a schoolhouse in his neighbourhood, about three miles distant from where I then was. During this meeting one backslider was reclaimed. This day I walked six miles, and preached twice to large congregations, both in the morning and evening. The Lord was with me, glory be to his holy name. I next went six miles and held a meeting in a coloured friend's house, at eleven o'clock in the morning, and preached to a well behaved congregation of both coloured and white. After service I again walked back, which was in all twelve miles in the same day. This was on Sabbath, or as I sometimes call it, seventh-day; for after my conversion I preferred the plain language of the quakers. On fourth-day, after this, in compliance with an invitation received by note, from the same magistrate who had heard me at the above place, I preached to a large congregation, where we had a precious time: much weeping was heard among the people. The same gentleman, now at the close of the meeting, gave out another appointment at the same place, that day week. Here again I had liberty, there was a move among the people. Ten years from that time, in the neighbourhood of Cape May, I held a prayer meeting in a school house, which was then the regular place of preaching for the Episcopal Methodists; after service, there came a white lady of the first distinction, a member of the Methodist Society, and told me that at the same school house, ten years before, under my preaching, the Lord first awakened her. She rejoiced much to see me, and invited me home with her, where I staid till the next day. This was bread cast upon the waters, seen after many days.

DOCUMENT 50:
Excerpt, Charles Ball, *Slavery in the United States:
A Narrative of the Life and Adventures of Charles Ball,
a Black Man* (Lewiston, PA: W. Shugert, 1836), 166.

Courtesy Library of Congress.

In this short excerpt, Ball details how male and female slaves were given small plots of land on larger plantations to harvest their own crops. This suggests a limited amount of autonomy within enslaved communities. Ball was born a slave on a tobacco plantation in Maryland around 1781. He was sold south to Georgia, and escaped from slavery in 1810. Though a fugitive, he returned to Maryland to his family. He published this narrative with the help of Isaac Fisher.

On every plantation with which I ever had any acquaintance the people are allowed to make patches, as they are called—that is gardens, in some remote and unprofitable part of the estate, generally in the woods, in which they plant corn, potatoes, pumpkins, melons etc. for themselves. These patches they must cultivate on Sunday, or let them go uncultivated.

DOCUMENT 51:
Excerpt, Solomon Northup, *Narrative of Solomon
Northup: Twelve Years a Slave* (Auburn, NY: Derby and
Miller, 1853).

Courtesy Library of Congress.

In the first excerpt, Solomon Northrup recounts the sale of a slave mother, owned by Elisha Berry, whom he identifies as "a rich man living in the neighborhood of Washington." This very personal narrative shows the inhumanity of slavery on a public stage. In the second excerpt, Northrup details Christmas for enslaved men and women, one of the few times each year that they had of restricted liberty from their masters. Northrup was born in New York to a freedman in 1808. He was kidnapped and enslaved at the age of thirty-three, living in Louisiana until his father's former owner

freed him. He published his memoir with the assistance of David
Wilson.

. . . I remained in Williams' slave pen about two weeks. The night previous to my departure a woman was brought in, weeping bitterly, and
leading by the hand a little child. They were Randall's mother and half-
sister. On meeting them he was overjoyed, clinging to her dress, kissing
the child. [Randall is a lad of about ten.]

Emily, the child, was seven or eight years old, of light complexion,
and with a face of admirable beauty . . . The woman also was arrayed
in silk, with rings upon her fingers, and golden ornaments suspended
from her ears. Her air and manners, the correctness and propriety of
her language—all showed, evidently, that she had sometime stood above
the common level of a slave . . . Her name was Eliza, and this was the
story of her life, as she afterwards related it.:

She was the slave of Elisha Berry, a rich man, living in the neighborhood of Washington. Years before he had . . . quarreled with his wife.
In fact, soon after Randall was born, they separated. Leaving his wife
and daughter in the house they had always occupied, he erected a new
one near by, on the estate. Into this house, he brought Eliza; and, on
condition of her living with him, she and her children were to be emancipated. She resided with him there nine years, with servants to attend
upon her, and provided with every comfort and luxury of life. Emily
was his child. . . . At length, for some cause beyond Berry's control, a
division of his property was made. She and her children fell to the share
of Mr. Brooks [Berry's son-in-law]. During the nine years she had lived
with Berry . . . she and Emily had become the object of Mrs. Berry's and
her daughter's hatred and dislike. . . .

The day she was led into the pen, Brooks had brought her from the
estate into the city, under pretence that the time had come when her
free papers were to be executed, in fulfillment of her master's promise.
Elated at the prospect of immediate liberty, she decked herself and
little Emily in their best apparel, and accompanied him with a joyful
heart. On their arrival in the city . . . she was delivered to the trader
Burch. The paper that was executed was a bill of sale. The hope of years
was blasted in a moment. . . .

A planter of Baton Rouge . . . purchased Randall. . . . All the time the trade was going on, Eliza was crying aloud, and wringing her hands. She besought the man not to buy him, unless he also bought herself and Emily. She promised, in that case, to be the most faithful slave that ever lived. . . . Freeman turned round to her, savagely, with his whip in his uplifted hand, ordering her stop her noise, or he would flog her. He would not have such work—such sniveling; and unless she ceased that minute, he would take her to the yard and give her a hundred lashes. . . . She kept on begging and beseeching them, most piteously, not to separate the three. . . . But it was no avail. . . . The bargain was agreed upon, and Randall must go alone. . . .

What has become of the lad, God knows. . . . I would have cried myself if I had dared. . . .

At length, one day . . . Freeman ordered us to our places, in the great room. A gentleman was waiting for us as we entered. After some further inspection . . . he finally offered Freeman one thousand dollars for me, nine hundred for Harry, and seven hundred for Eliza. . . . As soon as Eliza heard it she was in agony again. By this time she had become haggard and hollow-eyed with sickness and sorrow. . . . She broke from her place in the line of women, and rushing down where Emily was standing, caught her in her arms. . . . Freeman sternly ordered her to be quiet, but she did not heed him. He caught her by the arm and pulled her rudely, but she only clung closer to the child. Then, with the volley of great oaths, he struck her such a heartless blow, that she staggered backward. . . . "Mercy, mercy, master!" she cried, falling on her knees. "Please, master, buy Emily. I can never work any if she is taken from me; I will die."

Finally . . . the purchaser of Eliza stepped forward, evidently affected, and said to Freeman he would buy Emily, and asked him what her price was. . . .

But to this human proposal Freeman was entirely deaf. He would not sell her then on any account whatever. There were heaps and piles of money to be made of her, he said, when she was a few years older. There were men enough in New Orleans who would give five thousand dollars for such an extra, handsome, fancy piece as Emily would be. . . . No, no, he would not sell her then. . . .

When Eliza heard Freeman's determination not to part with Emily, she became absolutely frantic. . . . We waited some time, when, finally,

Freeman out of patience, tore Emily from her mother by the main force. . . .

"Don't leave me, mama—don't leave me," screamed the child, as its mother was pushed harshly forward. . . . But she cried in vain. Out of the door and into the street we were quickly hurried. Still we could hear her calling to her mother, "Come back—don't leave me . . ." until her infant voice grew faint and still more faint . . . and finally was wholly lost. . . . The only respite from constant labor the slave has through the whole year, is during the Christmas holidays. Epps allowed us three—others allow four, five and six days, according to the measure of their generosity. It is the only time to which they look forward with any interest or pleasure. They are glad when night comes, not only because it brings them a few hours repose, but because it brings them one day nearer Christmas. It is hailed with equal delight by the old and young; even Uncle Abram ceases to glorify Andrew Jackson, and Patsy forgets her many sorrows, amid the general hilarity of the holidays. It is a time of feasting, and frolicking, and fiddling—the carnival season with the children of bondage. They are the only days when they are allowed a little restricted liberty, and heartily indeed do they enjoy it.

It is custom for one planter to give a "Christmas supper," inviting the slaves from neighboring plantations to join his own on the occasion. . . . Usually from three to five hundred are assembled, coming together on foot, in carts, on horseback, on mules, riding double and triple, sometimes a boy and girl, and old woman. Uncle Abram astride a mule, with Aunt Phebe and Patsy behind him, trotting together towards a Christmas supper, would be no uncommon sight on Bayou Boeuf.

Then, too, "of all days i' the year," they array themselves in their best attire. The cotton coat has been washed clean, the stump of a tallow candle has been applied to their shoes, and if so fortunate as to possess a rimless or crownless hat, it is placed jauntily on the head. They are welcome with equal cordiality, however, if they come bare-headed and bare-footed to the feast. As a general thing, the women wear handkerchiefs tied about their heads, but if chance has thrown in their way a fiery red ribbon, or a cast-off bonnet of their mistress' grandmother, it is sure to be worn on such occasions. Red—the deep blood red—is decidedly the favorite color among the enslaved damsels of my acquaintance. If a red ribbon does not encircle the neck, you will be certain to find all the hair of their woolly heads tied up with red strings of one sort or another.

The table is spread in the open air, and loaded with varieties of meat and piles of vegetables. Bacon and corn meal at such times are dispensed with. Sometimes the cooking is performed in the kitchen on the plantation, at others in the shade of wide branching trees. In the latter case, a ditch is dug in the ground, and wood laid in and burned until it is filled with glowing coals, over which chickens, ducks, turkeys, pigs, and not unfrequently the entire body of a wild ox, are roasted. They are furnished also with flour, of which biscuits are made, and often with peach and other preserves, with tarts, and every manner and description of pies, except the mince, that being an article of pastry as yet unknown among them. Only the slave who has lived all the years on his scanty allowance of meal and bacon, can appreciate such suppers. White people in great numbers assemble to witness the gastronomical enjoyments . . . .

When the viands have disappeared, and the hungry maws of the children of toil are satisfied, then, next in the order of amusement, is the Christmas dance. My business on these gala days always was to play on the violin. The African race is a music-loving one, proverbially; and many there were among my fellow-bondsmen whose organs of tune were strikingly developed, and who could thumb the banjo with dexterity . . . .

On that particular Christmas I have now in my mind, Miss Lively and Mr. Sam, the first belonging to Stewart, the latter to Roberts, started the ball. It was well known that Sam cherished an ardent passion for Lively, as also did one of Marshall's and another of Carey's boys; for Lively was lively indeed, and a heart-breaking coquette withal. It was a victory for Sam Roberts, when, rising from the repast, she gave him her hand for the first "figure" in preference to either of his rivals. They were somewhat crest-fallen, and, shaking their heads angrily, rather intimated they would like to pitch into Mr. Sam and hurt him badly.

But not an emotion of wrath ruffled the placid bosom of Samuel as his legs flew like drum-sticks down the outside and up the middle, by the side of his bewitching partner. The whole company cheered them vociferously, and, excited with the applause, they continued "tearing down" after all the others had become exhausted and halted a moment to recover breath. But Sam's superhuman exertions overcame him finally, leaving Lively alone, yet whirling like a top. Thereupon one of Sam's rivals, Pete Marshall, dashed in, with might and main, leaped and shuffled and threw himself into every conceivable shape, as if determined to show Miss Lively and all the world that Sam Roberts was of no account . . . .

During the remaining holidays succeeding Christmas, they are provided with passes, and permitted to go where they please within a limited distance, or they may remain and labor on the plantation, in which case they are paid for it. It is very rarely, however, that the latter alternative is accepted. They may be seen at these times hurrying in all directions, as happy looking mortals as can be found on the face of the earth. They are different beings from what they are in the field; the temporary relaxation, the brief deliverance from fear, and from the lash, producing an entire metamorphosis in their appearance and demeanor. In visiting, riding, renewing old friendships, or, perchance, reviving some old attachment, or pursuing whatever pleasure may suggest itself, the time is occupied.

Such is "southern life as it is," three days in the year, as I found it—the other three hundred and sixty-two being days of weariness, and fear, and suffering, and unremitting labor.

DOCUMENT 52:
John Edward Bruce, "A Sketch of My Life," c. 1875.

Courtesy Bruce Manuscripts, Schomburg Center for Research in Black Culture, New York Public Library.

In this excerpt, J. E. Bruce recalls his mother, a slave owned by Mayor Harvey Griffin, who allowed her to work on her own if she gave him half her wages. Bruce's mother worked in the garrison in Fort Washington, Maryland, selling pies and coffee and later secondhand clothing. Bruce and his mother were freed in 1860 when Union forces came through Maryland. He went on to become a journalist, a historian, and a founder of the Negro Society for Historical Research in New York.

My mother was a slave. . . . owned by Mayor Harvey Griffin. . . . After my father was sold my master gave my mother permission to work for herself, provided she gave him one half she worked for which she agreed to do. She then obtained a situation as cook in the largest tavern in the village. . . . She did not stay there long because the mean brute threatened to whip her in one of his drunken sprees. . . .

My mother worked in the garrison [of Fort Washington, Maryland] a while then she carried on a little business for her self selling pies, hot coffee, etc. to the Marines and exchanging the same for their rations. Her business increased and it became necessary that she should buy a horse and wagon to convey her goods to the fort, which she did. . . . My mother then got along very comfortably for about three years. . . .

My mother got many presents from the Marines in the shape of old clothes, shoes, caps, stockings etc. . . . Our business increased twofold then, because mother was running a second hand clothing store on a small scale and made quite a respectable living. The poor white surrounding us became jealous in a body and waited on the Major and gave vent to their feeling. The Major would have nothing to say of any length but would only answer in monosyllables. . . .

Mother and I were freed in 1860 when the first regiment of Union soldiers passed through Maryland on their way to Washington . . . We marched with the soldiers.

DOCUMENT 53:
Narrative of Martha Jackson, *Alabama Narratives: Federal Works Project,* WPA for the State of Alabama, 1939.

Courtesy Library of Congress.

In this short excerpt, Jackson, who was born around 1850, discusses how women were treated as "breeders," expected to bear children every year to increase the slaveowner's property.

"Lawdy, Lawdy, them was tribbolashuns! Wunner dese here womans was my Antie en she say dat she skacely call to min' he e'r whoppin' her, 'cause she was er breeder woman en' brought in chillum ev'y twelve mont's jes lak a cow bringin' in a calf . . . He orders she can't be put to no strain 'casen uv dat."

DOCUMENT 54:

Excerpt, Kate E. R. Pickard, *The Kidnapped and the Ransomed. Being the Personal Recollections of Peter Still and his Wife "Vina," after Forty Years of Slavery* (New York and Auburn: Miller, Orton and Mulligan, 1856), 364–65.

Courtesy Documenting the American South, University Library, The University of North Carolina at Chapel Hill.

This memoir, written by Kate Pickard, documents the lives of two slaves, Vina from Alabama and Peter from Kentucky. This excerpt details Peter's attempts to purchase Vina by earning a portion of the sum and appealing to abolitionists to help support her purchase.

. . . About ten o'clock in the morning, Vina, who amid all the confusion, was watching for a messenger, saw her master coming up the hill from the river. He walked towards the cabins, and soon called— "Vina! O Vina!"

She strove to quell the tumultuous throbbings of her heart, and she suceeeded in subduing all appearance of emotion—so that when she reached the spot where the master stood, her face was calm, and her voice was clear as usual.

"Well, Vina," said he, "how would you like to see Peter?"

"Mons's well, Sir," replied she.

"Do you know where he is?"

"I reckon, sir, he's in Cincinnati."

"No—he lives in Philadelphia, and he's bought you all."

"Bought us?"

"Yes, he's bought you;—how would you like to go to him?"

"Why, if it's true, sir, I'd like to go mighty well."

"If it's true?—don't you believe it?"

"I don't know, sir, whether I believes it or not."

"Well, don't you suppose choose?—Don't you belong to me?"

"Yes, Sir, I know you can."

"Well, if you want to go, make haste and get yourselves ready; for I've got to carry you all over to Florence to-night. There's a man there, who has come for you—he can tell you all about Peter. You ought to have been there before now, but you are all so devilish hard to hear that I had to hallo there for a boat, 'till I'm right hoarse."

"We didn't hear you, Sir—the hogs kept such a fuss."

"I know—I know—but you all must hurry yourselves now."

He went to the boys, and told the news to them; but they, too, made strange of it, and seemed to doubt his words.

"Well," said he, "you all act like you don't believe me—now, I'm no ways anxious to sell you, and if you don't want to go, you must get ready devilish quick, for I must have you in Florence to-night; and we must cross the river before dark."

The mother and her sons entered their cabin, and hastily, gathering up such of their things as they could carry easiest, they hastened to the river. Among their fellow-slaves were many whom they counted friends, but even to these they had no time to say "Good bye." Crossing to the main land in a canoe, they sprang into the wagon which waited for them there, and drove toward home, the master riding by their side.

DOCUMENT 55:
Letter, Vilet Lester to Patsey Patterson, 1857.

Courtesy Joseph Allred Papers, Rare Book, Manuscript, and Special Collections Library, Duke University.

Information on Vilet Lester, a slave owned by the Patterson family in Randolph County, North Carolina, is limited. This letter, however, demonstrates the relationship between an enslaved black woman and a white woman who were, at one time, playmates.

Georgia Bullock Co August 29th 1857
My Loving Miss Patsy
I hav long bin wishing to imbrace this presant and pleasant opertunity of unfolding my Seans and fealings Since I was constrained to leav my Long Loved home and friends which I cannot never gave my Self the Least

promis of returning to. I am well and this is Injoying good hlth and has
ever Since I Left Randolph. whend I left Randolf I went to Rockingham
and Stad there five weaks and then I left there and went to Richmon vir-
gina to be Sold and I Stade there three days and was bought by a man by
the name of Groover and braught to Georgia and he kept me about Nine
months and he being a trader Sold me to a man by the name of Rimes
and he Sold me to a man by the name of Lester and he has owned me
four years and Says that he will keep me til death Siperates us without
Some of my old north Caroliner friends wants to buy me again. my Dear
Mistress I cannot tell my fealings nor how bad I wish to See youand old
Boss and Mss Rahol and Mother. I do not [k]now which I want to See the
worst Miss Rahol or mother I have thaugh[t] that I wanted to See mother
but never befour did I [k]no[w] what it was to want to See a parent and
could not. I wish you to gave my love to old Boss Miss Rahol and bailum
and gave my manafold love to mother brothers and sister and pleas to tell
them to Right to me So I may here from them if I cannot See them and
also I wish you to right to me and Right me all the nuse. I do want to now
whether old Boss is Still Living or now and all the rest of them and I want
to [k]now whether balium is maried or no. I wish to [k]now what has Ever
become of my Presus little girl. I left her in goldsborough with Mr. Walker
and I have not herd from her Since and Walker Said that he was going to
Carry her to Rockingham and gave her to his Sister and I want to [k]no[w]
whether he did or no as I do wish to See her very mutch and Boss Says he
wishes to [k]now whether he will Sell her or now and the least that can
buy her and that he wishes a answer as Soon as he can get one as I wis
himto buy her an my Boss being a man of Reason and fealing wishes to
grant my trubled breast that mutch gratification and wishes to [k]now
whether he will Sell her now. So I must come to a close by Escribing my
Self you long loved and well wishing play mate as a Servant until death

Vilet Lester
of Georgia
to Miss Patsey Padison
of North Caroliner

My Bosses Name is James B Lester and if you Should think a nuff of me
to right me which I do beg the faver of you as a Sevant direct your letter

to Millray Bullock County Georgia. Pleas to right me So fare you well in love.

DOCUMENT 56:
Letter, J. W. Loguen to Mrs. Sarah Logue, *The Liberator*, April 27, 1860.

Courtesy Library of Congress.

This letter from a former slave to his mistress reveals the deep anger felt by many who gained their freedom. The letter from Loguen, an Underground Railroad conductor and minister, is notable for its force and broad criticism of the mistress. The abolitionist William Lloyd Garrison published *The Liberator* from 1831 to 1865.

Mrs. Sarah Logue: Yours of the 20th of February is duly received, and I thank you for it. It is a long time since I heard from my poor old mother, and I am glad to know that she is yet alive, and, as you say, "as well as common." What that means, I don't know. I wish you had said more about her.

You are a woman; but had you a woman's heart, you never could have insulted a brother by telling him you sold his only remaining brother and sister, because he put himself beyond your power to convert him into money.

You sold my brother and sister, Abe and Anne, and twelve acres of land, you say, because I ran away. Now you have the unutterable mean-ness to ask me to return and be your miserable chattel, or, in lieu thereof, send you $1000 to enable you to redeem the land, but not to redeem my poor brother and sister! If I were to send you money, it would be to get my brother and sister, and not that you should get land. You say you are a cripple, and doubtless you say it to stir my pity, for you knew I was sus-ceptible in that direction. I do pity you from the bottom of my heart. Nevertheless, I am indignant beyond the power of words to express, that you should be so sunken and cruel as to tear the hearts I love so much all to pieces; that you should be willing to impale and crucify us all, out of compassion for your foot or leg. Wretched woman! Be it known to you that I value my freedom, to say nothing of my mother, brothers and sisters, more than your whole body; more, indeed, than my own life; more than all the lives of all the slaveholders and tyrants under heaven.

You say you have offers to buy me, and that you shall sell me if I do not send you $1000, and in the same breath and almost in the same sentence, you say, "Your know we raised you as we did our own children." Woman, did you raise your own children for the market? Did you raise them for the whipping-post? Did you raise them to be driven off, bound to a coffle in chains? Where are my poor bleeding brothers and sisters? Can you tell? Who was it that sent them off into sugar and cotton fields, to be kicked and cuffed, and whipped, and to groan and die; and where no kin can hear their groans, or attend and sympathize at their dying bed, or follow in their funeral? Wretched woman! Do you say you did not do it? Then I reply, your husband did, and you approved the deed—and the very letter you sent me shows that your heart approves it all. Shame on you!

But, by the way, where is your husband? You don't speak of him. I infer, therefore, that he is dead; that he has gone to his great account, with all his sins against my poor family upon his head. Poor man! gone to meet the spirits of my poor, outraged and murdered people, in a world where Liberty and Justice are Masters.

But you say I am a thief, because I took the old mare along with me. Have you got to learn that I had a better right to the old mare, as you call her, than Manasseth Logue had to me? It is a greater sin for me to steal his horse, than it was for him to rob my mother's cradle, and steal me? If he and you infer that I forfeit all my rights to you, shall I not infer that you forfeit all your rights to me? Have you got to learn that human rights are mutual and reciprocal, and if you take my liberty and life, you forfeit your own liberty and life? Before God and high heaven, is there a law for one man which is not a law for every other man?

If you or any other speculator on my body and rights, wish to know how I regard my rights, they need but come here, and lay their hands on me to enslave me. Did you think to terrify me by presenting the alternative to give my money to you, or give my body to slavery? Then let me say to you, that I meet the proposition with unutterable scorn and contempt. The proposition is an outrage and an insult. I will not budge one hair's breadth. I will not breathe a shorter breath, even to save me from your persecutions. I stand among a free people, who, I thank God, sympathize with my rights, and the rights of mankind; and if you emissaries and venders come here to re-enslave me, and escape the unshrinking vigor of my own right arm, I trust my strong and brave friends, in this city and State, will be my rescuers and avengers.

Yours, &c.,
J. W. LOGUEN.

DOCUMENT 57:
Article, *The Liberator,* October 26, 1860.

Courtesy Library of Congress.

This article, reprinted from an unnamed St. Louis newspaper, was published in William Lloyd Garrison's abolitionist newspaper, and illustrates how complicated and expensive it was to purchase the freedom of one's family members.

A St. Louis paper of a recent date has the following paragraph:—

In the foundry of Gaty, M'Cune & co., in this city, among its two hundred and seventy operatives are two negroes, who began life at the establishment, in 1849, as slaves. By dint of unlagging industry, in due course of time one of them bought himself, wife and five children, paying for himself $1400, and on an average for his wife and children $800 each. The negro is now supposed to be worth, in his own right, more than $5000 in real estate in that city. Another negro entered the factory about the same time, amassed sufficient money by his attention to duty to purchase himself at the price of $1500, his wife at $500, and four children at $400, and is now worth $6000 in real estate. These negroes were bought from their masters by Mr. Gray, with the understanding that they should work themselves free, and out of his own pocket he gave two per cent. interest on the deferred payments.

DOCUMENT 58:

Louisa Picquet, *The Octoroon: or Inside Views of Southern Domestic Life* (New York: Published by the Author, Nos. 5 & 7 Mercer Street, 1861), 36–38.

Courtesy Documenting the American South, University Library, The University of North Carolina at Chapel Hill.

Born in South Carolina, Louisa lived as a slave in Georgia, Texas, and Louisiana. In New Orleans, she was sold to Mr. Williams and bore him four children. The term "octoroon" was largely used in former French or Spanish colonies, and often denoted light-skinned people who were only one-eighth African American, as was Picquet. Many enjoyed privileges that their darker skinned counterparts did not. Upon his death, she was freed and moved to Ohio and sought to free her mother. The memoir, mainly an interview conducted by the Methodist minister Hiram Mattison, addresses the sexual exploitation of female slaves. This excerpt focuses on her sexual relationship with Mr. Williams.

CHAPTER VI.

THE FAMILY SOLD AT AUCTION—LOUISA BOUGHT BY A
"NEW ORLEANS GENTLEMAN," AND WHAT CAME OF IT.

Q.—"How did you say you come to be sold?"

A.—"Well, you see, Mr. Cook made great parties, and go off to watering-places, and get in debt, and had to break up [fail], and he took us to Mobile, and hired the most of us out, so the men he owe should not find us, and sell us for the debt. Then, after a while, the sheriff came from Georgia after Mr. Cook's debts, and found us all, and took us to auction, and sold us. My mother and brother was sold to Texas, and I was sold to New Orleans."

Q.—"How old were you, then?"

A.—"Well, I don't know exactly, but the auctioneer said I wasn't quite fourteen. I didn't know myself."

Q.—"How old was your brother?"

A.—"I suppose he was about two months old. He was little bit of baby."

Q.—"Where were you sold?"

A.—"In the city of Mobile."

Q.—"In a yard? In the city?"

A.—"No. They put all the men in one room, and all the women in another; and then whoever want to buy come and examine, and ask you whole lot of questions. They began to take the clothes off of me, and a gentleman said they needn't do that, and told them to take me out. He said he knew I was a virtuous girl, and he'd buy me, anyhow. He didn't strip me only just under my shoulders."

Q.—"Were there any others there white like you?"

A.—"Oh yes, plenty of them. There was only Lucy of our lot, but others!"

Q.—"Were others stripped and examined?"

A.—"Well, not quite naked, but just same."

Q.—"You say the gentleman told them to 'take you out.' What did he mean by that?"

A.—"Why, take me out of the room where the women and girls were kept; where they examine them—out where the auctioneer sold us."

Q.—"Where was that? In the street, or in a yard?"

A.—"At the market, where the block is?"

Q.—"What block?"

A.—"My! don't you know? The stand, where we have to get up?"

Q.—"Did *you* get up on the stand?"

A.—"Why, of course; we all have to get up to be seen."

Q.—"What else do you remember about it?"

A.—"Well, they first begin at upward of six hundred for me, and then some bid fifty more, and some twenty-five more, and that way."

Q.—"Do you remember any thing the auctioneer said about you when he sold you?"

A.—"Well, he said he could not recommend me for any thing else only that I was a good-lookin' girl, and a good nurse, and kind and affectionate to children; but I was never used to any hard work. He told them they could see that. My hair was quite short, and the auctioneer spoke about it, but said, 'You see it good quality, and give it a little time, it will grew out again. You see Mr. Cook had my hair cut off. My hair grew fast, and look so much better than Mr. Cook's daughter, and he fancy I had better hair than his daughter, and so he had it cut off to make a difference."

Q.—"Well, how did they sell you and your mother? that is, which was sold first?"

A.—"Mother was put up the first of our folks. She was sold for splendid cook, and Mr. Horton, from Texas, bought her and the baby, my brother. Then Henry, the carriage-driver, was put up, and Mr. Horton bought him, and then two field-hands, Jim and Mary. The women there tend mills and drive ox wagons, and plough, just like men. Then I was sold next. Mr. Horton run me up to fourteen hundred dollars. He wanted I should go with my mother. Then some one said 'fifty.' Then Mr. Williams allowed that he did not care what they bid, he was going to have me anyhow. Then he bid fifteen hundred.

Mr. Horton said 'twas no use to bid any more, and I was sold to Mr. Williams. I went right to New Orleans then."

Q.—"Who was Mr. Williams?"

A.—"I didn't know then, only he lived in New Orleans. Him and his wife had parted, some way—he had three children boys. When I was going away I heard some one cryin', and prayin' the Lord to go with her only daughter, and protect me. I felt pretty bad then, but hadn't no time only to say good-bye. I wanted to go back and get the dress I bought with the half-dollars, I thought a good deal of that; but Mr. Williams would not let me go back and get it. He said he'd get me plenty of nice dresses. Then I thought mother could cut it up and make dresses for my brother, the baby. I knew she could not wear it; and I had a thought, too, that she'd have it to remember me."

Q.—"It seems like a dream, don't it?"

A.—"No; it seems fresh in my memory when I think of it—no longer than yesterday. Mother was right on her knees, with her hands up, prayin' to the Lord for me. She didn't care who saw her: the people all lookin' at her. I often thought her prayers followed me, for I never could forget her. Whenever I wanted any thing real bad after that, my mother was always sure to appear to me in a dream that night, and have plenty to give me, always."

Q.—"Have you never seen her since?"

A.—"No, never since that time. I went to New Orleans, and she went to Texas. So I understood."

Q.—"Well, how was it with you after Mr. Williams bought you?"

A.—"Well, he took me right away to New Orleans."

Q.—"How did you go?"

A.—"In a boat, down the river. Mr. Williams told me what he bought me for, soon as we started for New Orleans. He said he was getting old, and when he saw me he thought he'd buy me, and end his days with me. He said if I behave myself he'd treat me well: but, if not, he'd whip me almost to death."

Q.—"How old was he?"

A.—"He was over forty; I guess pretty near fifty. He was gray headed. That's the reason he was always so jealous. He never let me go out anywhere."

Q.—"Did you never go to church?"

A.—"No, sir; I never darken a church door from the time he bought me till after he died. I used to ask him to let me go to church. He would accuse me of some object, and said there was more rascality done there than anywhere else. He'd sometimes say, 'Go on, I guess you've made your arrangements; go on, I'll catch up with you.' But I never dare go once."

Q.—"Had you any children while in New Orleans?"

A.—"Yes; I had four."

Q.—"Who was their father?"

A.—"Mr. Williams."

Q.—"Was it known that he was living with you?"

A.—"Every body knew I was housekeeper, but he never let on that he was the father of my children. I did all the work in his house—nobody there but me and the children."

Q.—"What children?"

A.—"My children and his. You see he had three sons."

Q.—"How old were his children when you went there?"

A.—"I guess the youngest was nine years old. When he had company, gentlemen folks, he took them to the hotel. He never have no gentlemen company home. Sometimes he would come and knock, if he stay out later than usual time; and if I did not let him in in a minute, when I would be asleep, he'd come in and take the light, and look under the bed, and in the wardrobe, and all over, and then ask me why I did not let him in sooner. I did not know what it meant till I learnt his ways."

Q.—"Were your children mulattoes?"

A.—"No, sir! They were all white. They look just like him. The neighbors all see that. After a while he got so disagreeable that I told him, one day, I wished he would sell me, or 'put me in his pocket'— that's the way we say—because I had no peace at all. I rather die than live in that way. Then he got awful mad, and said nothin' but death should separate us; and, if I run off, he'd blow my brains out. Then I thought, if that be the way, all I could do was just to pray for him to die."

Q.—"Where did you learn to pray?"

A.—"I first begin to pray when I was in Georgia, about whippin'— that the Lord would make them forget it, and not whip me: and it seems if when I pray I did not get so hard whippin'."

DOCUMENT 59:
Photograph, Slaves in front of cabin, 1861.

Courtesy Library of Congress, LC-USZCN-280.

This photograph shows a family of slaves in front of a wooden cabin, known as the Gaines' house. The house is either in Washington, D.C., or in Hampton, Virginia. At the Library of Congress, it was filed with a Civil War album kept by Larkin G. Mead.

DOCUMENT 60:
Excerpt, Bethany Veney, *The Narrative of Bethany Veney, A Slave Woman* (Worcester, MA: n.p., 1889), 38–39.

Courtesy Documenting the American South, University Library, The University of North Carolina at Chapel Hill.

Bethany Veney was born a slave in 1815 in Virginia and served numerous masters before being sold to G. J. Adams, who freed her in the North. Her memoir documents her early life and focuses in particular on the role of religion in her life. This excerpt focuses on her first taste of freedom in Rhode Island, which abolished slavery in 1774.

Document 59

CHAPTER IX.
NEW EXPERIENCES—HOME IN THE NORTH.

THE feelings with which I entered my Northern home, 22 Chares-Field Street, Providence, R.I., on a bright pleasant morning in August, 1858, can be more easily fancied than described. A new life had come to me. I was in a land where, by its laws, I had the same right to myself that any other woman had. No jailer could take me to prison, and sell me at auction to the highest bidder. My boy was my own, and no one could take him from me. But I had left behind me every one I had ever known. I did not forget the dreadful hardships I had endured, and yet somehow I did not think of them with half the bitterness with which I had endured them. I was a stranger in a strange land; and it was no wonder, perhaps, that a dreadful loneliness and homesickness came over me.

The family were just rising when Mr. Adams, with his night-key, opened the door, and showed me the way to the sitting-room, and then went to find his wife. I had only a moment to look about me, when the girl from the kitchen came in, and in a very friendly manner asked me to go there with her. Then, in a few minutes more, Mrs. Adams came, and, in her smiling, motherly way, held out her hand to me, saying, "Good-morning, Betty." She met me as if I were an old acquaintance. At any rate, she made me feel that I was with friends.

It was not easy at first to accommodate myself to the new surroundings. In the Southern kitchen, under slave rule, there was little thought of convenience or economy. Here I found all sorts of Yankee inventions and improvements to make work easy and pleasant. There were dishes and pans of every description, clean and distinct cloths for all purposes, brushes and brooms for different uses. I couldn't help feeling bewildered sometimes at the difference in so many ways, and for a moment wished myself back in "old Virginny," with my own people; and I very, very often longed to see the old familiar faces and hear the old sounds, but never could I forget to be grateful for my escape from a system under which I had suffered so much.

DOCUMENT 61:
Excerpt, S. J. McCray, *Life of Mary F. McCray, Born and Raised a Slave in the State of Kentucky. By Her Husband and Son* (Lima, OH: n.p., 1898), 10–13.

Courtesy Documenting the American South, University Library, The University of North Carolina at Chapel Hill.

Little is known about Mary McCray (1838–1894) or the circumstances of the publication of her memoir. This excerpt focuses on the role of religion in her life, which was one arena in which she had control over her time.

CHAPTER III.
HER COMMISSION.

In those days there were no churches for the slaves on the plantation, but they were compelled to go from one plantation to another to hold their meetings in their log cabins. She used to go with her aunt and others to those prayer meetings. The mighty power of God would be in the meetings. They would hold their meetings sometimes nearly all night. Many would fall under the mighty power of God, and many of them would get soundly converted.

Our subject was greatly urged to seek the Lord. She went forward and soon found that she was a lost sinner without the blood of Jesus to wash away all her sins.

They would work hard all day in the corn fields and nearly every night would go two or three miles from home to attend meeting. Many were converted every night. She was somewhat discouraged because she was so slow to believe. Her cousin fell under the mighty power of God, and was happily converted, coming through shouting and praising God, and commenced at once to preach to the people, telling them to flee from the wrath to come. She said to our subject to believe and she would be converted. This encouraged her to go on.

She was trying to get converted shouting, like her cousin, but the Dear Lord did not come to her in that way. She did reason with the devil for some time, who told her that if she did not shout she would not have religion. She had a terrible struggle to get over that. After that terrible struggle about getting converted shouting, her faith was greatly increased, and while she was praying one day she was wonderfully blessed. She told her cousin how she felt. Her cousin told her that she had religion. She said, "Oh, no, I am just getting in a good way." She did not understand the scheme of the devil, so she was defeated and had to do her work all over again . But the Holy Spirit still strove with her. The meetings were still going on with increased power. She attended nearly ever night. The old people encouraged her, and then she began to take part in speaking and praying. By so doing the same blessing came to her again, but she was not satisfied. She went on in that state quite a long time. Finally one night she went to bed and fell into a dream, or trance, she did not know which. However a man came to her while she was in that vision. She was trying to cross a clear stream of water. The man she believed to be a white man. He threw a narrow board in the middle of the stream of water, and there was also a broad board in the stream. The man told her to make her choice. She stepped on the narrow one and went across. As soon as she was across he showed her a beautiful place and told her it was heaven. She saw her cousin there and she was with all the angels. They were all just alike. She turned to come back, when she heard a voice saying: "You have just as much religion as those who shout." After that she woke up. She felt very strange and told her aunt about the vision. Her aunt said that she would get through all right. In a short time afterwards she received the witness of the Holy Spirit that her sins were all forgiven. She was then a happy girl. She knew that her sins were all washed away by the blood of Jesus. She could sing this song:

"Oh! happy day, that fixed my choice,

On Thee, my Savior and my God;

Well may this glowing heart rejoice,

And tell its rapture all abroad."

"Happy day! Happy day!

When Jesus washed my sins away.

He taught me how to watch and pray,

And live rejoicing every day,

Happy day! Happy day!

When Jesus washed my sins away."

The meeting spread from one plantation to another, and many of the poor slaves' hearts were made to rejoice, for the Lord Jesus visited them, notwithstanding they were treated only as cattle and horses. Thanks be unto the Lord God of Heaven, who did look down upon them in their helpless condition in tender mercy.

The subject of this sketch was a faithful young Christian, laboring in the prayer meetings from house to house. They did not have churches of their own. She related that one night their prayer meeting continued until daylight, the power of God having fallen upon the people in such a wonderful manner that they fell on the floor like dead men and women. Many of them had to go one, two and three miles to their homes, and some of them were greatly punished for being away from their houses at that late hour of night, for most all of them were, compelled to go to work before daylight. But in spite of all this cruel treatment they would pray and sing so that it would disturb their old masters so that they could not sleep and they would whip them, but still the poor slaves would continue to serve the Lord.

CHAPTER 4

Resisting Slavery

The documents in this section examine women's wide range of responses to slavery and attempts to ameliorate its affects, escape from it, and bring about its demise.

DOCUMENT 62:
Portrait of Phillis Wheatley, 1773.

Courtesy Library of Congress, LC-USZ62–12533.

Born in Senegal and brought to Massachusetts at the age of seven, Phillis Wheatley (1753–1784) was purchased by John and Susannah Wheatley. Phillis learned to read and write, and by the age of twelve she was fluent in Greek and Latin. In 1773, she published this volume of poetry, only the second such volume published by a woman in the colonies. This poem, reflecting on her being brought as a slave from Africa, presents a powerful commentary on the relationship between religion and slavery. Wheatley's accomplishments countered the widespread belief that slaves were subhuman and incapable of intellectual pursuits.

DOCUMENT 63:
Phillis Wheatley, "On Being Brought from Africa to America," from *Poems on Various, Subjects, Religions and Moral* (London and Philadelphia: Joseph Cruckshank, 1773).

Courtesy Library of Congress.

Document 62

'Twas mercy brought me from my Pagan land,
Taught my benighted soul to understand
That there's a God, that there's a Saviour too:
Once I redemption neither sought nor knew.
Some view our sable race with scornful eye,
"Their colour is a diabolic die."
Remember, Christians, Negros, black as Cain,
May be refin'd and join th'angelic train.

DOCUMENT 64:
Advertisement placed by Stephen Dence, *Virginia Gazette* (Williamsburg), March 26, 1787.

Courtesy Library of Congress.

Stephen Dence placed this advertisement in the local newspaper regarding "a small yellow Negro wench named Hannah" to help in her capture. The advertisement concludes that anyone who assists in her recapture will be "rewarded according to their trouble."

Run away about the 15th of December last, a small yellow Negro wench named Hannah, about 35 years of age; had on when she went away a green plains petticoat, and sundry other clothes, but what sort I do not know, as she stole many from the other Negroes. She has remarkable long hair, or wool, is much scarified under the throat from one ear to the other, and has many scars on her back, occasioned by whipping. She pretends much to the religion the Negroes of late have practised, and may probably endeavour to pass for a free woman, as I understand she intended when she went away, by the Negroes in the neighbourhood. She is supposed to have made for Carolina. Whoever takes up the said slave, and secures her so that I get her again, shall be rewarded according to their trouble, by

STEPHEN DENCE.

DOCUMENT 65:
Letter, Abigail Adams, 1774.

Courtesy Historical Society of Massachusetts.

Abigail Adams wrote this short letter in response to a petition that was signed in June 1774 that was presented to Thomas Gage, the governor of Massachusetts. With her usual keen eye and sense of irony, Adams points out to her husband that "it always appeared a most iniquitous scheme to me to fight ourselves for what we are daily robbing and plundering from those who have as good a right to freedom as we have." Abigail Adams (1744–1818) was the wife of John Adams, second president of the United States from 1797 to 1801. When this letter was written, he was a member of the Continental Congress.

Boston [. . .] Sep 22 1774

I have just returnd from a visit to my Brother, with my Father who carried me there the day before yesterday—and called here in my return to see this much injured Town. I view it with much the same sensations that I should the body of a departed friend—only [put]of its present glory—for to [irk] finally to a more happy state. I will not despair, but will believe that our cause being good we shall finally prevail. The [mascine] in time of peace prepair for war—(if this may be called a time of peace) resounds throughout the Country, [. . .] [. . .] they are [warned] at Braintree all above 14 and under 60 to attend with their arms and to train once a fortnight from that time is a Scheme which lays much at heart with many.

Scot has arrived, and brings news that he expected to find all peace and quietness here as he left them at home—you will have more particulars than I am able to send you from much better hands. There has been in Town conspiracy of the Negroes—at present it is kept pretty private and was discovered by one who endeavourd to disuaid them from it—he being threatened with his life applied to justice Quincy for protection—they conducted in this ways—got an [. . .] man to draw up a petition to the Govener telling him they would fight for him provided he would arm them and engage to liberate them if he conquerd—and it is said that he attended so much to it as to [consuet] [. . .] upon it—and one [. . .] has been very busy and active—there is but little said, and what steps they will take in consequence of it I know not—I wish most sincerely there was not a slave in the province—it allways appeard a most iniquitous scheme to me. fight ourselfs for what we are daily [ebbing] and plundering from those who have as good a right freedom as we have—you know my mind upon this subject. I left all our little ones well, and shall return to them to night. I hope to hear from you by the return of the heaven of this and by [Revere]—I long for the Day of your return, yet look upon you much safer where you are, but know it will not do for you—not one action has been brought to this court, no briefings of any fort in your way—all law [. . .]. and the [. . .] will soon follow—for they are supporters of each other—adieu my father hurries me Yours most sincerely

---

DOCUMENT 66:
Portrait, Portrait of Elizabeth "Mumbet" Freeman, 1811.

Courtesy Historical Society of Massachusetts.

Document 66

DOCUMENT 67:
Brom & Bett vs. J. Ashley, 1781.

Elizabeth Freeman (known as Mum Bett) was born into slavery in 1742 in New York. After a violent incident with her mistress, she asked Theodore Sedgewick, a local lawyer, to help her sue for freedom. In *Brom & Bett vs. J. Ashley,* Bett won, and she became one of the first slaves freed under the Massachusetts constitution of 1780. The court required her owner, John Ashley, to pay thirty shillings and court costs. This municipal case ultimately led to the abolition of slavery in Massachusetts. When she was nearly seventy years old, Susan Ridley Sedgewick painted a miniature portrait of Mum Bett in watercolor on ivory. Her gravestone reads: "She was born a slave and remained a slave for nearly thirty years. She could neither read nor write yet in her own sphere she had no superior or equal. She neither wasted time nor property. She never violated a trust nor failed to perform a duty. In every situation of domestic trial, she was the most efficient helper, and the tenderest friend. Good mother, farewell." W. E. B. Du Bois was one of her great-grandchildren.

Brom & Bett vs. Ashley

Transcript of Case No. 1
Brom & Bett vs. J. Ashley Esq.
Book 4A, page 55
Inferior Court of Common Pleas
Berkshire County
Great Barrington, Massachusetts
1781
Transcribed by Brady Barrows at Berkshire County Courthouse 1998
Sponsored by http://www.mumbet.com

Begin Record:
Brom A Negro Man and Bett a Negro Woman both of Sheffield in said County of Berkshire. Plaintiffs against John Ashley of Sheffield aforesaid Esq. Defendant In a plea of replevin wherein the [aF] Brom and Bett prayed out a plevinces writ of Replevin, signed by the Clerk of our said court, dated the twenty eighth day of May in the year of our Lord one

thousand seven hundred & eighty one which is as follows (to wit) The
Commonwealth of Massachusetts. To the Sheriff of our county of
Berkshire his under Sheriff or Deputy Greeting. When we have often
commanded you that justly and without delay you should cause to be
replevied Brom a Negro man of Sheffield in our said county Laborerer,
and Bett a Negro Woman of Sheffield aforesaid. spinster, whom John
Ashley Esq. and John Ashley, JurR. Esq. both of Sheffield aforesaid have
taken and being [~o] taken detain (as it is said) unleys they were taken
by our special command, or by the command of our Chief Justice, or
for Homicide, or for any other just cause, whereby according to the
Usage of this Commonwealth they are not Replevigable, or that you
should signify to us the cause, wherefore the said John Ashley and John
Ashley Jun. have taken & detained said Brom & Bett and you having
returned unto us that you have repaired unto the houses of John Ashley
and John Ashley Jun. Esqs to Replevy the said Brom & Bett according
to the tenor of our aforesaid Writ but the said John Ashley Esq did not
permit a delivery of the aforesaid Brom & Bett to be made because he
attested the said Brom & Bett were his servants for life, thereby claiming
a right of servitude [*es*ons] at the said Brom & Bett. We unwilling that
the s. Brom if he be a Freman and the said Bett if she be a Free Woman,
by such taking and claim should be deprived of the Common law, command you if the said Brom & Bett shall find you Sufficient Security of
being before our Justices of our Inferior Court of common Pleas to be
holden at Great Barrington within & for our s. County of Berkshire on
the third Tuesday of August next to answer unto the aforesaid John
Ashley Esq. if they shall find you such sufficient Security then in the
meantime that you cause to be replevied the aforesaid Brom and Bett
according to the tenor of oure aforesaid writs; and besides if the said.
Brom & Bett shall have made you secure of their complaint as aforesaid
then summon by good summoners the said John Ashley Esq that he be
before the Justices of our s. Court on the third Tuesday of August next
to answer unto the said Brom & Bett of the takeing and claim aforesaid,
and have there then the names of the Pledges in this Writ tested by Wm
Whiting Esq. at G. Barrington this twenty eighth day of May as aforesaid.
Then did Brom & Bett appear by their attorneys Tappin Reeve and
Theodore Sedgwick Esq and the said John Ashley Esq. Comes also (by
his attorneys John Canfield Esq & David Noble Gental) and says that the
s. Brom & Bett ought not to have and maintain their suit aforesaid

against him but that the same ought to be abated and dismissed, because he says that the said Brom & Bett are & were at the time of Receiving the original Writ the legal Negro servants of him the s. John Ashley during their lives, and this the said John is ready to verify and hereof prays the Judgment of this Court, and that the said Suit may be abolished. and the said Brom & Bett by their said attorneys (John Reeve and Theodore Sedgwick Esqs) say that their suit aforesaid ought not to be abated because they say that they are not, nor are either of them, nor were they, or either of them, at the time of the giving the original Writ, the Negro servants or servants of him aforesaid John Ashley during their lives and this they pray may be inquired of by the County and the said John Ashley (by his a.f Attorneys) like=wise both the same and after a full hearing of this case the evidence therein being produced. the same case is committed to the Jury Jonathan Holcom Foreman and his fellows who being duly sworn return this verdict that in this case the Jury find that the aforesaid Brom & Bett are not and were not at the time of the purchase of the original writ the legal Negro servants of him the said John Ashley during their life and [afsefs] thirty shillings damages wherefore it is considered by the Court Adjudged and determined that the said Brom & Bett are not, nor were they at the time of the purchase of the original writ the legal Negro of the said John Ashley during life, and that the said Brom & Bett do recover against the said John Ashley the sum of thirty shillings lawful silver Money, Damages, and the Costs of this suit Paned at five pounds fourteen shillings and four pence like Money and hereof the s. Brom & Bett may have their Executions. The said John Ashley appeals from the Judgment of this Court to the Supreme Judicial Court to be holden at Great Barrington within and for the County of Berkshire upon the first Tuesday of October next: and John Ashley Jun. Esq. Recognizes with [sureties] as the law Directs for the said John Ashley his prosecuting with assest this appeal at the said Supreme Court & c. as on file_____

End of Record
[ ] brackets indicate uncertain word
The original was written in script
This transcribed copy made available by:
http://www.mumbet.com

DOCUMENT 68:

"Unnatural and Horrid Murder," *Southern Statesman* (Jackson, TN), September 10, 1831.

Courtesy Tennessee State Library and Archives, Nashville.

This short article describes how a "negro woman, the property of Col. Thomas Loftin, near this place destroyed three of her children by drowning." Murdering one's children was an extreme but powerful form of resistance available to women. Many of these women were called modern-day Medeas, for the Greek tragic figure who murdered her own children for revenge.

Unnatural and horrid Murder.—on Wednesday night last, a negro woman, the property of Col. Thomas Loftin, near this place, destroyed three of her children by drowning; one a boy aged about seven years, and two girls, one an infant at the breast. On the evening of that day, she had been chastized by her master, the first time it is said, that he had ever corrected her. At a late hour of the night, she, according to her own acknowledgements, deliberately took them to a pool of water, one at a time, and held them in it, until life became extinct. In the act of taking her fourth child for the same purpose, she was discovered by her husband, when an alarm was made. The drowned children were found about two hours after the act was committed, but, every exertion to resuscitate them proved ineffectual. The woman stand committed for trial.

DOCUMENT 69:

Advertisement submitted by James Norcom for the capture of Harriet Jacobs, American Beacon (Norfolk, VA), July 4, 1835.

Courtesy Library of Congress.

James Norcom, in trying to recapture his slave Harriet Jacobs, posted this advertisement in a local newspaper. It promised a one-hundred-dollar reward and describes Jacobs as one who "speaks easily and fluently, and has an agreeable carriage and address."

Jacobs would go on to write *Incidents in the Life of a Slave Girl,* one of the best-known autobiographies in American literature.

$100 REWARD

WILL be given for the apprehension and delivery of my Servant Girl HARRIET. She is a light mulatto, 21 years of age, about 5 feet 4 inches high, of a thick and corpulent habit, having on her head a thick covering of black hair that curls naturally, but which can be easily combed straight. She speaks easily and fluently, and has an agreeable carriage and address. Being a good seamstress, she has been accustomed to dress well, has a variety of very fine clothes, made in the prevailing fashion, and will probably appear, if abroad, tricked out in gay and fashionable finery. As the girl absconded from the plantation of my son without any known cause or provocation, it is probable she designs to transport herself to the North.

The above reward, with all reasonable charges, will be given for apprehending her or securing her in any prison or jail within the U. States.

All persons are hereby forewarned against harboring or entertaining her, or being in any way instrumental in her escape, under the most rigorous penalties of the law.

JAMES NORCOM.
Edenton, N.C. June 30

DOCUMENT 70:
Excerpt, Catharine E. Beecher, *Essay on Slavery and Abolitionism, with Reference to the Duty of American Females* (Philadelphia: Perkins, 1837).

Courtesy Library of Congress.

Catharine Beecher was the eldest child of Lyman Beecher, a prominent New England minister, and sister to Harriet Beecher Stowe, author of *Uncle Tom's Cabin.* She wrote widely about women's domestic sphere, but was largely unsympathetic to the suffrage movement. This essay is a response to the abolitionist Angelina

Grimké's *Appeal to the Christian Women of the South,* which was printed a year earlier. In the reply, Beecher focuses on the real but often informal nature of women's power and wholeheartedly accepts women's subordinate position to men. Far more moderate than Grimké (1805–1879), Beecher (1800–1878) advocated change through education and reform, not direct action.

MY DEAR FRIEND:

Your public address to Christian females of the South has reached me, and I have been urged to aid in circulating it at the North. I have also been informed, that you contemplate a tour, during the ensuing year, for the purpose of exerting your influence to form Abolition Societies among ladies of non-slave-holding States.

Our acquaintance and friendship give me a claim to your private ear; but there are reasons why it seems more desirable to address you, who now stand before the public as an advocate of Abolition measures, in a more public manner.

The object I have in view, is to present some reasons why it seems unwise and inexpedient for ladies of the non-slave-holding States to unite themselves in Abolition Societies; and thus, at the same time, to exhibit the inexpediency of the course you propose to adopt. . . .

Now Abolitionists are before the community, and declare all slavery is sin, which out to be immediately forsaken; and that it is their object and intention to promote the *immediate emancipation* of all the slaves in this nation . . . [R]eproaches, rebukes, and sneers, were employed to convince whites that their prejudices were sinful . . .

[T]he severing of the Union by the present mode of agitating the question . . . may be one of the results, and, if so, what are the probabilities for a Southern republic that has torn itself off for the purpose of excluding foreign interference, and for the purpose of perpetuating slavery? . . .

Heaven has appointed to one sex the superior, and to the other the subordinate station, and this without any reference to the character or conduct of either. It is therefore as much for the dignity as it is for the interest of females, in all respects to conform to the duties of this relation. . . . But while woman holds a subordinate relation in society to the other sex, it is not because it was designed that her duties or her influence should be any less important, or all-pervading. But it was designed that the mode of gaining influence and of exercising power should be altogether different and peculiar. . . .

Woman is to win every thing by peace and love; by making herself so much respected, esteemed and loved, that to yield to her opinions and to gratify her wishes, will be the free-will offering of the heart. But this is to be all accomplished in the domestic and social circle. . . . But the moment woman begins to feel the promptings of ambition, or the thirst for power, her aegis of defence is gone. All the sacred protection of religion, all the generous promptings of chivalry, all the poetry of romantic gallantry, depend upon woman's retaining her place as dependent and defenceless, and making no claims, and maintaining no right but what are the gifts of honour, rectitude and love.

A woman may seek the aid of co-operation and combination among her own sex, to assist her in her appropriate offices of piety, charity, maternal and domestic duty; but whatever, in any measure, throws a woman into the attitude of a combatant, either for herself or others—whatever binds her in a party conflict—whatever obliges her in any way to exert coercive influences, throws her out of her appropriate sphere. . . .

If it is asked, "May not woman appropriately come forward as a suppliant for a portion of her sex who are bound in cruel bondage?" It is replied, that, the rectitude and propriety of such measure, depend entirely on its probable results. If petitions from females will operate to exasperate; if they will be deemed obtrusive, indecorous, and unwise, by those to whom they are addressed; . . . if they will be the opening wedge, that will eventually bring females as petitioners and partisans into every political measure that may tend to injure and oppress their sex . . . then it is neither appropriate nor wise, nor right, for a woman to petition for the relief of oppressed females. . . .

In this country, petitions to congress, in reference to the official duties of legislators, seem, IN ALL CASES, to fall entirely without the sphere of female duty. Men are the proper persons to make appeals to the rulers whom they appoint, and if their female friends, by arguments and persuasions, can induce them to petition, all the good that can be done by such measures will be secured. But if females cannot influence their nearest friends, to urge forward a public measure in this way, they surely are out of their place, in attempting to do it themselves. . . .

It is allowed by all reflecting minds, that the safety and happiness of this nation depends upon having the *children* educated, and not only intellectually, but morally and religiously. There are now nearly two millions of children and adults in this country who cannot read, and who have no schools of any kind. To give only a small supply of teachers to these destitute children, who are generally where the population is sparse, will demand *thirty thousand teachers* at the moment and an addition of *two thousand every year*. Where is this army of teachers to be found? Is it at all probable that the other sex will afford even a moderate portion of this supply? . . . Men will be educators in the college, in the high school, and in some of the most honourable and lucrative common schools, but the *children,* the *little children* of this nation must, to a wide extent, be taught by females, or remain untaught. . . . And as the value of education rises in the public mind . . . women will more and more be furnished with those intellectual advantages which they need to fit them for such duties.

The result will be, that America will be distinguished above all other nations, for well-educated females and for the influence they will exert on the general interests of society. But if females, as they approach the other sex, in intellectual elevation, begin to claim, or to exercise in any manner, the peculiar prerogatives of that sex, education will prove a doubtful and dangerous blessing. But this will never be the result. For the more intelligent a woman becomes, the more she can appreciate the wisdom of that ordinance that appointed her subordinate station.

But it may be asked, is there nothing to be done to bring this national sin of slavery to an end? Must the internal stave-trade, a trade now ranked as piracy among all civilized nations, still prosper in our bounds? Must the very seat of our government stand as one of the chief slave-markets of the land; and must not Christian females open their lips, nor lift a finger, to bring such a shame and sin to an end? To this it may be replied, that Christian females may, and can say and do much to bring these evils to an end; and the present is a time and occasion when it seems most desirable that they should know, and appreciate, and *exercise* the power which they possess for so desirable an end. . . .

In the present aspect of affairs among us, when everything seems to be tending to disunion and distraction, it surely has become the duty of every female instantly to relinquish the attitude of a partisan, in every matter of clashing interests, and to assume the office of a mediator, and an advocate of peace. And to do this, it is not necessary that a woman should in any manner relinquish her opinion as to the evils or the benefits, the right or the wrong, of any principle of practice. But, while quietly holding her own opinions, and calmly avowing them, when conscience and integrity make the duty imperative, every female can employ her influence, not for the purpose of exciting or regulating public sentiment, but rather for the purpose of promoting a spirit of candour, forbearance, charity, and peace.

DOCUMENT 71:

Speech, Angelina Grimké Weld, "History of Pennsylvania Hall which was Destroyed by a Mob on the 17th of May, 1838."

Along with her sister Sarah, Angelina was active in abolitionist and suffragist causes, though she was born into a slaveholding family. To an audience in Pennsylvania Hall, South Carolina-born Grimké discusses the "demoralizing influence" of slavery and its "destructiveness to human happiness." Outside the hall, a mob was shouting and throwing rocks through the windows to protest her message. Grimké periodically addressed herself to the women in the audience: "Women of Philadelphia! allow me as a Southern woman, with much attachment to the land of my birth, to entreat you to come up to this work. Especially let me urge you to petition. *Men* may settle this and other questions at the ballot-box, but you have no such right; it is only through petitions that you can reach the Legislature. It is therefore peculiarly *your* duty to petition."

Men, brethren and fathers—mothers, daughters and sisters, what came ye out for to see? A reed shaken with the wind? Is it curiosity merely, or a deep sympathy with the perishing slave, that has brought this large audience together? [A yell from the mob without the building.] Those voices without ought to awaken and call out our warmest sympathies. Deluded beings! "they know not what they do." They know not that they are undermining their own rights and their own happiness, temporal and eternal. Do you ask, "what has the North to do with slavery?" Hear it—hear it.

Those voices without tell us that the spirit of slavery is *here,* and has been roused to wrath by our abolition speeches and conventions: for surely liberty would not foam and tear herself with rage, because her friends are multiplied daily, and meetings are held in quick succession to set forth her virtues and extend her peaceful kingdom. This opposition shows that slavery has done its deadliest work in the hearts of our citizens. Do you ask, then, "what has the North to do?" I answer, cast out first the spirit of slavery from your own hearts, and then lend your aid to convert the South. Each one present has a work to do, be his or her situation what it may, however limited their means, or insignificant their supposed influence. The great men of this country will not do this work; the church will never do it. A desire to please the world, to keep the favor of all parties and of all conditions, makes them dumb on this and every other unpopular subject. They have become worldly-wise, and therefore God, in his wisdom, employs them not to carry on his plans of reformation and salvation. He hath chosen the foolish things of the world to confound the wise, and the weak to overcome the mighty.

As a Southerner I feel that it is my duty to stand up here to-night and bear testimony against slavery. I have seen it—I have seen it. I know it has horrors that can never be described. I was brought up under its wing: I witnessed for many years its demoralizing influences, and its destructiveness to human happiness. It is admitted by some that the slave is not happy under the *worst* forms of slavery. But I have *never* seen a happy slave. I have seen him dance in his chains, it is true; but he was not happy. There is a wide difference between happiness and mirth. Man cannot enjoy the former while his manhood is destroyed, and that part of the being which is necessary to the making, and to the enjoyment of happiness, is completely blotted out. The slaves, however, may be, and sometimes are, mirthful. When hope is extinguished, they say, "let us eat and drink, for tomorrow we die." [Just then stones were thrown at the windows,—a great noise without, and commotion within.] What is a mob? What would the breaking of every window be? What would the levelling of this Hall be? Any evidence that we are wrong, or that slavery is a good and wholesome institution? What if the mob should now burst in upon us, break up our meeting and commit violence upon our persons—would this be any thing compared with what the slaves endure? No, no: and we do not remember them "as bound with them," if we shrink in the time of peril, or feel unwilling to sacrifice ourselves, if need be, for their sake. [Great noise.] I thank the Lord that there is yet life left enough to feel the truth, even though it rages at it—that conscience is not so completely seared as to be unmoved by the truth of the living God.

Many persons go to the South for a season, and are hospitably entertained in the parlor and at the table of the slave-holder. They never enter the huts of the slaves; they know nothing of the dark side of the picture, and they return home with praises on their lips of the generous character of those with whom they had tarried. Or if they have witnessed the cruelties of slavery, by remaining silent spectators they have naturally become callous—an insensibility has ensued which prepares them to apologize even for barbarity. Nothing but the corrupting influence of slavery on the hearts of the Northern people can induce them to apologize for it; and much will have been done for the destruction of Southern slavery when we have so reformed the North that no one here will be willing to risk his reputation by advocating or even excusing the holding of men as property. The South know it, and acknowledge that as fast as our principles prevail, the hold of the master must be relaxed. [Another outbreak of mobocratic spirit, and some confusion in the house.]

How wonderfully constituted is the human mind! How it resists, as long as it can, all efforts made to reclaim from error! I feel that all this disturbance is but an evidence that our efforts are the best that could have been adopted, or else the friends of slavery would not care for what we say and do. The South know what we do. I am thankful that they are reached by our efforts. Many times have I wept in the land of my birth, over the system of slavery. I knew of none who sympathized in my feelings—I was unaware that any efforts were made to deliver the oppressed—no voice in the wilderness was heard calling on the people to repent and do works meet for repentance—and my heart sickened within me. Oh, how should I have rejoiced to know that such efforts as these were being made. I only wonder that I had such feelings. I wonder when I reflect under what influence I was brought up that my heart is not harder than the nether millstone. But in the midst of temptation I was preserved, and my sympathy grew warmer, and my hatred of slavery more inveterate, until at last I have exiled myself from my native land because I could no longer endure to hear the wailing of the slave. I fled to the land of Penn; for here, thought I, sympathy for the slave will surely be found. But I found it not. The people were kind and hospitable, but the slave had no place in their thoughts. Whenever questions were put to me as to his condition, I felt that they were dictated by an idle curiosity, rather than by that deep feeling which would lead to effort for his rescue. I therefore shut up my grief in my own heart. I remembered that I was a Carolinian, from a state which framed this iniquity by law. I knew that throughout her territory was continual suffering, on the one part, and continual brutality and sin on the other. Every Southern breeze wafted to me the discordant tones of weeping and wailing, shrieks and groans, mingled with prayers and blasphemous curses. I thought there was no hope; that the wicked would go on in his wickedness, until he had destroyed both himself and his country. My heart sunk within me at the abominations in the midst of which I had been born and educated. What will it avail, cried I in bitterness of spirit, to expose to the gaze of strangers the horrors and pollutions of slavery, when there is no ear to hear nor heart to feel and pray for the slave. The language of my soul was, "Oh tell it not in Gath, publish it not in the streets of Askelon." But how different do I feel now! Animated with hope, nay, with an assurance of the triumph of liberty and good will to man, I will lift up my voice like a trumpet, and show this people their transgression, their sins of omission towards the slave, and what they can do towards affecting Southern mind, and overthrowing Southern oppression.

We may talk of occupying neutral ground, but on this subject, in its present attitude, there is no such thing as neutral ground. He that is not for us is against us, and he that gathereth not with us, scattereth abroad. If you are on what you suppose to be neutral ground, the South look upon you as on the side of the oppressor. And is there one who loves his country willing to give his influence, even indirectly, in favor of slavery—that curse of nations? God swept Egypt with the besom of destruction, and punished Judea also with a sore punishment, because of slavery. And have we any reason to believe that he is less just now?—or that he will be more favorable to us than to his own "peculiar people?" [Shoutings, stones thrown against the windows, &c.]

There is nothing to be feared from those who would stop our mouths, but they themselves should fear and tremble. The current is even now setting fast against them. If the arm of the North had not caused the Bastile of slavery to totter to its foundation, you would not hear those cries. A few years ago, and the South felt secure, and with a contemptuous sneer asked, "Who are the abolitionists? The abolitionists are nothing?"—Ay, in one sense they were nothing, and they are nothing still. But in this we rejoice, that "God has chosen things that are not to bring to nought things that are." [Mob again disturbed the meeting.]

We often hear the question asked, What shall we do?" Here is an opportunity for doing something now. Every man and every woman present may do something by showing that we fear not a mob, and, in the midst of threatenings and revilings, by opening our mouths for the dumb and pleading the cause of those who are ready to perish.

To work as we should in this cause, we must know what Slavery is. Let me urge you then to buy the books which have been written on this subject and read them, and then lend them to your neighbors. Give your money no longer for things which pander to pride and lust, but aid in scattering "the living coals of truth" upon the naked heart of this nation,—in circulating appeals to the sympathies of Christians in behalf of the outraged and suffering slave. But, it is said by some, our "books and papers do not speak the truth." Why, then, do they not contradict what we say? They cannot. Moreover the South has entreated, nay commanded us to be silent; and what greater evidence of the truth of our publications could be desired?

Women of Philadelphia! allow me as a Southern woman, with much attachment to the land of my birth, to entreat you to come up to this work. Especially let me urge you to petition. *Men* may settle this and other questions at the ballot-box, but you have no such right; it is only through petitions that you can reach the Legislature. It is therefore peculiarly *your* duty to petition. Do you say, "It does no good?" The South already turns pale at the number sent. They have read the reports of the proceedings of Congress, and there have seen that among other petitions were very many from the women of the North on the subject of slavery. This fact has called the attention of the South to the subject. How could we expect to have done more as yet? Men who hold the rod over slaves, rule in the councils of the nation: and they deny our right to petition and to remonstrate against abuses of our sex and of our kind. We have these rights, however, from our God. Only let us exercise them: and though often turned away unanswered, let us remember the influence of importunity upon the unjust judge, and act accordingly. The fact that the South look with jealousy upon our measures shows that they are effectual. There is, therefore, no cause for doubting or despair, but rather for rejoicing.

It was remarked in England that women did much to abolish Slavery in her colonies. Nor are they now idle. Numerous petitions from them have recently been presented to the Queen, to abolish the apprenticeship with its cruelties nearly equal to those of the system whose place it supplies. One petition two miles and a quarter long has been presented. And do you think these labors will be in vain ? Let the history of the past answer. When the women of these States send up to Congress such a petition, our legislators will arise as did those of England, and say, "When all the maids and matrons of the land are knocking at our doors we must legislate." Let the zeal and love, the faith and works of our English sisters quicken ours—that while the slaves continue to suffer, and when they shout deliverance, we may feel the satisfaction of *having done what we could.*

DOCUMENT 72:
Excerpt, William Lloyd Garrison, "Rights of Women,"
The Liberator, January 12, 1838.

Courtesy Library of Congress.

In this excerpt of a speech, the famous abolitionist and editor William Lloyd Garrison appeals to fellow abolitionists to support women's rights, though he faced a great deal of resistance. Many argued that fighting for women's equality undermined the antislavery movement and even the stability of marriage. The Grimké sisters mentioned in this letter are Angelina Emily (1805–1879) and Sarah Moore (1792–1873), abolitionists who came from a large slaveholding family in South Carolina. Garrison published his antislavery newspaper *The Liberator* from 1831 to 1865.

On Thursday of last week, a large assemblage of both sexes filled the spacious Odeon, to listen to a debate on the part of the Boston Lyceum, whether it would be better for society if equal rights and duties were enjoyed by women as well as men. Two individuals spoke on the affirmative, and three on the negative side of the question. It was almost unanimously decided against the women—of course; although, if we can appreciate simple truth and sound logic, in our opinion those who sustained the affirmative (Messrs. Amasa Walker and J. A. Bolles) were victorious in every point of view. The speech of Mr. Walker was a mass of pertinent facts and forcible illustrations, in vindication of the intellectual, moral and social equality of woman with man. The question under discussion, he said, was a bold one, affecting as it did the happiness and interest of one half of the human race directly; but what questions of reform had ever been proposed to mankind, that was not at first regarded as a bold one? He related an anecdote that is worth preservation. Some twelve years since, a few individuals held a meeting in Boston for the purpose of considering the practicability of not only forming but sustaining a Lyceum. A distinguished citizen, who was present, seemed to regard the project as Utopian; it would answer very well in theory, but not in practice; it might survive a few months, but as soon as its novelty was lost, it would go down. The reply to him was, "We intend to hitch on to it a powerful locomotive, —viz. the attendance and influence of woman,—and then it will be sure to go ahead." This was a new idea. Up to that time, it had not entered into the minds of men, that women could be either interested in or benefitted by scientific lectures. The plan was adopted, and the result had far surpassed the prediction. Mr. Walker said that women had always been found on the side of humanity and religion, foremost in every good work; and the nearer they approximated to an equality of rights with the men, the better it would be for society.

Mr. Bolles made a very neat, ingenious, and argumentative speech. It was claimed, he said, that priority of creation established the superiority of man over woman. If that were true, then the beasts of the field were superior to Adam; for they had precedence in creation over him. Adam was made from the dust of the ground; but it was not until the breath of Jehovah had quickened his inanimate form, and immortality had been united to that which was mortal, that Eve was created from his side. The order of creation was from the imperfect to the perfect. The climax of divine wisdom and benevolence was attained in the creation of woman. He reminded the audience, that the translators of the Bible did not attach to the words, "*help* meet for him," the Yankee meaning of "help"—that is, a servant or domestic—but simply a companion and equal. The idea was not that Eve was to be useful merely in doing the kitchen and chamber work in Paradise, but that she should be the solace, the "better half," of the twain made one. As to the eating of the forbidden fruit, Mr. B. said it was a remarkable circumstance, that Eve was induced to eat thereof, in consequence of her strong intellectual aspirations. The language of the serpent to her was—"Ye shall not surely die: for God doth know, that in the day ye eat thereof, then your eyes shall be opened; and ye shall be as gods, knowing good and evil." But Adam ate of the fruit obviously to gratify his appetite, or manifest his affection for his wife. To the objection that the punishment of Eve was that her desire should be to her husband, and he should rule over her, Mr. B. replied, that this punishment was *hers,* not necessarily or justly her *posterity,* by transmission or bequest of personal guilt, (and here he clashed with certain doctrinal notions)—and again, that it went only to show, that no such subjection to man was enjoined in Paradise, and consequently, in the restoration of our race from the fall by a common Savior, all inequalities, the fruits of that fall, ought to cease between the sexes. "In Christ Jesus, there is neither male nor female, neither bond nor free, but all are ONE." The instructions of Paul, on this subject, he argued, were clearly local and temporary in their application. Who were disposed to regard the apostle, when he said, "He that giveth in marriage doeth well, but he that giveth not in marriage doeth better," as enjoining celibacy, in preference to matrimony, upon people of every nation, and through all time? "For myself," said Mr. B., "I am one of those *unfortunate* men who have been able only to *do well.* I leave those who contend on the negative side of this question to *do better,* if they can."

Mr. B. said that an equality of rights is not an identity of duties. The duties of men and women might be correlative, reciprocal, equal, but are not necessarily identical. There are some employments, which men can better follow than women. The average physical strength, and muscular energy of men exceed those of the other sex; and yet women, in some countries, perform nearly all the drudgery and toil. But, as a moral and intellectual being, woman is entitled to exercise the same rights and enjoy the same privileges as man.

Whether Mr. B. argued merely for the occasion, as a disputant, or with sincere convictions of the truth of what he uttered we do not know; but his speech was a good one.

Those who spoke in the negative were very careful to express a high regard for woman—of course; but then, she must keep (one of them said, in his haste, "she ought to be *made to keep*") in her "appropriate sphere,"—a phraseology too indefinite to enable anyone to know how much or how little was intended by it, except by observing the spirit of those impounders of stray women. Bad illustrations and worse witticisms supplied the place of sound arguments; and "chimeras dire" [wild, dreadful fancies and fantasies] were conjured up as the inevitable consequences that must arise in admitting the sex to equal rights and privileges. It was thought a capital joke to suppose a frigate "manned, no *womanned*" for a cruise upon the ocean. It was asked, how would it look to see the delicate hands of women managing thirty-two pounders in a conflict with the enemy, and these feminine warriors wading up to their knees in blood? Why, shockingly, no doubt. And so it is a shocking sight to see *men* engaged in such a horrid work. But the gospel of peace forbids our race, without distinction of sex, fighting under any circumstances. It commands every human being to love, not to kill his enemies; and when smitten by the hand of violence on one cheek, to turn the other also. The argument was a barbarous one, and therefore not entitled to christian consideration. We were told that woman's empire is the heart, in which it is her privilege to sway the sceptre of dominion. A most unmeaning flourish of words! Can any reason be given, why a man may not jointly rule in the same empire? why he should not govern solely by love as well as woman?

Though the arguments, in the discussion, were all on the side of the women, yet these were powerless against the prejudices, the pride and love of supremacy, the monopoly of power, on the part of the men. The unanimity with which the question was decided in the negative, and the uncourteous exultation which followed the decision, only revealed how feebly Christianity—that grand leveller of arbitrary and unnatural distinctions,—is apprehended even in republican, Christian America. Observe—women were not allowed to speak or vote on the occasion. There were at least two present (A. E. and S. M. Grimké) who, if they could have been permitted to speak on behalf of their sex, would have made a noble defence. It was like a meeting of slaveholders to discuss with all gravity the question, whether their slaves, if emancipated, would be in a better condition than if kept in bondage: and having muzzled their victims, so that their wishes could not be expressed or known, coming to the rational conclusion that to extend their "appropriate sphere" beyond the boundaries of a plantation, would be injurious to them and destructive to the welfare of society!

However, there is nothing like agitation. Free discussion will finally break all fetters, and put down all usurpation. The discussion of this question respecting the Rights of Woman is very important—its decision, at the Odeon, is of no consequence. Both sexes are ultimately to stand upon the dead level of humanity, equal in rights, in dominion, in honor, in dignity, in renown. They are far from occupying this position now. Even by the laws of this boasted republic, women are almost regarded as nonentities, as household appendages.—Their rights and liberties are entrusted, to a fearful extent, to proud and tyrannical men. If they would be emancipated, they must achieve their own deliverance; for when have the usurpers of mankind voluntarily surrendered their ill-gotten power? They must respect themselves; learn to despise outward ornament, and covet inward worth; cultivate their minds, and inform their understandings; and vindicate their cause in the light of a pure and resplendent Christianity.

DOCUMENT 73:
Excerpt, Theodore D. Weld, *American Slavery As It Is: Testimony of a Thousand Witnesses* (New York: American Anti-Slavery Society, 1839).

Courtesy Library of Congress.

The noted abolitionist Sarah M. Grimké contributes the story of a mulatto seamstress who frequently ran away from her master in Charleston, South Carolina. This excerpt details her punishment in a white family where "the mistress daily read the scriptures." Theodore Weld (1803–1895) was a noted abolitionist, editor, speaker, and author. Married to Sarah's sister Angelina, he is best known for his publication of this volume that helped influence Harriet Beecher Stowe's *Uncle Tom's Cabin*.

A handsome mulatto woman, about 18 or 20 years of age, whose independent spirit could not brook the degradation of slavery, was in the habit of running away; for this offence she had been repeatedly sent by her master and mistress to be whipped by the keeper of the Charleston workhouse. This had been done with such inhuman severity, as to lacerate her back in a most shocking manner; a finger could not be laid between the cuts. But the love of liberty was too strong to be annihilated by torture; and, as a last resort, she was whipped at several different times, and kept a close prisoner. A heavy iron collar, with three prongs projecting from it, was placed round her neck, and a strong and sound front tooth was extracted, to serve as a mark to describe her, in case of escape.

Her sufferings at this time were agonizing; she could lie in no position but on her back, which was sore from scroungings, as I can testify from personal inspection, and her only place of rest was the floor, on a blanket. These outrages were committed in a family where the mistress daily read the scriptures, and assembled her children for family worship. She was accounted, and was really, so far as alms-giving was concerned, a charitable woman, and tender-hearted to the poor; and yet this suffering slave, who was the seamstress of the family was continually in her presence, sitting in her chamber to sew, or engaged in her other household work, with her lacerated and bleeding back, her mutilated mouth, and heavy iron collar without, so far as appeared, exciting any feelings of compassion.

DOCUMENT 74:
Letter, William Wells Brown to William Lloyd Garrison, *The Liberator,* January 12, 1849.

Courtesy Library of Congress.

In this excerpt of a letter, Brown recounts the story of Ellen and William Craft, whose escape from their owners in Georgia became an important story told by abolitionists in the first half of the nineteenth century. Ellen, who was light skinned, dressed as white man, and her husband dressed as his servant. They managed to flee from Georgia to Philadelphia. The letter ends with the line: "Ellen is truly a heroine." William Wells Brown (1816–1884) was born into slavery and escaped north to become a noted abolitionist and novelist. William Lloyd Garrison (1805–1879) was a prominent abolitionist and editor of the antislavery newspaper, *The Liberator,* in print from 1831 to 1865.

An Ingenious Escape

We shook hands, said farewell, and started in different directions for the railway station. I took the nearest possible way to the train, for fear I should be recognized by someone, and got into the negro car in which I knew I should have to ride; but my master (as I will now call my wife) took a longer way round, and only arrived there with the bulk of the passengers. He obtained a ticket for himself and one for his slave to Savannah, the first port, which was about two hundred miles off. My master then had the luggage stowed away, and stepped into one of the best carriages. . . .

As soon as the train had left the platform, my master looked round in the carriage, and was terror-stricken to find a Mr. Cray—an old friend of my wife's master, who dined with the family the day before, and knew my wife from childhood-sitting on the same seat. . . . My master's first impression, after seeing Mr. Cray, was, that he was there for the purpose of securing him. However, my master thought it was not wise to give information respecting himself, and for fear that Mr. Cray might draw him into conversation and recognize his voice, my master resolved to feign deafness as the only means of self-defense.

After a little while, Mr. Cray said to my master, "It is a very fine morning, sir." The latter took no notice, but kept looking out of the window. Mr. Cray soon repeated this remark, in a little louder tone, but my master remained as before. This indifference attrected the attention of the passengers near, one of whom laughed out. This, I suppose, annoyed the old gentleman; so he said, "I will make him hear"; and in a loud tone of voice repeated, "It is a very fine morning, sir."

My master turned his head, and with a polite bow said, "Yes," and commenced looking out of the window again.

One of the gentlmen remarked that it was a very great deprivation to be deaf. "Yes," replied Mr. Cray, "and I shall not trouble that fellow any more." This enabled my master to breathe a little easier, and to feel that Mr. Cray was not his pursuer after all.

The gentlemen then turned the conversation upon the three great topics of discussion in first-class circles in Georgia, namely, Niggers, Cotton, and the Abolitionists.

My master had often heard of abolitionists, but in such a connection as to cause him to think that they were a fearful kind of wild animal. But he was highly delighted to learn, from the gentlemen's conversation, that the abolitionists were persons who were opposed to oppression; and therefore, in his opinion, not the lowest, but the very highest, of God's creatures. . . .

We arrived at Savannah early in the evening, and got into an omnibus. . . . Soon after going on board, my master turned in; and as the captain and some of the passengers seemed to think this strange, and also questioned me respecting him, my master thought I had better get out the flannels and opodeloc which we had prepared for the rheumatism, warm then quickly by the stove in the gentleman's saloon, and bring them to his berth. We did this as an excuse for my master's retiring to bed so early. . . .

There was no place provided for colored passengers, whether slave or free. So I paced the deck till a late hour, then mounted some cotton bags, in a warm place near the funnel, sat there till morning, and then went and assisted my master to get ready for breakfast. . . .

By this time we were near Charleston. . . . There were a large number of persons on the quay waiting the arrival of the steamer: but we were afraid to venture out for fear that someone might recognize me; or that they had heard that we were gone, and had telegraphed to have us stopped. . . . We had our luggage placed on a fly, and I took my master by the arm. . . . he hobbled on shore, got in and drove off to the best hotel. . . .

On arriving at the house the landlord ran out and opened the door: but judging, from the poultices and green glasses, that my master was an invalid, he took him very tenderly by one arm and ordered his man to take the other. . . .

My master asked for a bedroom. The servant was ordered to show a good one, into which we helped him. . . . My master then handed me the bandages, I took them. . . . and told the landlord my master wanted two hot poultices as quickly as possible. . . .

In a few minutes the smoking poultices were brought in. I placed them in white hankerchiefs, and hurried upstairs, went into my master's apartment, shut the door, and laid them on the mantlepiece. As he was alone for a little while, he thought he could rest a great deal better with the poultices off. However, it was necessary to have them to complete. . . . the journey. . . .

When we left Macon, it was our intention to take a steamer at Charleston through Philadelphia; but on arriving there we found that the vessels did not run during the winter, and I have no doubt it was well for us that they did not; for on the very last voyage the steamer made that we intended to go by, a fugitive was discovered secreted on board, and sent back to slavery. However, as we had also heard of the Overland Mail Route, we were all right. I ordered a fly to the door, had the luggage placed on it; we got in, and drove down to the Custom House Office, which was near the wharf where we had to obtain tickets, to take a steamer for Wilmington, North Carolina. When we reached the building, I helped my master into the office, which was crowded with passengers. He asked for a ticket for himself and one for his slave to Philadelphia. This caused the principle officer—a very mean-looking, cheese colored fellow, who was sitting there—to look up at us very suspiciously, and in a fierce tone of voice he said to me, "Boy, do you belong to that gentleman?" I quickly replied, "Yes, sir" (which was quite correct). The tickets were handed out, and as my master was paying for them the chief said to him, " I wish you to register your name here, sir, and also the name of your nigger, and pay a dollar duty on him."

My master paid the dollar, and pointing to the hand that was in the poultice, requested the officer to register his name for him. This seemed to offend the "high-bred" South Carolinian. he jumped up, shaking his head, and, cramming his hands almost through the bottom of his trousers pockets, with a slave-bullying air, said, " I shan't do it."

This attracted the attention of all the passengers. Just then the young military officer with whom my master travelled and conversed on the steamer from Savannah stepped in, somewhat the worse for brandy; he shook hands with my master, and pretended to know all about him. He said, "I know his kin (friends) like a book"; and as the officer was known in Charleston, and was going to stop there with friends, the recognition was very much in my master's favor.

The captain of the steamer, a good-looking jovial fellow, seeing that the gentleman appeared to know my master, and perhaps not wishing to lose us as passengers, said in an offhand sailor-like manner, "I will register the gentleman's name, and take the responsibility upon myself." He asked my master's name. He said, "William Johnson." The names were put down, I think, "Mr. Johnson and slave." . . .

We left our cottage on Wednesday morning, the 21st of December, 1848, and arrived at Baltimore, Saturday evening, the 24th (Christmas Eve). Baltimore was the last slave port of any note at which we stopped. . . .

They are particularly watchful at Baltimore to prevent slaves from escaping into Pennsylvania, which is a free State. . . .

[Editor's note: The story continues when the two realized that they had to prove that the owner had clear title to the slave.]

On entering the room we found the principle man, to whom my master said, "Do you wish to see me, sir?" "Yes," said this eagle-eyed officer; and he added, "It is against our rules, sir, to allow any person to take a slave out of Baltimore into Philadelphia, unless he can satisfy us that he has a right to take him along." "Why is that?" asked my master, with more firmness than could be expected. "Because, sir," continued he, in a voice and manner that almost chilled our blood, "if we should suffer any gentlemen to take a slave past here into Philadelphia; and should the gentlman with whom the slave might be traveling turn out not to be his rightful owner, and should the proper master come and prove that his slave escaped on our road, we shall have him to pay for; and, therefore, we cannot let any slave pass here without receiving security to show, and to satisfy us, that it is all right."

[Editor's note: The following letter was published in the December 17, 1852, issue of *The Liberator*.]

Ockham School, near Ripley, Surrey
Oct. 26, 1852.

DEAR SIR,—I feel very much obliged to you for informing me of the erroneous report which has been so extensively circulated in the American newspapers: "That I had placed myself in the hands of an American gentleman in London, on condition that he would take me back to the family who held me a slave in Georgia.' So I write these few lines merely to say that the statement is entirely unfounded, for I have never had the slightest inclination whatever of returning to bondage; and God forbid that I should ever be so false to liberty as to prefer slavery in its stead. In fact, since my escape from slavery, I have got on much better in every respect than I could have possibly anticipated. Though, had it been to the contrary, my feelings in regard to this would have been just the same, for I had much rather starve in England, than be a slave for the best man that ever breathed upon the American continent.

Yours very truly,
ELLEN CRAFT
The Liberator, Dec. 17, 1852

DOCUMENT 75:
The Case of Mrs. Margaret Douglass, 1853, 7 Am. State Trials 45 (1853).

The literacy of slaves was a hotly contested issue in the mid-nineteenth century. Margaret Douglass, a white woman in Norfolk, Virginia, began teaching African American children to read, claiming she did not know it was illegal to do so. She was taken to court, indicted, and sentenced to a month in prison. Judge Baker, who sought to make an example of her, "as an example to all others in like cases," warned that educating blacks made it possible for them to read "abolition pamphlets and inflammatory documents."

The case of Mrs. Margaret Douglass, 1853: The Verdict and Sentence

November 13 [1853]

The Jury this morning returned into court with a verdict of *Guilty,* and fixing the penalty at a fine of one dollar. The Court then adjourned for the term.

January 10, 1854

After the adjournment of the Court on November 13, Mrs. Douglass obtained permission from the Judge and the Sheriff to visit New York, where she remained several weeks, returning to Norfolk with her daughter. She appeared today for sentence.

JUDGE BAKER . . .

There are persons, I believe, in our community, opposed to the policy of the law in question. They profess to believe that universal intellectual culture is necessary to religious instruction and education, and that such culture is suitable to a state of slavery; and there can be no misapprehension as to your opinions on this subject, judging from the indiscreet freedom with which you spoke of your regard for the colored race in general. Such opinions in the present state of our society I regard as manifestly mischievous. It is not true that our slaves cannot be taught religious and moral duty, without being able to read the Bible and use the pen. Intellectual and religious instruction often go hand in hand, but the latter may well be exist without the former; and the truth of this is abundantly vindicated by the well-known fact in many parts of our own Commonwealth, as in other parts of the county in which among the whites one-fouth or more are entirely without a knowledge of letters, respect for the law, and for moral and religious conduct and behavior, are justly and propely appreciated and practiced.

A valuable report or document recently published in the city of New York by the Southern Aid Society sets forth many valuable and important truths upon the condition of Southern slaves, and the utility of moral and religious instruction, apart from a knowledge of books. I recommend the careful perusal of it to all whose opinions concur with your own. It shows that a system of catechetical instruction, with a clear and simple exposition of Scripture, has been employed with gratifying success; that the slave population of the South are peculiarly susceptible of good religious influences. Their mere residence among a Christian people has wrought a great and happy change in their condition: they have been raised from the night of heathenism to the light of Christianity, and thousands of them have been brought to a saving knowledge of the Gospel.

Of the one hundred millions of the negro race, there cannot be found another so large a body as the three millions of slaves in the United States, at once so intelligent, so inclined to the Gospel, and so blessed by the elevating influence of civilization and Christianity. Occasional instances of cruelty and oppression, it is true, may sometimes occur, and probably will ever continue to take place under any system of laws: but this is not confined to wrongs committed upon the negro; wrongs are committed and cruelly practiced in a like degree by the lawless white man upon his own color; and while the negroes of our town and State are known to be surrounded by most of the substantial comforts of life, and invited both by precept and example to participate in proper, moral and religious duties, it argues, it seems to me, a sickly sensibility towards them to say their persons, and feelings, and interests are not sufficiently respected by our laws, which, in effect, tend to nullify the act of our Legislature passed for the security and protection of their masters.

The law under which you have been tried and found guilty is not to be found among the original enactments of our Legislature. The first legislative provision upon this subject was introduced in the year 1831, immediately succeeding the bloody scenes of the memorable Southampton insurrection; and that law being found not sufficiently penal to check the wrongs complained of, was re-enacted with additional penalties in the year 1848, which last mentioned act, after several years' trial and experience, has been re-affirmed by adoption, and incorporated into our present code. After these several and repeated recognitions of the wisdom and propriety of the said act, it may well be said that bold and open opposition to it is a matter not to be slightly regarded, especially as we have reason to believe that every Southern slave state in our country, as a measure of self-preservation and protection, has deemed it wise and just to adopt laws with similar provisions.

There might have been no occasion for such enactments in Virginia, or elsewhere, on the subject of negro education, but as a matter of self-defense against the schemes of Northern incendiaries, and the outcry against holding our slaves in bondage. Many now living well remember how, and when, and why, the anti-slavery fury began, and by what means its manifestations were made public. Our mails were clogged with abolition pamphlets and inflammatory documents, to be distributed among our Southern negroes to induce them to cut our throats. Sometimes, it may be, these libelous documents were distributed by Northern citizens professing Southern feelings, and at other times, by Southern people professing Northern feelings. These, however, were not the only means resorted to by the Northern fanatics to stir up insubordination among our slaves. They scattered far and near pocket handkerchiefs, and other similar articles, with frightful engravings, and printed over with anti-slavery nonsense, with the view to work upon the feeling and ignorance of our negroes, who otherwise would have remained comfortable and happy. Under such circumstances there was but one measure of protection for the South, and that was adopted. . . .

For these reasons, as an example to all others in like cases disposed to offend, and in vindication of the policy and justness of our laws, which every individual should be taught to respect, the judgment of the Court is, in addition to the proper fine and costs, that you be imprisoned for the period of one month in the jail of this city.

DOCUMENT 76:

"The Rescue of Jane Johnson" from William Still, *Underground Railroad* (Philadelphia: Porter & Croates, 1872), 86–97.

This affidavit, taken from Jane Johnson by the State of New York, tells of an abolitionist who helped save Johnson from her owner, Colonel John H. Wheeler, while traveling in 1855 to New York.

The Rescue of Jane Johnson

AFFIDAVIT AND TESTIMONY OF JANE JOHNSON
STATE OF NEW YORK, CITY AND COUNTY OF NEW YORK.

Jane Johnson being sworn, makes oath and says—
My name is Jane—Jane Johnson: I was the slave of Mr. Wheeler of Washington; he bought me and my two children, about two years ago, from Mr. Cornelius Crew, of Richmond, Va.; my youngest child is between six and seven years old, the other between ten and eleven; I have one other child only, and he is in Richmond; I have not seen him for about two years; never expect to see him again; Mr. Wheeler brought me and my two children to Philadelphia, on the way to Nicaragua, to wait on his wife; I didn't want to go without my two children, and he consented to take them; we came to Philadelphia by the cars; stopped at Mr. Sully's, Mr. Wheeler's father-in-law, a few moments; then went to the steamboat for New York at 2 o'clock, but were too late; we went into Bloodgood's Hotel; Mr. Wheeler went to dinner; Mr. Wheeler had told me in Washington to have nothing to say to colored persons, and if any of them spoke to me, to say I was a free women traveling with a minister; we staid at Bloodgood's till 5 o'clock; Mr. Wheeler kept his eye on me all the time except when he was at dinner; he left his dinner to

come and see if I was safe, and then went back again; while he was at dinner, I saw a colored woman and told her I was a slave woman, that my master had told me not to speak to colored people, and that if any of them spoke to me to say that I was free; but I am not free; but I want to be free; she said: 'poor thing, I pity you;' after that I saw a colored man and said the same thing to him, he said he would telegraph to New York, and two men would meet me at 9 o'clock and take me with them; after that we went on board the boat, Mr. Wheeler sat beside me on the deck; I saw a colored gentleman come on board, he beckoned to me; I nodded my head, and could not go; Mr. Wheeler was beside me and I was afraid; a white gentleman then came and said to Mr. Wheeler, 'I want to speak to your servant, and tell her of her rights;' Mr. Wheeler rose and said, 'If you have anything to say, say it to me—she knows her rights;' the white gentleman asked me if I wanted to be free; I said 'I do, but I belong to this gentleman and I can't have it;' he replied, 'Yes, you can, come with us, you are as free as your master, if you want your freedom come now; if you go back to Washington you may never get it;' I rose to go, Mr. Wheeler spoke, and said, 'I will give you your freedom,' but he had never promised it before, and I knew he would never give it to me; the white gentleman held out his hand and I went toward him; I was ready for the word before it was given me; I took the children by the hands, who both cried, for they were frightened, but both stopped when they got on shore; a colored man carried the little one, I led the other by the hand. We walked down the street till we got to a hack; nobody forced me away; nobody pulled me, and nobody led me; I went away of my own free will; I always wished to be free and meant to be free when I came North; I hardly expected it in Philadelphia, but I thought I should get free in New York; I have been comfortable and happy since I left Mr. Wheeler, and so are the children; I don't want to go back; I could have gone in Philadelphia if I had wanted to; I could go now; but I had rather die than go back. I wish to make this statement before a magistrate, because I understand that Mr. Williamson is in prison on my account, and I hope the truth may be of benefit to him.

her

Jane X Johnson

mark

DOCUMENT 77:
Wood Engraving, "Effect of John Brown's Invasion at the South," 1859.

Courtesy Library of Congress, LC-USZ62–79478.

This cover image from *Harper's Weekly* featured three scenes that satirized Brown's legacy in the South—mainly focused on weapons that would be given to enslaved men and women. The caption reads: "Much obliged to dar ar Possum Wattomie for dese pikes he gin us—Dey's turrible handy to dig taters wid"—"What's dem fool niggers fraid on? I'd like 'ter see one o' dem folks ondertake to carry me off, I would!"—"A Southern planter arming his slaves to resist invasion."

DOCUMENT 78:
Photograph, John Brown, "Meeting the slave-mother and her child on the steps of Charlestown jail on his way to execution," 1863.

Courtesy Library of Congress, LC-USZ62–2890.

Printed in the North during the Civil War, this romanticized image shows Brown as a martyr for the abolitionist cause. Brown is depicted pausing to address a woman and kiss a child as he calmly faces his death. Notable symbols, such as the figure with a hat marked with a '76 and the flag of Virginia with the motto *Sic simper tyrannis*, suggest the gravity of his cause. Additionally, the statue of Justice is shown to be broken and cast aside, a clear commentary on the injustice of Brown's execution.

Document
77

DOCUMENT 79:

Photograph, Susan B. Anthony.

Courtesy Library of Congress, LC-USZ62–88968.

Susan B. Anthony (1820–1906) was a noted supporter of women's suffrage and well remembered for giving antislavery speeches. Many suffragists became involved in the movement through temperance and antislavery societies and were mobilized to fight for their own

JOHN BROWN

Meeting the Slave mother and her Child on the steps of Charlestown jail on his way to execution.
The Artist has represented Capt Brown regarding with a look of compassion a Slave mother and Child who obstructed
the passage on his way to the Scaffold.... Capt Brown stooped and kissed the Child... then met his Fate.

FROM THE ORIGINAL PAINTING BY LOUIS RANSOM.

Document 78

rights. An 1859 speech, "Make the Slaves Case Our Own," was writ-
ten when Anthony worked for William Lloyd Garrison's American
Anti-Slavery Society. Born into an abolitionist family in 1820 in
Massachusetts, Anthony joined an illustrious group of activists,
Elizabeth Cady Stanton, Lucretia Mott, and Lucy Stone, in establish-
ing the American Equal Rights Association in 1866. In 1869 Anthony

Document 79

and Stanton established the National Woman Suffrage Association (NWSA) to protest the overt sexism of the Fourteenth and Fifteenth Amendments. Anthony regularly toured the country advocating for women's rights. In 1890, the NWSA and the American Women Suffrage Association merged. Anthony served as the second president after Stanton.

DOCUMENT 80:
Photograph, Portrait of Harriet Tubman, c. 1860.

Courtesy Library of Congress, LC-USZ62–7816.

Harriet Tubman (1819–1913) was a runaway slave from Maryland who led hundreds of slaves to freedom through the Underground Railroad, earning her the nickname "Moses." During the Civil War, she served as a spy and nurse for the Union forces in South Carolina.

DOCUMENT 81:
Excerpt, Sarah H. Bradford, *Scenes in the Life of Harriet Tubman* (Auburn: W. J. Moses, Printer, 1869), 10–20.

Courtesy Documenting the American South, University Library, The University of North Carolina at Chapel Hill.

This excerpt, from the chapter entitled "Some Scenes in the Life of Harriet Tubman," tells the story of Harriet Tubman's escape to freedom in 1849. She was born a slave in Maryland and became a noted antislavery activist and conductor on the Underground Railroad, making nineteen trips south to free more than three hundred slaves, including members of her family.

The first person by whom she was hired was a woman who, though married and the mother of a family, was still "Miss Susan" to her slaves, as is customary at the South. This woman was possessed of the good things of this life, and provided liberally for her slaves—so far as food and clothing went. But she had been brought up to believe, and to act upon the belief, that a slave could be taught to do nothing, and *would* do nothing but under the sting of the whip. Harriet, then a young girl, was taken from her life in the field, and having never seen the inside of a house better than a cabin in the negro quarters, was put to house-work without being told how to do anything. The first thing was to put a parlor in order. "Move these chairs and tables into the middle of the room, sweep the carpet clean, then dust everything, and put them back in their places!" These were the directions given, and Harriet was left alone to do her work.

Document 80

The whip was in sight on the mantel-piece, as a reminder of what was to be expected if the work was not done well. Harriet fixed the furniture as she was told to do, and swept with all her strength, raising a tremendous dust. The moment she had finished sweeping, she took her dusting cloth, and wiped everything "so you could see your face in 'em, de shone so," in haste to go and set the table for breakfast, and do her other work. The dust which she had set flying only settled down again on chairs, tables, and the piano. "Miss Susan" came in and looked around. Then came the call for "Minty"—Harriet's name was Araminta at the South.

She drew her up to the table, saying, "What do you mean by doing my work this way, you—!" and passing her finger on the table and piano, she showed her the mark it made through the dust. "Miss Susan, I done sweep and dust jus' as you tole me." But the whip was already taken down, and the strokes were falling on head and face and neck. Four times this scene was repeated before breakfast, when, during the fifth whipping, the door opened, and "Miss Emily" came in. She was a married sister of "Miss Susan," and was making her a visit, and though brought up with the same associations as her sister, seems to have been a person of more gentle and reasonable nature. Not being able to endure the screams of the child any longer, she came in, took her sister by the arm, and said, "If you do not stop whipping that child, I will leave your house, and never come back!" Miss Susan declared that "she *would* not mind, and she slighted her work on purpose." Miss Emily said, "Leave her to me a few moments;" and Miss Susan left the room, indignant. As soon as they were alone, Miss Emily said: "Now, Minty, show me how you do your work." For the sixth time Harriet removed all the furniture into the middle of the room; then she swept; and the moment she had done sweeping, she took the dusting cloth to wipe off the furniture. "Now stop there," said Miss Emily; "go away now, and do some of your other work, and when it is time to dust, I will call you." When the time came she called her, and explained to her how the dust had now settled, and that if she wiped it off now, the furniture would remain bright and clean. These few words an hour or two before, would have saved Harriet her whippings for that day, as they probably did for many a day after.

While with this woman, after working from early morning till late at night, she was obliged to sit up all night to rock a cross, sick child. Her mistress laid upon her bed with a whip under her pillow, and slept; but if the tired nurse forgot herself for a moment, if her weary head dropped, and her hand ceased to rock the cradle, the child would cry out, and then down would come the whip upon the neck and face of the poor weary creature. The scars are still plainly visible where the whip cut into the flesh. Perhaps her mistress was preparing her, though she did not know it then, by this enforced habit of wakefulness, for the many long nights of travel, when she was the leader and guide of the weary and hunted ones who were escaping from bondage.

"Miss Susan" got tired of Harriet, as Harriet was determined she should do, and so abandoned intention of buying her, and sent her back to her master. She was next hired out to the man who inflicted upon her the lifelong injury from which she is suffering now, by breaking her skull with a weight from the scales. The injury thus inflicted causes her often to fall into a state of somnolency from which it is almost impossible to rouse her. Disabled and sick, her flesh all wasted away, she was returned to her *owner*. He tried to sell her, but no one would buy her. "Dey said dey wouldn't give a sixpence for me," she said.

"And so," she said, "from Christmas till March I worked as I could, and I *prayed* through all the long nights—I groaned and prayed for ole master: 'Oh Lord, convert master!' 'Oh Lord, change dat man's heart!' 'Pears like I prayed all de time,'" said Harriet; "'bout my work, everywhere, I prayed an' I groaned to de Lord. When I went to de horse-trough to wash my face, I took up de water in my han' an' I said, 'Oh Lord, wash me, make me clean!' Den I take up something to wipe my face, an' I say, 'Oh Lord, wipe away all my sin!' When I took de broom and began to sweep, I groaned, 'Oh Lord, wha'soebber sin dere be in my heart, sweep it out, Lord, clar an' clean!'" No words can describe the pathos of her tones, as she broke out into these words of prayer, after the manner of her people. "An' so," said she, "I prayed all night long for master, till de first of March; an' all de time he was bringing people to look at me, an' trying to sell me. Den we heard dat some of us was gwine to be sole to go wid de chain-gang down to de cotton an' rice fields, and dey said I was gwine, an' my brudders, an' sisters. Den I changed my prayer. Fust of March I began to pray, 'Oh Lord, if you ant nebber gwine to change dat man's heart, kill him, Lord, an' take him out ob de way.'

"Nex' ting I heard old master was dead, an' he died jus' as he libed. Oh, then, it 'peared like I'd give all de world full ob gold, if I had it, to bring dat poor soul back. But I couldn't pray for him no longer."

The slaves were told that their master's will provided that none of them should be sold out of the State. This satisfied most of them, and they were very happy. But Harriet was not satisfied; she never closed her eyes that she did not imagine she saw the horsemen coming, and heard the screams of women and children, as they were being dragged away to a far worse slavery than that they were enduring there. Harriet was married at this time to a free negro, who not only did not trouble himself about her fears, but did his best to betray her, and bring her back after she escaped. She would start up at night with the cry, "Oh, dey're comin', dey're comin', I mus' go!"

Her husband called her a fool, and said she was like old Cudjo, who when a joke went round, never laughed till half an hour after everybody else got through, and so just as all danger was past she began to be frightened. But still Harriet in fancy saw the horsemen coming, and heard the screams of terrified women and children. "And all that time, in my dreams and visions," she said, "I seemed to see a line, and on the other side of that line were green fields, and lovely flowers, and beautiful white ladies, who stretched out their arms to me over the line, but I couldn't reach them nohow. I always fell before I got to the line."

One Saturday it was whispered in the quarters that two of Harriet's sisters had been sent off with the chain-gang. That morning she started, having persuaded three of her brothers to accompany her, but they had not gone far when the brothers, appalled by the dangers before and behind them, determined to go back, and in spite of her remonstrances dragged her with them. In fear and terror, she remained over Sunday, and on Monday night a negro from another part of the plantation came privately to tell Harriet that herself and brothers were to be carried off that night. The poor old mother, who belonged to the same mistress, was just going to milk. Harriet wanted to get away without letting her know, because she knew that she would raise an uproar and prevent her going, or insist upon going with her, and the time for this was not yet. But she must give some intimation to those she was going to leave of her intention, and send such a farewell as she might to the friends and relations on the plantation. Those communications were generally made by singing. They sang as they walked along the country roads, and the chorus was taken up by others, and the uninitiated knew not the hidden meaning of the words—

> When dat ar ole chariot comes,
> I'm gwine to lebe you;
> I'm boun' for de promised land,
> I'm gwine to lebe you.

These words meant something more than a journey to the Heavenly Canaan. Harriet said, "Here, mother, go 'long; I'll do the milkin' to-night and bring it in." The old woman went to her cabin. Harriet took down her sun-bonnet, and went on to the "big house," where some of her relatives lived as house servants. She thought she could trust Mary, but there were others in the kitchen, and she could say nothing. Mary began to frolic with her. She threw her across the kitchen, and ran out, knowing that Mary would follow her. But just as they turned the corner of the house, the master to whom Harriet was now hired, came riding up on his horse. Mary darted back, and Harriet thought there was no way now but to sing. But "the Doctor," as the master was called, was regarded with special awe by his slaves; if they were singing or talking together in the field, or on the road, and "the Doctor" appeared, all was hushed till he passed. But Harriet had no time for ceremony; her friends must have a warning; and whether the Doctor thought her *"imperen"* or not, she must sing him farewell. So on she went to meet him, singing:

> I'm sorry I'm gwine to lebe you,
> Farewell, oh farewell;
> But I'll meet you in the mornin',
> Farewell, oh farewell.

The Doctor passed, and she bowed as she went on, still singing:

> I'll meet you in the mornin',
> I'm boun' for de promised land,
> On the oder side of Jordan,
> Boun' for de promised land.

She reached the gate and looked round; the Doctor had stopped his horse, and had turned around in the saddle, and was looking at her as if there might be more in this than "met the ear." Harriet closed the gate, went on a little way, came back, the Doctor still gazing at her. She lifted up the gate as if she had not latched it properly, waved her hand to him, and burst out again:

> I'll meet you in the mornin,'
> Safe in de promised land,
> On the oder side of Jordan,
> Boun' for de promised land.

And she started on her journey, "not knowing whither she went," except that she was going to follow the north star, till it led her to liberty. Cautiously and by night she traveled, cunningly feeling her way, and finding out who were friends; till after a long and painful journey she found, in answer to careful inquiries, that she had at last crossed that magic "line" which then separated the land of bondage from the land of freedom; for this was before *we* were commanded by law to take part in the iniquity of slavery, and aid in taking and sending back those poor hunted fugitives who had manhood and intelligence enough to enable them to make their way thus far towards freedom.

"When I found I had crossed dat *line,*" she said, "I looked at my hands to see if I was de same pusson. There was such a glory ober ebery ting; de sun came like gold through the trees, and ober the fields, and I felt like I was in Heaben."

But then came the bitter drop in the cup of joy. She said she felt like a man who was put in State Prison for twenty-five years. All these twenty-five years he was thinking of his home, and longing for the time when he would see it again. At last the day comes—he leaves the prison gates—he makes his way to his old home, but his old home is not there. The house has been pulled down, and a new one has been put up in its place; his family and friends are gone nobody knows where; there is no one to take him by the hand, no one to welcome him.

"So it was with me," she said. "I had crossed the line. I was *free;* but there was no one to welcome me to the land of freedom. I was a stranger in a strange land; and my home, after all, was down in Maryland; because my father, my mother, my brothers, and sisters, and friends were there. But I was free, and *they* should be free. I would make a home in the North and bring them there, God helping me. Oh, how I prayed then," she said; "I said to de Lord, 'I'm gwine to hole stiddy on to *you,* an' I *know* you'll see me through.'"

DOCUMENT 82:
Letter, Abraham Lincoln to Mrs. Horace Mann, April 5, 1864. Roy P. Basler, Marian Delores Pratt, and Lloyd A. Dunlap, eds., *Collected Works of Abraham Lincoln,* 8 volumes (Piscataway, NJ: Rutgers University Press, 1953).

Courtesy Rutgers University Press.

President Abraham Lincoln writes this letter to the wife of Horace
Mann, the noted Massachusetts educator, and insists that he does
not have the authority to emancipate the slaves. It is an important
document that reflects the complexity of federal versus state power
as well as Lincoln's ambivalent views on slavery.

Mrs. Horace Mann,

Madam,

The petition of persons under eighteen, praying that I would free all
slave children, and the heading of which petition it appears you wrote,
was handed me a few days since by Senator [Charles] Sumner. Please
tell these little people I am very glad their young hearts are so full of
just and generous sympathy, and that, while I have not the power to
grant all they ask, I trust they will remember that God has, and that, as
it seems, He wills to do it.

Yours truly
A. LINCOLN

DOCUMENT 83:
Illustration, The Underground Railroad, by Charles T. Webber, c. 1893.

Library of Congress, LC-USZ62-28860.

This photograph, reproduced from a painting by Charles T. Webber,
depicts enslaved men, women, and children escaping from bondage.
The Underground Railroad was a network of people who helped
slaves escape to the North and into Canada. It began in the late eighteenth century and remained active until the end of the Civil War.
Many women served as "conductors," such as Harriet Tubman, who
made nineteen trips South to free more than three hundred slaves.

Document 83

DOCUMENT 84:
Martha Harrison, "I Wasn't Crying 'Bout Mistress, I Was Crying 'Cause The White Bread Was Gone," from Ophelia Settle Egypt, J. Masouka, and Charles S. Johnson, eds., "Unwritten History of Slaves, Autobiographical Accounts of Negro Ex-Slaves," Social Science Source Documents No. 1 (Nashville, TN: Fisk University, Social Science Institute, 1946).

Courtesy Fisk University Franklin Library Special Collections.

This interview, completed when Harrison was quite old, recounts multiple forms of resistance in which slaves engaged, including sustaining stable marriages in the face of uncertainty and violence.

They had cradles of the little nigger babies, and long before the War I was big enough to rock them babies, and old Cunningan would come in and tell ole Miss that they was gonna have a war to free the niggers, and I heard 'em talking, but I didn't know what they were talking 'bout. Mother come in with her steers, from hauling rails, and I told her what they said, and she made like it wasn't nothing, 'cause she was scared I'd tell them if she made like it was important . . .

I didn't do nothing but play and pick up chips for old Aunt Fanny. She fed us. They had these round wooden bowls, and Aunt Fanny would take that and pour the licker in it, and put bread in it for the chillen to eat. It was a great big bowl, big as that dish pan there. That's what we had for dinner, and milk and bread for supper. Mistress would say, "Go pick up some chips for old Aunt Fan to put on the lid," and I would run and break out to get the chips first, 'cause I was crazy about white bread, and when we all got back with the chips, Mistress would give us some white bread, but she would make me wait till they all got there. I liked it 'cause mammy 'nem didn't get white bread but once a week—that was Sunday, and the rest of the time they just had corn bread or shorts. I was so foolish! When she died (Mistress) it liked to killed me; I just cried and cried, and mammy say, "What's the matter with you, gal?" I said, "Ole Miss is dead, and I won't get no more white bread." She said, "Shet our mouth, gal." I thought when she died she carried all the white bread with her. Folks was saying, "Look at that poor little nigger crying 'bout her Mistress," but I wasn't crying 'bout mistress, I was crying 'cause the white bread was gone. . . .

I couldn't tell you how many niggers he [*her master*] did have; he had so many and his wife had so many. The place was full; times sho' was hard, sho' as you born. Chillen was just as lousy as pigs. They had these combs that was just like cards you "card" cotton with, and they would comb your head with them. They wouldn't get lice out, but it would make it feel better. They had to use larkspur to get 'em out; that would always get lice out of your head. But there wasn't no chillen would get sick before the War. I reckon the lice musta kept 'em healthy. . . .

Lawd, the times we did have. I know that when the War got over and we got free they put me in the field to work. I never went to school a day in my life; what I learned to read, I learned myself. My children all went to school, though. . . .

[The] overseer . . . went to my father one morning and said, "Bob, I'm gonna whip you this morning." Daddy said, "I ain't done nothing," and he said, "I know it, I'm gonna whip you to keep you from doing nothing," and he hit him with that cowhide—you know it would cut the blood out of you with every lick if they hit you hard—and daddy was chopping cotton, so he just took up his hoe and chopped right down on that man's head and knocked his brains out. Yes'm, it killed him, but they didn't put colored folks in jail then, so when old Charlie Merrill, the nigger trader, come along they sold my daddy to him, and he carried him way down in Mississippi. Ole Merrill would buy all the time, buy and sell niggers just like hogs. They sold him Aunt Phoebe's little baby that was just toddling along, and Uncle Dick—that was my mammy's brother.

The way they would whip you was like they done my oldest sister. They tied her, and they had a place just like they're gonna barbecue a hog, and they would strip you and tie you and lay you down. . . . Old Aunt Fanny had told marster that my sister wouldn't keep her dress clean, and that's what they was whipping her 'bout. So they had her down in the cellar whipping her, and I was real little. I couldn't say "Big Sis," but I went and told Mammy, "Old Marster's got "'Big Jim' down there in the cellar beating her," and mammy got out of bed and went in there and throwed Aunt Fan out the kitchen door, and they had to stop whipping Big Sis and come and see about Aunt Fan. You see, she would tell things on others, trying to keep from getting whipped herself. I seed mistress crack her many a time over the head with a broom, and I'd be so scared she was gonna crack me, but she never did hit me, 'cept slap me when I'd turn the babies over. I'd get tired and make like I was sleep, and would ease the cradle over and throw the baby out. I never would throw mammy's out, though. Old Miss would be setting there just knitting and watching the babies; they had a horn and every woman could tell when it was time to come and nurse her baby by the way they would blow the horn. The white folks was crazy 'bout their nigger babies, 'cause that's whre they got their profit. . . . When I'd get tired, I would just ease that baby over and Mistress would slap me so hard; I didn't know a hand could hurt so bad, but I'd take the slap and get to go out to play. She would slap me hard and say, "Git on out of here and stay till you wake up," and that was just want I wanted, 'cause I'd play then. . . .

My husband never did like for me to work; he used to ask me how come I work when he was doing all he could to give me what I wanted. "Looks like you don't 'preciate what I'm trying to do for you." But I'd say, "Yes, I do, honey. I jest help you 'cause I don't want you to break down. If you put a load on one horse it will pull him down, but two horses can pull it jest as easy." . . .

DOCUMENT 85:

Susie King Taylor, "Sneaking an Education: Memories of a Contraband," from *Reminiscences of My life in Camp with the 33rd United States Colored Troops* (Boston: Author, 1902), 5–6.

Courtesy Library of Congress.

Susie Taylor, born in Georgia in 1848, tells how she learned to read from a widowed free African American woman in Savannah. Her education helped her write passes for her enslaved grandmother and other free people of color.

I was born under the slave law in Georgia in 1848 and was brought up by my grandmother in Savannah. There were three of us with her, my youngest sister and brother. My brother and I being the two eldest, we were sent to a friend of my grandmother, a Mrs. Woodhouse, a widow, to learn to read and write. She was a free woman and lived on Bay Lane between Habersham and Price Streets, about half a mile from my house. We went every day with our books wrapped in paper to prevent the police or white persons from seeing them. We went in, one at a time, through the gate into the yard to the kitchen, which was the school room. She had 25 or 30 children whom she taught, assisted by her daughter, Mary Jane. The neighbors would see us going in some time, but they supposed we were there learning trades, as it was the custom to give children a trade of some kind. After school, we left the same way we entered, one by one and we would go to a square about a block from the school and wait for each other. We would gather laurel leaves and pop them in our hands, on our way home. I remained at her school for two years or more, when I was sent to a Mrs. Mary Beasley, where I continued until May 1860, when she told my grandmother she had taught me all she knew, and grandmother had better get someone else who could teach me more, so I stopped my studies for a while.

I had a white playmate about this time, named Katie O'Connor, who lived on the next corner of the street from my house and who attended a convent. One day she told me, if I would promise not to tell her father, she would give me some lessons. On my promise not to do so, and gaining her mother's consent, she gave me lessons about four months every evening. At the end of this time she was put into the convent permanently, and I've never seen her since.

A month after this James Blouis, our landlord's son, was attending the high school and was very fond of grandmother, so she asked him to give me a few lessons which he did until the middle of 1861, when the Savannah Volunteer Guards, to which he and his brother belonged were ordered to the front under General Barton. In the first battle of Mannassas his brother Eugene was killed and James deserted over to the Union side and at the close of the war went to Washington, D.C., where he has since resided.

I often wrote passes for my grandmother, for all colored persons, free or slave were compelled to have a pass; free colored persons having a guardian in place of a master. These passes were good until 10 or ten-thirty P.M. for one night or every night for one month. . . .

DOCUMENT 86:

Sojourner Truth, "Ar'n't I a Woman," 1851.

Sojourner Truth (1797–1883) is believed to have delivered this speech to the 1851 Women's Convention in Akron, Ohio. The original account of her speech was published in the June 21, 1851, issue of the *Anti-Slavery Bugle*, edited by Marcus Robinson. Many other versions subsequently appeared, and Nell Irvin Painter offers discussion of the debate surrounding this speech in *Sojourner Truth: A Life, A Symbol* (New York: W. W. Norton, 1997). Sojourner Truth was born Isabella Baumfree in New York into slavery in 1787 and escaped to freedom in 1826. In 1843, she changed her name to Sojourner Truth and published *The Narrative of Sojourner Truth: A Northern Slave* in 1850. Income from that publication gave her the ability to travel and speak at antislavery and women's rights conventions.

Well, children, where there is so much racket there must be something out of kilter. I think that 'twixt the negroes of the South and the women at the North, all talking about rights, the white men will be in a fix pretty soon. But what's all this here talking about?

That man over there says that women need to be helped into carriages, and lifted over ditches, and to have the best place everywhere. Nobody ever helps me into carriages, or over mud-puddles, or gives me any best place! And ain't I a woman? Look at me! Look at my arm! I have ploughed and planted, and gathered into barns, and no man could head me! And ain't I a woman? I could work as much and eat as much as a man—when I could get it—and bear the lash as well! And ain't I a woman? I have borne thirteen children, and seen most all sold off to slavery, and when I cried out with my mother's grief, none but Jesus heard me! And ain't I a woman?

Then they talk about this thing in the head; what's this they call it? [member of audience whispers, "intellect"] That's it, honey. What's that got to do with women's rights or negroes' rights? If my cup won't hold but a pint, and yours holds a quart, wouldn't you be mean not to let me have my little half measure full?

Then that little man in black there, he says women can't have as much rights as men, 'cause Christ wasn't a woman! Where did your Christ come from? Where did your Christ come from? From God and a woman! Man had nothing to do with Him.

If the first woman God ever made was strong enough to turn the world upside down all alone, these women together ought to be able to turn it back , and get it right side up again! And now they is asking to do it, the men better let them.

Obliged to you for hearing me, and now old Sojourner ain't got nothing more to say.

DOCUMENT 87:
Photograph, Abraham Lincoln and Sojourner Truth, 1864.

Courtesy Library of Congress, LC-USZ62–16225.

In this image, Lincoln is showing Truth "a Bible presented by the colored people of Baltimore," October 29, 1864, a year before the Civil War ended. After her famous "Ar'n't I a Woman" speech in 1851, Truth, a former slave, became a powerful and visible figure in the abolition movement.

Document 87

DOCUMENT 88:
Wood Engraving, Modern Day Medea—Margaret Garner, 1867.

Courtesy Library of Congress, LC-USZ62–84545.

Margaret Garner and her family attempted to escape from slavery in Kentucky over the frozen Ohio River into Cincinnati. They were apprehended by slave catchers and Garner killed two of her children and tried to kill them all instead of allowing them to remain enslaved. Medea was a figure in Greek mythology who killed two of her children as a form of revenge for her husband's abandonment. This image is a photograph of a painting by Thomas Noble.

Document 88

DOCUMENT 89:
Excerpt, Sarah R. Levering, *Memoirs of Margaret Jane Blake of Baltimore, Md., and Selections in Prose and Verse* (Philadelphia: Press of Innes and Son, 1897), 14–17.

Courtesy University of North Carolina at Chapel Hill.

Blake was born in 1811 to a free father and enslaved mother. This memoir is written by Sarah Levering, the white woman who was raised by and whose family owned Margaret. It reveals as much about white attitudes toward slavery and Reconstruction as it does about Margaret's life. The memoir includes only a handful of direct quotes from Margaret, all critical of Northern whites and abolitionists. The publication of the memoir in 1897 was intended to support "a manual labor school for the benefit of Afro-American citizens, as they prefer being called." This excerpt tells the story of the escape of Ann Dutton (Duncan), one of Levering's slaves who was rebellious and mistreated by the family.

. . . After a few years, death and reverse of fortune caused changes in our family which were displeasing to Margaret, and she was allowed to choose a home for herself, and the wages paid for her services went to pay for her clothes and her physician's bills. She had much suffering from the tumor and often was obliged to return to her old home for rest and to be nursed back to ordinary health. The first place where she hired was in the family of Mr. J. B., and her record there was one of obedience and faithfulness. She claimed some indulgence and it was granted her, for they knew she had been allowed many privileges. The second place where she hired was in the family of Mr. H. G. Here, too, she claimed her privileges, and they were granted her, for she was liked and the family desired to retain her. During this time with Mrs. G., Blake was much annoyed by the abolitionists. She complained very much of them. They tormented her. She would say: "I want my freedom, but I do not want to *steal* it." Mrs. G. went one summer to the North to visit her husband's relatives and gained the consent of Margaret and her mistress that she could attend her as lady's maid. Mother consented to the trip being taken, hoping the change of scene and climate might benefit Margaret's health, knowing that the moment she set foot on that soil she was free, and if she pleased to do so she might stay there. But Margaret was of a different mind. Upon the arrival of the party in the city of New York lodgings were taken in a hotel, and the Irish waiters belonging to the establishment immediately bothered the lady's maid with attentions, inviting her to walk out with them to view the city. Icily she repelled them. "No," she replied, "I will not walk out with you in the streets of New York. I shall not do in New York what I would be ashamed to do in Baltimore. Colored women are disgraced in Baltimore if they are seen in the company of white men on the streets." "Are you free?" asked the waiters. "I am as free as you are," she rejoined; "I come and go as I please." Thus the free slave rebuffed her white suitors. She was afraid of them.

When night came on she begged Mrs. G. to have a bed laid on her bedroom floor, that she might be safe from the impudent Irish waiters. She was afraid they might steal her off and sell her to Georgia. That arrangement was made to Blake's satisfaction. She was safe from the much-dreaded Irish waiters. The party she was traveling with proceeded on their way and soon reached one of the New England States to spend the summer among relatives who were permanent residents there.

The pleasant visit ended, and Mrs. G. prepared to turn Southward. And Margaret? How was it with her? She, too, was ready to return to Baltimore. The free slave? Yes; the free slave returned to face her mistress and her young ladies, not ashamed to show her face to her people!

Ann Dutton, or Duncan, as she preferred to be called, was of a different mind. One day she informed her mistress that she was desirous of attending a funeral to take place that afternoon. Permission was given her to attend the funeral, and she was much helped in her work that she might be there in proper time. When she was ready to leave the house it was noticed that she wore a wadded merino cloak, a long cloak with a large cape to it. Her mistress said to her: "Ann, why do you wear that heavy cloak this warm afternoon?" "Oh!" she replied, "the evenings are cool, and I shall need it before I get back."

So she departed. Night fell, and Ann still out! The family became anxious about her and feared she might be ill-treated by rough crowds on the streets. It was the night of the day of General William H. Harrison's election to the Presidency, and much excitement prevailed. Wait! wait! and no Ann Duncan in sight yet! At last it occurred to one of the family, in consideration of the strange freak of the donning of her heavy cloak, to go to her room and examine her bureau. Her room was looked over and not a garment was to be seen that belonged to her. All gone! We never saw her more. It was a cleverly-managed escape.

DOCUMENT 90:
Excerpts, Elsie Clews Parsons, *Folk-Lore of the Sea Islands, South Carolina* (Cambridge and New York: American Folk-Lore Society, 1932), 61–63.

These brief stories recount slaves who outwitted their master or mistress and were modeled on "hag" stories that were common in the Caribbean and Africa. Storytelling, like song, was an important form of resistance. The American Folk-Lore Society was founded in Cambridge, Massachusetts, in 1888 by humanities scholars, as well as author Mark Twain and President Rutherford B. Hayes.

[I]

Wen' to a witch-man. When his master 'mence to whip him, eve'y cut he give de man, his *[master's]* wife way off at home feel de cut. Sen' wor' please stop cut lick de man. When he *[master]* got home, his wife was wash down wid blood.

[II]

His master beat him so sevare, so de man went to a witch. De witch said, "Never min'! you go home. Tomorrow you will see me." When de man got up in de mornin', de white man was jus' as happy as happy as happy can be; but de more de sun goes down, he commence ter sleep. At de same time he call to his Negro, "Tomorrow you go an' do such an' such a tas'." Givin' out his orders kyan hardly hol' up his head. As soon as de sun was down, he down too, he down yet. De witch done dat. He *[witch]* come, but he stay in his home an' done dat.

[III]

A white man had a wife. Eve'y night his wife go, but he don' know where his wife go to. He had a servant to wait on dem. So de servant whispered to his master, "Master, don' you know mistress kill all my chil'run?" Say, "Mistress is a hag."—"You think you can prove it? You think you can ketch her?"—"Yes, suh! you let me sleep here one night. I kyan ketch her." So de servant an' his master make de agreement how to ketch 'em. He said to his servan', "Don' you go home tonight. You sleep hyere. I'm goin' away soon in de mornin'." Dey bof (de man an' de wife) dey went to baid, de servan' on de watch. Late in de night de mistress woke up. De servan' watch her. Somet'in' she put on her flesh an' take off her skins. After take off her skins, she roll it up an' put it in her dirty clo'es in de back o' de baid. An' she gone out. After she gone out, de servan' call to her master, said, "Master, mistress is gone. To proof to you dat mistress is a hag, I come now an' show you what she done." She went back ob de baid an' get de clo'es what de skin in, an' bring it to her master, an' say, "Here is mistress skin." An' he said to his servan', "What shall we do wid de skin to ketch her?" She said, "Put black pepper an' salt in de skin on de inside." So de master did dat. So later on de mistress came an' get her skin. An' she 'mence to put it on; an' eve'y time de skin bu'n her so much, she said to de skin, "Skin, skin, you don' know me?

'Tis me." Still she couldn' get it on. So she went to her baid an' wrapped up. Master was out now. She lay down till late. Her husband 'mence to p'ovoke her to get up. Still she won't get up. Jus' keep po'vokin'. All at oncet he snatched off de cover off her, an' dere she was raw like a beef. So he called witnesses to prove it. So dey make a kil' of lime an' put her in it, an' bu'n her down. But as much as de fire a-bu'nin', she never holler 'til dey t'row de skin in. De skin 'mence to scream. So dat was de en' of his wife.

[IV]

Once upon a time there was a old man in slavery. He told his master that he was cripple and couldn't work. So the man let him stay home to take care of his children. One day the master went away. When he came home, he find the man play on his banjo,—

"I was fooling my master seventy-two years ago,
And I am fooling him now."

He was singing this song away on his banjo. His master caught him, and start to kill him by whipping him. So the old man went to the doctor Negro. The next day he was to be kill'. When his master started to whip him, every time the man start to whip him, none of the licks touch. And he had freedom.

CHAPTER 5

The Meaning of Freedom

The documents in this section examine the period after the Civil War when the nation sought to reconcile the North and South and determine the status of freedmen and -women. The meaning of freedom often varied from region to region.

DOCUMENT 91:

Theodore Weld to Lewis Tappan, March 18, 1834, in Gilbert H. Barnes and Dwight L. Dumond, eds., *Weld-Grimke Letters,* Vol. I (New York, 1934), 134.

Courtesy Library of Congress.

This letter details the complicated and often expensive process by which members of enslaved families tried to free each other. Theodore Weld (1803–1895) was a noted abolitionist, editor, speaker, and author. He is best known for his 1838 publication of *American Slavery As It Is: Testimony of a Thousand Witnesses,* which helped to influence Harriet Beecher Stowe's *Uncle Tom's Cabin.*

I visited this week about 30 black families, and found some members of more than half these families were still in bondage, and the father, mother and children were struggling to lay up money enough to purchase their freedom. I found one man who had just finished paying for his wife and five children. Another man and wife bought themselves some years ago, and have been working night and day to purchase their children; they had just redeemed the last and had paid for themselves and children 1,400 dollars! Another woman had recently paid the last installment of the purchase money for her husband. She had purchased him by taking in washing, and working late at night, after going out and performing as help at hard labor. . . .

DOCUMENT 92:
Letter, Frederick Douglass, *The Liberator,* October 6, 1848.

Courtesy Library of Congress.

In this letter, Douglass writes Horatio G. Warner, editor of the *Rochester Courier,* to complain that his daughter was denied entry into a school because of his prejudice. This letter illustrates that even in freedom, African Americans faced discrimination and hostility. Douglass, born a slave in Maryland in 1818 and escaped to freedom in 1838, became a noted author and orator. During the Civil War, he conferred with President Abraham Lincoln and helped recruit African American soldiers for the Union cause. *The Liberator* was an antislavery newspaper published by William Lloyd Garrison from 1831 to 1865.

Sir:—My reasons—I will not say my apology, for addressing you this letter, will become evident, by perusing the following brief statement of facts.

About the middle of August of the present year—deeply desiring to give my daughter, a child between nine and ten years old, the advantages of a good school—and learning that "Seward Seminary" of this city was an institution of that character—I applied to its principal, Miss Tracy, for the admission of my daughter into that Seminary. The principal—after making suitable enquiries into the child's mental qualifications, and informing me of the price of tuition per term, agreed to receive the child into the school at the commencement of the September term. . . . But instead of receiving her into the school according to agreement—and as in honor the principal was bound to do, she was merely thrust into a room separate from all other scholars, and in this prison-like solitary confinement received the occasional visits of a teacher appointed to instruct her. On my return home, I found her still going to school, and not knowing the character of the treatment extended to her, I asked with a light heart, as I took her to my side, well my daughter, how do you get on at the Seminary? She answered with tears in her eyes, *"I get along pretty well, but father, Miss Tracy does not allow me to go into the room with the other scholars because I am colored."*

Stung to the heart's core by this grievous statement, and suppressing my feelings as well as I could, I went immediately to the Seminary to remonstrate with the principal against the cruelty and injustice of treating my child as a criminal on account of her color—subjecting her to solitary confinement because guilty of a skin not colored like her own. In answer to all that I could say against such treatment, I was answered by the principal, that since she promised to receive the child into school, she had consulted with the trustees, (a body of persons I believe unknown to the public,) and that they were opposed to the child's admission to the school—that she thought at first of disregarding their opposition, but when she remembered how much they had done for her in sustaining the institution, she did not feel at liberty to do so; but she thought if I allowed her to remain and be taught separately for a term or more, that the prejudice might be overcome, and the child admitted into the school with the other young ladies and misses.

At a loss to know what to do for the best interest of the child, I consulted with Mrs. Douglass and others, and the result of the consultation was, to take my child from the Seminary, as allowing her to remain there in such circumstances, could only serve to degrade her in her own yes, and those of the other scholars attending the school. Before, however, carrying out my determination to withdraw the child from the Seminary, Miss Tracy, the principal, submitted the question of the child's reception to each scholar individually, and I am sorry to say, in a manner well calculated to rouse their prejudices against her. She told them if there was one objection to receiving her, she should be excluded . . . Each scholar was then told by the principal, that the question must be submitted to their parents, that if one parent objected, the child would not be received into the school . . .

. . . Out of all the parents to whom the question of her admission was submitted, no one, excepting yourself objected. You are in a minority of *one* . . .

. . . You have already done serious injury to Seward Seminary. Three young ladies left the school immediately after the exclusion of my daughter, and I have heard of three more, who had intended to go, but who have now declined going to that institution, because it has given its sanction to that antidemocratic, and ungodly caste. I am also glad to inform you that you have not succeeded as you hoped to do, in depriving my child of the means of a decent education, or the privilege of going to an excellent school. She had not been excluded from Seward Seminary five hours, before she was welcomed into another quite as respectable and *equally* Christian to the one from which she was excluded. She now sits in a school among children as pure, and as white as you or yours, and no one is offended. Now I should like to know how much better you are than me, and how much better your children than mine? We are both worms of the dust, and our children are like us. We differ in color, it is true, (and not much in that respect,) but who is to decide which color is most pleasing to God, or most honorable among men? But I do not wish to waste words or argument on one whom I take to be as destitute of honorable feeling, as he has shown himself full of pride and prejudice.

DOCUMENT 93:
Julia Ward Howe, Battle Hymn of the Republic, 1862.

Julia Howe (1819–1910) wrote the poem that became the now-famous song in 1861 after visiting a Union army camp. The poem was first published in the February issue of the *Atlantic Monthly* the following year, and it was set to music composed by William Steffe. It soon became a popular Union hymn. Howe was born in New Jersey and became a noted author and abolitionist. She is also remembered as the first person to proclaim Mother's Day in 1870. Editions of the hymn vary slightly.

Mine eyes have seen the glory of the coming of the Lord:
He is trampling out the vintage where the grapes of wrath are stored;
He hath loosed the fateful lightning of His terrible swift sword:
His truth is marching on.
Glory! Glory! Hallelujah! Glory! Glory! Hallelujah!
Glory! Glory! Hallelujah! His truth is marching on.

I have seen Him in the watch-fires of a hundred circling camps,
They have builded Him an altar in the evening dews and damps;
I can read His righteous sentence by the dim and flaring lamps:
His day is marching on.
Glory! Glory! Hallelujah! Glory! Glory! Hallelujah!
Glory! Glory! Hallelujah! His day is marching on.

I have read a fiery gospel writ in burnished rows of steel:
"As ye deal with my contemners, so with you my grace shall deal;
Let the Hero, born of woman, crush the serpent with his heel,
Since God is marching on."
Glory! Glory! Hallelujah! Glory! Glory! Hallelujah!
Glory! Glory! Hallelujah! Since God is marching on.

He has sounded forth the trumpet that shall never call retreat;
He is sifting out the hearts of men before His judgment-seat;
Oh, be swift, my soul, to answer Him! be jubilant, my feet!
Our God is marching on.
Glory! Glory! Hallelujah! Glory! Glory! Hallelujah!
Glory! Glory! Hallelujah! Our God is marching on.

In the beauty of the lilies Christ was born across the sea,
With a glory in his bosom that transfigures you and me:
As He died to make men holy, let us die to make men free,
While God is marching on.
Glory! Glory! Hallelujah! Glory! Glory! Hallelujah!
Glory! Glory! Hallelujah! While God is marching on.

He is coming like the glory of the morning on the wave,
He is wisdom to the mighty, He is succor to the brave;
So the world shall be His footstool, and the soul of time His slave,
Our God is marching on.
Glory! Glory! Hallelujah! Glory! Glory! Hallelujah!
Glory! Glory! Hallelujah! Our God is marching on.

DOCUMENT 94:
Letter, Charlotte Forten (Grimké), *The Liberator,*
November 20, 1862.

Courtesy Library of Congress.

Charlotte Forten was born in Philadelphia to a prominent free family. She was well educated, became an active abolitionist, and befriended William Lloyd Garrison, William Wells Brown, and Ralph Waldo Emerson. She worked as a teacher and became one of the first African American women to come south during the Civil War to teach in the Sea Islands. In 1864 she married the nephew of Angelina and Sarah Grimké. She wrote essays about her experience in the *Atlantic Monthly* in June 1864. Two years earlier, she detailed first arriving in the Sea Islands for Garrison's newspaper, *The Liberator.*

St. Helena's island, on which I am, is about six miles from the mainland of Beaufort. I must tell you that we were rowed hither from Beaufort by a crew of Negro boatmen, and that they sung for us several of their own beautiful songs. There is a peculiar wildness and solemnity about them which cannot be described, and the people accompanying the singing with a singular swaying motion of the body, which seems to make it more effective. How much I enjoyed that row in the beautiful, brilliant southern sunset, with no sounds to be heard but the musical murmur of the water, and the wonderfully rich, clear tones of the singers! But all the time I did not realize that I was actually in South Carolina! And indeed I believe I do not quite realize it now. But we are far from feeling fear,—we were in a very excited, jubilant state of mind, and sang the John Brown song with spirit, as we drove through the pines and palmettos. Ah! it was good to be able to sing that *here,* in the very heart of Rebeldom!

There are no white soldiers on this island. It is protected by gunboats, and by Negro pickets who do their duty well. These men attacked and drove back a boat-load of rebels who tried to land here one night, several weeks ago. General [Rufus] Saxton is forming a colored regiment at Beaufort, and many of the colored men from this and the adjacent islands have joined it. The General is a noble-hearted man, who has a deep interest in the people here, and he is generally loved and trusted by them. I am sorry to say that some other officers treat the freed people and speak of them with the greatest contempt. They are consequently disliked and feared.

As far as I have been able to observe—and although I have not been here long, I have seen and talked with many of the people—the Negroes here seem to be, for the most part, an honest, industrious, and sensible people. They are eager to learn; they rejoice in their new-found freedom. It does one good to see how *jubilant* they are over the downfall of their "secesh" masters, as they call them. I do not believe there is a man, woman, or even a child that is old enough to be sensible, that would submit to being made a slave again. There is evidently a deep determination in their souls that *that* shall never be. Their hearts are full of gratitude to the Government; and to the "Yankees." . . .

My school is about a mile from here, in the little Baptist church . . . There are two ladies in the school beside myself—Miss T. and Miss M., both of whom are most enthusiastic teachers. They have done a great deal of good here. At present, our school is small,—many of the children on the island being ill with whooping cough,—but in general it averages eighty or ninety. I find the children generally well-behaved, and eager to learn; yea, they are nearly all most eager to learn, many of them make most rapid improvement. It is a great happiness to teach them. I wish some of those persons at the North, who say the race is hopelessly and naturally inferior, could see the readiness with which these children, so long oppressed and deprived of every privilege, learn and understand.

I have some grown pupils—people on our own plantation—who take lessons in the evenings. It will amuse you to know that one of them—our man-of-all work—is named *Cupid*. (Venusus and Cupids are very common here.) He told he me was "feared" he was almost too old to learn; but I assured him that was not the case, and now he is working diligently at the alphabet. One of my people—Harry—is a scholar to be proud of. He makes most wonderful improvement. I never saw any one so determined to learn. I enjoy having him and Cupid talk about the time that the rebels had to flee from this place. The remembrance of it is evidently a source of the most exquisite happiness and amusement. There are several families living here, and it is very pleasant to visit their cabins and talk with them. They are very happy now. They never weary of contrasting their present with their former condition, and they work for the Government now, and receive wages and rations in return. I am very happy here, but wish I was able to do a great deal more. I wish some one would write a little Christmas hymn for our children to sing. I want to have a kind of festival for them on Christmas, if we can. The children have just learned the John Brown song, and next week they are going to learn the song of the "Negro Boatman." The little creatures love to sing. They sing with the great enthusiasm. I wish you could hear them.

DOCUMENT 95:
Letter, My Dear Amelia, 1863. From Carter G. Woodson, *Mind of the Negro as Reflected in Letters Written During the Crisis, 1800–1860* (Washington, D.C.: The Association for the Study of Negro Life and History, Inc., c. 1926).

Courtesy Association for the Study of African American Life and History.

In this short letter, Lewis Douglass, the son of the noted abolitionist Frederick Douglass, writes to his future wife, from Morris Island, South Carolina, on July 20, 1863. Lewis writes immediately after the 54th Massachusetts Infantry Regiment unsuccessfully stormed Fort Wagner, named for Lieutenant Colonel Thomas Wagner, where he was wounded. He achieved the rank of sergeant major, the highest rank available to African American soldiers at that time. This letter was collected in a volume by Carter G. Woodson, a noted African American historian who founded the Association for the Study of African American Life and History and the *Journal of Negro History*.

A letter from the front . . . 1863

MY DEAR AMELIA:

I have been in two fights, and am unhurt. I am about to go in another I believe tonight. Our men fought well on both occasions. The last was desperate. We charged that terrible battery on Morris island known as Fort Wagner, and were repulsed . . . . De Forest of your city is wounded, George Washington is missing, Jacob Carter is missing,

Charles Reason wounded, Charles Whiting, Charles Creamer all wounded.

I escaped unhurt from amidst that perfect hail of shot and shell. It was terrible. I need not particularize, the papers will give a better [account] than I have time to give. My thoughts are with you often, you are as dear as ever, be good to remember it as I no doubt you will. As I said before we are on the eve of another fight and I am very busy and have just snatched a moment to write you. I must necessarily be brief. Should I fall in the next fight killed or wounded I hope I fall with my face to the foe.

This regiment has established its reputation as a fighting regiment, not a man flinched, though it was a trying time. Men fell all around me. A shell would explode and clear a space of twenty feet. Our men would close up again, but it was no use, we had to retreat, which was a very hazardous undertaking. How I got out of that fight alive I cannot tell, but I am here.

My Dear girl I hope again to see you. I must bid you farewell should I be killed. Remember if I die I die in a good cause. I wish we had a hundred thousand colored troops we would put an end to this war.

Good Bye to all. Your own loving—Write soon—
LEWIS

DOCUMENT 96:
Charlotte Ann Jackson from the Chase Family Papers,
Lucy Chase Manuscript Collection.

Courtesy American Antiquarian Society.

Lucy and Sarah Chase were members of a Quaker family in the North involved in reform efforts. At the beginning of the Civil War, they joined the New England Educational Association and helped establish and supervise schools. After the war, the two women continued to promote educational reform. Little is known about Jackson except that she was one of the Chase sisters' students. The letter in this collection does not have information about the date or place it was written.

When i was liveing with White People i was tide down hand and foot and they tide me to the Post and whip me till i Could not stand up and they tide my Close over my head and whip me much as they want and they took my Brother and sent him to Richmond to stay one year And sent my Aunt my Sister my farther away too and said if he did not go away they would kill him they said they was Goin to Put me in Prisens But the light has come the Rebles is put down and Slavry is dead God Bless the union Forever more and they was puting people in tubs and they stead me to Death and i hope slavry shall be no more and they said that the yankees had horns and said that the yankees was Goin to kill us and something told me not to Believe them and somthing told me not to Be afraid and when they Come hare they would not let me Come out to see them and when i was out in the Street they was Stead i would go away from them and they said I Better stay whith them for the yankees would kill me I would Better stay

---

DOCUMENT 97:
Anonymous Diary, 1863 (attributed to Kate D. Foster).

Courtesy Mississippi Department of Archives and History, Z/0869.000/F.

This diary, written by a white woman in Natchez (Adams County), Mississippi, details the events of the summer of 1863 during the Civil War. It offers a glimpse of life on the home front and reveals her opinions of slaves, mostly as they left their farm.

July 14, 1863

. . . This morning when we were at breakfast Rose came running to tell us the Yankees were coming. We went to the front of the house and looking out saw over a hundred cavalry passing along the road talking, laughing and seeming to enjoy themselves. Their destination seemed to be Col. Brigiman's pasture where our government has over four thousand head of cattle. They did not come in and I hope if they do visit us they will remember that they have mothers, wives & sisters at home and treat us as they would wish them to be by our men. We intend to be as quiet as we can and not give them any cause for ill treatment. God can take care of us if we trust in Him. It is so still no one would suppose we were so closely attended by our enemy. I don't love them and never shall but my feelings are indescribable towards them now they are here. I know I hate them . . .

July 25, 1863

. . . We went to Grandma's—her maid & Maud's sister have left and a more arrant hypocrite I never heard of than Harriet. Grandma does not seem to care at all about the negroes leaving—she is right too for if they go let them and reap the benefit of it too. Pa's boy Allen has gone, fooled off by some old fool. Fred the carriage driver has gone to what they all think a better place but poor deluded creatures they will find out too late who are their best friends, Master or Massa. Mrs. Dunbar's two house servants Nancy and Mary Ann left Thursday morning and the latter took all of her children. Now Mrs. D. has to do the house cleaning and nearly all the house work. It seems that if the rest who are here if they had any feeling they would feel sorry for Mrs. D. and remain faithful. . . . I saw Mrs. William Dunbar and two daughters yesterday afternoon and they have to clean up the house. Taking *all* the negroes is not whipping us as the enemy will see.

July 28, 1863

. . . When the services were nearly ended a negro man in any by Sunday clothes came up the middle aisle to the pulpit, stopped a little while there, walked to the right hand side of the church. Mr. Carradine got up & demanded what he wanted. The impudent scamp said he came to church and wanted a seat. All of the congregation looked astounded as did Mr. Stratton. Mr. C. showed him into the gallery where the servants sit. I was so angry. Miss Lucie Struve says she looked around and the Yankees were laughing heartily to themselves. I should not be surprised if some one of our enemies had sent him in the church as an insult to us. . . . I think negroes are a lot of ingrates and God punishes us for ingratitude as much as for any other sin. Let the foe take all the negroes—they are welcome to them and the sooner we are rid of them the quicker we will whip our enemy. The federals who are here are quite condescending. When they take *all* from us, we will rally around the sacred tombs of our honored dead & fight the last battle for freedom on their consecrated graves. And think you will not be successful? Ask our "honored dead" if souls such as theirs could rest, and know the insolent invader had a Southern home, rendered holy by their loving presence in days gone by. No! though they seem to have us in durance vile we will come out of the furnace doubly purified for the good work & fight that God has given us to do. For to the people of this Confederacy is given the sublime mission of maintaining the supremacy of our Father in Heaven. Even now day is breaking and some hopes of our once more basking in the sunshine of God's smile. . . .

July 30, 1863
These many days have passed. Ned & May are still with us but they do no work. Ned goes to town ever day after something connected with the Devil no doubt. Matilida left last night. We think all will go whensoever it pleases their majesties. Rose is sick so for the last two mornings we have been obliged to do a greater part of the house work. It is not hard to do. Taking out the slops is the only part that I do not like. I am going to help Sarah iron to-day as she has so much to do with Matilda's work. I do hope some of them will be faithful for if they are not, I shall lose entire faith in the whole race. Mr. Dunbar's Joe left Monday. He was a consummate hypocrite, in fact they all are. . . .

August 23, 1863
Celia left last Saturday afternoon with her two children. She was very cool about it, had a wagon to come out for her things. I wish that I had ordered the men away and then made her go, but I was fearful I should bring trouble upon Aunt Jenny. Any way she is gone and I have been helping old Emmeline to cook. . . .

November 15, 1863
. . . John, Sarah & Rose have left and I did the washing for six weeks, came near ruining myself for life as I was too delicately raised for such hard work.

DOCUMENT 98:
Woodcut, Freedom to the Slaves, Currier and Ives, 1863.

Courtesy Library of Congress, LC-USZC2–2366.

This lithograph, published the year President Abraham Lincoln issued the Emancipation Proclamation, depicts Lincoln as a savior of enslaved men and women.

FREEDOM TO THE SLAVES
Proclaimed January 1st 1863, by ABRAHAM LINCOLN, President of the United States.
"Proclaim liberty throughout All the land unto All the inhabitants thereof." ___ LEV XXV 10.

Document 98

DOCUMENT 99:
Lithograph, Reading the Emancipation Proclamation, 1864.

Courtesy Library of Congress, LC-USZ62–5334.

This lithograph accompanied a pamphlet published on January 1, 1864, by Lucius Stebbins in Hartford, Connecticut. It shows a romanticized vision of enslaved men and women reading this important document around the hearth of their home.

DOCUMENT 100:
The Emancipation Proclamation, January 1, 1863.

Issued by President Abraham Lincoln during the third year of the Civil War, the proclamation held "that all persons held as slaves" within the rebellious states "are, and henceforward shall be free." Though symbolic for some, the proclamation did not affect slavery in the border states or areas of the Confederacy under Union control. Real freedom for slaves, then, depended upon a Union victory. Though Lincoln did not support slavery, he was not an abolitionist. He believed African Americans should not be part of mainstream white society.

January 1, 1863

By the President of the United States of America: A Proclamation.

Whereas, on the twenty-second day of September, in the year of our Lord one thousand eight hundred and sixty-two, a proclamation was issued by the President of the United States, containing, among other things, the following, to wit:

"That on the first day of January, in the year of our Lord one thousand eight hundred and sixty-three, all persons held as slaves within any State or designated part of a State, the people whereof shall then be in rebellion against the United States, shall be then, thenceforward, and forever free; and the Executive Government of the United States, including the military

Document 99

and naval authority thereof, will recognize and maintain the freedom of such persons, and will do no act or acts to repress such persons, or any of them, in any efforts they may make for their actual freedom.

"That the Executive will, on the first day of January aforesaid, by proclamation, designate the States and parts of States, if any, in which the people thereof, respectively, shall then be in rebellion against the United States; and the fact that any State, or the people thereof, shall on that day be, in good faith, represented in the Congress of the United States by members chosen thereto at elections wherein a majority of the qualified voters of such State shall have participated, shall, in the absence of strong countervailing testimony, be deemed conclusive evidence that such State, and the people thereof, are not then in rebellion against the United States."

Now, therefore I, Abraham Lincoln, President of the United States, by virtue of the power in me vested as Commander-in-Chief, of the Army and Navy of the United States in time of actual armed rebellion against the authority and government of the United States, and as a fit and necessary war measure for suppressing said rebellion, do, on this first day of January, in the year of our Lord one thousand eight hundred and sixty-three, and in accordance with my purpose so to do publicly proclaimed for the full period of one hundred days, from the day first above mentioned, order and designate as the States and parts of States wherein the people thereof respectively, are this day in rebellion against the United States, the following, to wit:

Arkansas, Texas, Louisiana, (except the Parishes of St. Bernard, Plaquemines, Jefferson, St. John, St. Charles, St. James Ascension, Assumption, Terrebonne, Lafourche, St. Mary, St. Martin, and Orleans, including the City of New Orleans) Mississippi, Alabama, Florida, Georgia, South Carolina, North Carolina, and Virginia, (except the forty-eight counties designated as West Virginia, and also the counties of Berkley, Accomac, Northampton, Elizabeth City, York, Princess Ann, and Norfolk, including the cities of Norfolk and Portsmouth[)], and which excepted parts, are for the present, left precisely as if this proclamation were not issued.

And by virtue of the power, and for the purpose aforesaid, I do order and declare that all persons held as slaves within said designated States, and parts of States, are, and henceforward shall be free; and that the Executive government of the United States, including the military and naval authorities thereof, will recognize and maintain the freedom of said persons.

And I hereby enjoin upon the people so declared to be free to abstain from all violence, unless in necessary self-defence; and I recommend to them that, in all cases when allowed, they labor faithfully for reasonable wages.

And I further declare and make known, that such persons of suitable condition, will be received into the armed service of the United States to garrison forts, positions, stations, and other places, and to man vessels of all sorts in said service.

And upon this act, sincerely believed to be an act of justice, warranted by the Constitution, upon military necessity, I invoke the considerate judgment of mankind, and the gracious favor of Almighty God.

In witness whereof, I have hereunto set my hand and caused the seal of the United States to be affixed.

Done at the City of Washington, this first day of January, in the year of our Lord one thousand eight hundred and sixty three, and of the Independence of the United States of America the eighty-seventh.

By the President: ABRAHAM LINCOLN
WILLIAM H. SEWARD, Secretary of State.

DOCUMENT 101:
Letter from Harriet and Louisa Jacobs to Lydia Maria Child, March 26, 1864. Published in the *National Anti-Slavery Standard,* April 16, 1864.

Courtesy Library of Congress.

Harriet Jacobs (1813–1897) was born into slavery in North Carolina, escaped in 1835 to New York, hiding in her grandmother's attic for seven years, and published *Incidents in the Life of a Slave Girl* under the name Linda Brent detailing the sexual abuse she endured under slavery. She became an abolitionist and supportive of education for freed men and women. Here she writes of her experiences to Lydia Maria Child (1802–1880), a noted novelist, editor, scholar, and well-known abolitionist who helped Jacobs with her memoir.

FRIEND JOHNSON: I last night received letters from Mrs. Jacobs and her daughter, who you know are employed by the Society of Friends in New York to teach the emancipated slaves in the region of Alexandria, Virginia[.] I send you extracts from their letters, because I am sure your readers will feel gratified, as I do, to see these two highly intelligent women laboring so zealously and faithfully for the good of their long-oppressed people; and also because the account they give of the conduct of the freedmen is so cheering to the friends, who are praying and laboring for their growth in knowledge, and virtue, and worldly comfort.

L. MARIA CHILD.
ALEXANDRIA, March 26, 1864.

DEAR MRS. CHILD: When I went to the North, last Fall, the Freedmen here were building a school-house, and I expected it would have been finished by the time I returned. But when we arrived, we found it uncompleted. Their funds had got exhausted, and the work was at a stand-still for several weeks. This was a disappointment; but the time did not hang idle on our hands, I assure you. We went round visiting the new homes of the Freedmen, which now dot the landscape, built with their first earnings as free laborers. Within the last eight months seven hundred little cabins have been built, containing from two to four rooms. The average cost was from one hundred to two hundred and fifty dollars. In building school-houses or shelters for the old and decrepid [sic], they have received but little assistance. They have had to struggle along and help themselves as they could. But though this has been discouraging, at times, it teaches them self reliance; and that is good for them, as it is for everybody. We have over seven thousand colored refugees in this place, and, including the hospitals, less than four hundred rations are given out. This shows that they are willing to earn their own way, and generally capable of it. Indeed, when I look back on the condition in which I first found them, and compare it with their condition now, I am convinced they are not so far behind other races as some people represent them. The two rooms we occupy were given to me by the Military Governor, to be appropriated to the use of decrepid [sic] women, when we leave them.

When we went round visiting the homes of these people, we found much to commend them for. Many of them showed marks of industry, neatness, and natural refinement. In others, chaos reigned supreme. There was nothing about them to indicate the presence of a wifely wife or a motherly mother. They bore abundant marks of the half-barbarous, miserable condition of Slavery, from which the inmates had lately come. It made me sad to see their shiftlessness and discomfort; but I was hopeful for the future. The consciousness of working for themselves, and of having a character to gain, will inspire them with energy and enterprise, and a higher civilization will gradually come.

Children abounded in these cabins. They peeped out from every nook and corner. Many of them were extremely pretty and bright look-ing. Some had features and complexions purely Anglo-Saxon; showing plainly enough the slaveholder's horror of amalgamation. Some smiled upon us and were very ready to be friends. Others regarded us with shy, suspicious looks, as is apt to be the case with children who have had a cramped childhood. But they all wanted to accept our invitation to go to school, and so did all the parents for them.

In the course of our rounds, we visited a settlement which had received no name. We suggested to the settlers that it would be proper to name it for some champion of Liberty. We told them of the Hon. Chas. Sumner, whose large heart and great mind had for years been devoted to the cause of the poor slaves. We told how violent and cruel slaveholders had nearly murdered him for standing up so manfully in defence of Freedom. His claim to their gratitude was at once recognized, and the settlement was called Sumnerville.

Before we came here, a white lady, from Chelsea, Mass., was labor-ing as a missionary among the Refugees; and a white teacher, sent by the Educational Commission of Boston, accompanied us. One of the freedmen, whose cabin consisted of two rooms, gave it up to us for our school. We soon found that the clamor of little voices begging for admit-tance far exceeded the narrow limits of this establishment.

Friends at the North had given us some articles left from one of the Fairs. To these we added what we could, and got up a little Fair here, to help them in the completion of the school-house. By this means we raised one hundred and fifty dollars, and they were much gratified by the result. With the completion of the school-house our field of labor widened, and we were joyful over the prospect of extended usefulness. But some diffi-culties occurred, as there always do in the settlement of such affairs. A question arose whether the white teachers or the colored teachers should be superintendents. The freedmen had built the school-house for their children, and were Trustees of the school. So, after some discussion, it was decided that it would be best for them to hold a meeting, and settle the question for themselves. I wish you could have been at that meeting. Most of the people were slaves, until quite recently, but they talked sensibly, and I assure you that they put the question to vote in quite parliamentary style. The result was a decision that the colored teachers should have charge of the school. We were gratified by this result, because our sympathies are closely linked with our oppressed race. These people, born and bred in slavery, had always been so accustomed to look upon the white race as their natural superiors and masters, that we had some doubts whether they could easily throw off the habit; and the fact of their giving preference to colored teachers, as managers of the establishment, seemed to us to indicate that even their brief possession of freedom had begun to inspire them with respect for their race.

On the 11th of January we opened school in the new school-house, with seventy-five scholars. Now, we have two hundred and twenty-five. Slavery has not crushed out the animal spirits of these children. Fun lurks in the corners of their eyes, dimples their mouths, tingles at their fingers' ends, and is, like a torpedo, ready to explode at the slightest touch. The war-spirit has a powerful hold upon them. No one turns the other cheek for a second blow. But they evince a generous nature. They never allow an older and stronger scholar to impose upon a younger and weaker one; and when they happen to have any little delicacies, they are very ready to share them with others. The task of regulating them is by no means an easy one; but we put heart, mind, and strength freely into the work, and only regret that we have not more physical strength. Their ardent desire to learn is very encouraging, and the improvement they make consoles us for many trials. You would be astonished at the progress many of them have made in this short time. Many who less than three months ago scarcely knew the A. B. C. are now reading and spelling in words of two or three syllables. When I look at these bright little boys, I often wonder whether there is not some Frederick Douglass among them, destined to do honor to his race in the future. No one can predict, now-a-days, how rapidly the wheels of progress will move on.

There is also an evening-school here, chiefly consisting of adults and largely attended; but with that I am not connected.

On the 10th of this month, there was considerable excitement here. The bells were rung in honor of the vote to abolish slavery in Virginia. Many did not know what was the cause of such a demonstration. Some thought it was an alarm of fire; others supposed the rebels had made a raid, and were marching down King st. We were, at first, inclined to the latter opinion; for, looking up that street we saw a company of the most woe-begone looking horsemen. It was raining hard, and some of them had dismounted, leading their poor jaded skeletons of horses. We soon learned that they were a portion of Kilpatrick's cavalry, on their way to

Culpepper. Poor Fellows! They had had a weary tramp, and must still tramp on, through mud and rain, till they reached their journey's end. What hopeless despondency would take possession of our hearts, if we looked only on the suffering occasioned by this war, and not on the good already accomplished, and still grander results shadowed forth in the future. The slowly-moving ambulance often passes by, with low beat of the drum, as the soldiers convey some comrade to his last resting-place. Buried on strange soil, far away from mother, wife, and children! Poor fellows! But they die, the death of brave men in a noble cause. The Soldier's Burying Ground here is well cared for, and is a beautiful place.

How nobly are the colored soldiers fighting and dying in the cause of Freedom! Our hearts are proud of the manhood they evince, in spite of the indignities heaped upon them. They are kept constantly on fatigue duty, digging trenches, and unloading vessels. Look at the Massachusetts Fifty-Fourth! Every man of them a hero! marching so boldly and steadily to victory or death, for the freedom of their race, and the salvation of their country! *Their* country! It makes my blood run warm to think how that country treats her colored sons, even the bravest and the best. If merit deserves reward, surely the 54th regiment is worthy of shoulder-straps. I have lately heard, from a friend in Boston, that the rank of second-lieutenant has been conferred. I am thankful there is a beginning. I am full of hope for the future. A Power mightier than man is guiding this revolution; and though justice moves slowly, it will come at last. The American people will outlive this mean prejudice against complexion. Sooner or later, they will learn that "a man's a man for a' that."

We went to the wharf last Tuesday, to welcome the emigrants returned from Hayti. It was a bitter cold day, the snow was falling, and they were barefooted and bareheaded, with scarely [sic] rags enough to cover them. They were put in wagons and carried to Green Heights. We did what we could for them. I went to see them next day, and found that three had died during the night. I was grieved for their hard lot; but I comforted myself with the idea that this would put an end to colonization projects. They are eight miles from here, but I shall go to see them again to-morrow. I hope to obtain among them some recruits for the Massachusetts Cavalry. I am trying to help Mr. Downing and Mr. Remond; not for money, but because I want to do all I can to strengthen the hands of those who are battling for Freedom.

Thank you for your letter. I wish you could have seen the happy group of faces round me, at our little Fair, while I read it to them. The memory of the grateful hearts I have found among these freed men and women, will cheer me all my life.

Yours truly,

H. JACOBS AND L. JACOBS

DOCUMENT 102:
Eliza Frances Andrews, *The War-Time Journal of a Georgia Girl,* 1864–1865 (New York: D. Appleton and Company, 1908), 10–15.

Courtesy Documenting the American South, University Library, The University of North Carolina at Chapel Hill.

Born into a wealthy white family in Washington, Georgia, in 1840, Eliza graduated in 1857 from LaGrange Female College. While her parents supported the Union, she was an ardent defender of the Confederacy. She published "A Romance of Robbery," about the poor treatment of whites during Reconstruction for the *New York World,* and began a career as a writer and teacher. In 1908, she published this memoir, which begins with Sherman's advance into Atlanta in 1864. The difficulty elite whites had as refugees in southern Georgia during the war is an important theme that runs throughout the text. The excerpted section focuses on her unwavering defense of the Southern cause.

Introduction

. . . That is the sentiment of the new South and of the few of us who survive from the old. We look back with loving memory upon our past, as we look upon the grave of the beloved dead whom we mourn but would not recall. We glorify the men and the memories of those days and would have the coming generations draw inspiration from them. We teach the children of the South to honor and revere the civilization of their fathers, which we believe has perished not because it was evil or vicious in itself, but because, like a good and useful man who has lived out his allotted time and gone the way of all the earth, it too has served its turn and must now lie in the grave of the dead past. The Old South, with its stately feudal *régime*, was not the monstrosity that some would have us believe, but merely a case of belated survival, like those giant sequoias of the Pacific slope that have lingered on from age to age, and are now left standing alone in a changed world. Like every civilization that has yet been known since the primitive patriarchal stage, it was framed in the interest of a ruling class; and as has always been, and always will be the case until mankind shall have become wise enough to evolve a civilization based on the interests of all, it was doomed to pass away whenever changed conditions transferred to another class the economic advantage that is the basis of all power. It had outlived its day of usefulness and was an anachronism in the end of the nineteenth century—the last representative of an economic system that had served the purposes of the race since the days when man first emerged from his prehuman state until the rise of the modern industrial system made wage slavery a more efficient agent of production than chattel slavery.

It is as unfair to lay all the onus of that institution on the Southern States of America as it would be to charge the Roman Catholic Church with the odium of all the religious persecutions of the sixteenth and seventeenth centuries. The spirit of intolerance was in the air; everybody persecuted that got the chance even the saints of Plymouth Rock, and the Catholics did the lion's share only because there were more of them to do it, and they had more power than our Protestant forefathers.

In like manner, the spirit of chattel slavery was in the race, possibly from its prehuman stage, and through all the hundreds of thousands of years that it has been painfully traveling from that humble beginning toward the still far-off goal of the superhuman, not one branch of it has ever awakened to a sense of the moral obliquity of the practice till its industrial condition had reached a stage in which that system was less profitable than wage slavery. Then, as the ethical sentiments are prone to follow closely the line of economic necessity, the conscience of those nations which had adopted the new industrialism began to awaken to a perception of the immorality of chattel slavery. Our Southern States, being still in the agricultural stage, on account of our practical monopoly of the world's chief textile staple, were the last of the great civilized nations to find chattel slavery less profitable than wage slavery, and hence the "great moral crusade" of the North against the perverse and unregenerate South. It was a pure case of economic determinism, which means that our great moral conflict reduces itself, in the last analysis, to a question of dollars and cents, though the real issue was so obscured by other considerations that we of the South honestly believe to this day that we were fighting for States Rights, while the North is equally honest in the conviction that it was engaged in a magnanimous struggle to free the slave.

It is only fair to explain here that the action of the principle of economic determinism does not imply by any means that the people affected by it are necessarily insincere or hypocritical. As enunciated by Karl Marx, under the cumbrous and misleading title of "the materialistic interpretation of history," it means simply that the economic factor plays the same part in the social evolution of the race that natural selection and the survival of the fittest are supposed to play in its physical evolution. The influence of this factor is generally so subtle and indirect that we are totally unconscious of it. If I may be pardoned an illustration from my own experience, I remember perfectly well when I myself honestly and conscientiously believed the institution of slavery to be as just and sacred as I now hold it to be the reverse. It was according to the Bible, and to question it was impious and savored of "infidelity." Most of my contemporaries would probably give a similar experience. Not one of us now but would look upon a return to slavery with horror, and yet not one of us probably is conscious of ever having been influenced by the economic factor!

The truth of the matter is that the transition from chattel to wage slavery was the next step forward in the evolution of the race, just as the transition from wage slavery to free and independent labor will be the next. Some of us, who see our own economic advantage more or less clearly in this transformation, and others who do not see it so clearly as they see the evils of the present system, are working for the change with the zeal of religious enthusiasts, while the capitalists and their retainers are fighting against it with the desperation of the old Southern slave-holder against the abolitionist. But here, in justice to the Southerner, the comparison must end. He fought a losing battle, but he fought it honestly and bravely, in the open—not by secret fraud and cunning. His cause was doomed from the first by a law as inexorable as the one pronounced by the fates against Troy, but he fought with a valor and heroism that have made a lost cause forever glorious. He saw the civil fabric his fathers had reared go down in a mighty cataclysm of blood and fire, a tragedy for all the ages—but better so than to have perished by slow decay through ages of sloth and rottenness, as so many other great civilizations of history have done, leaving only a debased and degenerate race behind them. It was a mediæval civilization, out of accord with the modern tenor of our time, and it had to go; but if it stood for some outworn customs that should rightly be sent to the dust heap, it stood for some things, also, that the world can ill afford to lose. It stood for gentle courtesy, for knightly honor, for generous hospitality; it stood for fair and honest dealing of man with man in the common business of life, for lofty scorn of cunning greed and ill-gotten gain through fraud and deception of our fellowmen—lessons which the founders of our New South would do well to lay to heart.

DOCUMENT 103:
"Memphis Riot and Massacres," U.S. Document, 1274, 39th Congress, 1st Session, 1865–1866, House Report, Vol. 3, No. 101.

This excerpt from witness testimony details the conflict between African American militias and white police forces during Reconstruction, suggesting how tenuous freedom was for many at the end of the Civil War. In Memphis, a three-day riot (May 1–3, 1866) required federal forces to quell. Dozens of people were injured, African American churches, schools, and homes were burned, which prompted the House of Representatives to appoint a three-person committee to investigate the incident.

FRANCES THOMPSON *(colored) sworn and examined.*
By the CHAIRMAN:

2919. State what you know or saw of the rioting. [Witness] Between one and two o'clock Tuesday night seven men, two of whom were policemen, came to my house. I know they were policemen by their stars. They were all Irishmen. They said they must have some eggs, and ham, and biscuit. I made them some biscuit and some strong coffee, and they all sat down and ate. A girl lives with me; her name is Lucy Smith; she is about 16 years old. When they had eaten supper, they said they wanted some women to sleep with. I said we were not that sort of women, and they must go. They said "that didn't make a damned bit of difference." One of them then laid hold of me and hit me on the side of my face, and holding my throat, choked me. Lucy tried to get out of the window, when one of them knocked her down and choked her. They drew their pistols and said they would shoot us and fire the house if we did not let them have their way with us. All seven of the men violated us two. Four of them had to do with me, and the rest with Lucy.

2913. Were you injured? I was sick for two weeks. I lay for three days with a hot, burning fever.

LUCY SMITH *(colored) sworn and examined.*
By the CHAIRMAN:

2925. State what you know of the late riots. (Witness) On Tuesday, the first night of the riots, some men came to our house. We were in bed. They told us to get up and get some supper for them. We got up, and made a fire, and got them supper.

2926. What else took place? What was left of the sugar, and coffee, and ham they threw into the bayou.

2927. How many men were there? There were seven of them; but I was so scared I could not be certain.

2928. Did they rob you? We had two trunks. They did not unlock them, but just jerked them open. They took $100 belonging to Frances, and $200 belonging to a friend of Frances, given to her to take care of. They took all the money and clothes and carried them off.

2929. Did you know any of the men? There were two policemen with the men; I saw their stars.

2930. What else took place? They tried to take advantage of me, and did. I told them I did not do such things, and would not. One of them said he would make me, and choked me by the neck. My neck was swollen up next day, and for two weeks I could not talk to anyone. After the first man had connexion with me, another got hold of me and tried to violate me, but I was so bad he did not. He gave me a lick with his fist and said that I was so damned near dead he would not have anything to do with me.

2931. Were you injured? I bled from what the first man had done to me. The man said, "Oh, she is so near dead I won't have anything to do with her." I was injured right smart, and kept my bed for two weeks after.

LUCY TIBBS *(colored) sworn and examined.*
By the CHAIRMAN:

2151. How old are you? [Witness] I do not know exactly. I suppose about twenty-four.

2152. Have you a husband? Yes; my husband is on a steamboat. We came here from Jackson, Arkansas, when the rebellion broke out.

2153. Were you here during the riots? Yes, sir. . . .

2178. Did they come into your house? Yes; a crowd of men came in that night; I do not know who they were. They just broke the door open and asked me where was my husband; I replied he was gone; they said I was a liar; I said, "Please do not do anything to me; I am just here with two little children."

2179. Did they do anything to you? They done a very bad act.

2180. Did they ravish you? Yes, sir.

2181. How many of them? There was but one that did it. Another man said, "Let that woman alone—that she was not in any situation to be doing that." They went to my trunk, burst it open, and took this money that belonged to my brother.

2182. Did they violate your person against your consent? Yes, sir; I had just to give up to them. They said they would kill me if I did not. They put me on the bed, and the other men were plundering the house while this man was carrying on.

2183. Were any of them policemen? I do not know; I was so scared I could not tell whether they were policemen or not; I think there were folks that knew all about me, who knew that my brother had not been long out of the army and had money.

2184. Where were your children? In bed.

2185. Were you dressed or undressed when these men came to you? I was dressed.

2186. Did you make any resistance? No, sir; the house was full of men. I thought they would kill me; they had stabbed a woman near by the night before.

2187. How old are your children? One of them will soon be five, and the other will be two years old in August.

2188. What did they mean by saying you were not in a condition to be doing that? I have been in the family way ever since Christmas.

2189. Who was this woman stabbed the night before? I do not know. I heard a woman and a man who went over there and saw her talking about it.

2190. Was she violated too? I suppose she was; they said she was. The next night they burned all those shanties down. Where they went to I could not tell.

2191. How many houses did they burn down? Three or four.

2192. Would you know this man who committed violence upon you if you should see him? I do not think I would.

2193. What countryman was he? I could not tell.

2194. What countrymen did the crowd appear to be? They appeared to be like Irishmen.

2195. How many rooms were there in your house? Only one.

2196. And this took place in the presence of all these men? Yes, sir. . . .

CYNTHIA TOWNSEND *(colored) sworn and examined.*
By the CHAIRMAN:

2209. Have you been a slave? [Witness] Yes; but I worked and bought myself. I finished paying for myself a few days before they took this place. . . .

2215. Have you a husband? Yes. My husband and son are about seven miles in the country at work. I sent word to them not to come back until this fuss was over. . . .

2219. Did they rob your house? Yes; they took my clothes, and fifty dollars in money, but I did not consider that much. . . .

2220. Who did the money belong to? It belonged to my son who was in the army, Frank King.

2221. Do you know of any violence being committed on the women in your neighborhood? Yes, sir; I know of some very bad acts. . . .

2223. State the circumstances? There is a woman who lives near me by the name of Harriet; Merriweather was her name before she married; I do not know what her husband's name is. There were as many as three or four men at a time had connexion with her; she was lying there by herself. They all had connexion with her in turn around, and then one of them tried to use her mouth.

2224. Was this during the riot? Yes, sir; it was on Monday evening.

2225. Did you see these men go in the house? Yes; I saw them going into the house and saw them coming out, and afterwards she came out and said they made her do what I told you they did; she has sometimes been a little deranged since then, her husband left her for it. When he came out of the fort, and found what had been done, he said he would not have anything to do with her any more. They drew their pistols before her and made her submit. There were white people right there who knew what was going on. One woman called me to go and look in and see what they were doing; that was when this thing was going on. She is the woman who came and made a complaint to Charley Smith; she is a very nice woman. . . .

MARY JORDAN (*colored*) *sworn and examined.*
By the CHAIRMAN:

3861. How old are you? [Witness] I am thirty-three years old.

3862. Are you married? Yes, sir; but my husband is dead.

3863. Have you been a slave? Yes, sir.

3864. Were you here when the rioting took place? Yes, sir; I lived on Aiken street. . . .

3869. What else did you see? After they went away we thought it was all over; but they came back again and set the colored saloon on fire. It was kept by a man by the name of Robinson. When they set the saloon on fire I ran out. I was very much alarmed, as it was so near. My husband was just dead and buried, and I had a sick child in my arms, and they had begun shooting at the colored people.

3870. Did you see anyone shot? I saw one shot, but I don't know his name.

3871. Did they set fire to your house? After that I went back to my house. I was so afraid, expecting every minute I would be shot down or my house set on fire and burned. Then they set fire to it, when we were all there.

3872. How many of you were there in the house? There was my little babe, seven months old, my little girl, eight years old, and my eldest daughter, about sixteen. We were all in there when it was set on fire. . . .

3874. Did you go out when your house caught on fire? They would not let us out.

3875. How long did you remain in there? They would not let us out until the house was all in flames.

3876. What did you save? I saved my children. I took up my shoes, but I was so scared I could not put them on.

3877. Do you say they shot at you when you first went out of your house? Yes, sir. When they set fire to the saloon I ran out and they shot at me when I had my little babe in my arms. The bullets came all around me, and I would have been shot if I had not run around the corner.

3878. What else do you know of this rioting? When I was running away with my babe a man put a pistol to my breast, and said he, "What are you doing" "I am trying to save my babe." "Sit down," said he, and I sat down, and they did not trouble me any more.

3879. Was your child injured? It rained, and my babe got wet and it afterwards died.

3880. Did you know any of these men? No, sir; I did not. Some of them had stars.

3881. What did you lose by the fire? I lost everything I had. I lost my clothes and my children's clothes, my bedstead and furniture.

3882. How much was it all worth? I had been working for three years, and trying to save, and my losses, I guess, would be $200.

3883. Had you any money? No, sir; I had no money.

3884. What else do you know about these troubles? When the flames were all around our house I told my children to follow me. My daughter said, "Mother, you will be shot." I said, "Better be shot than burned." It was raining, and I could get no shelter. We stayed out till they were all gone, and they did not disturb us any more. After a while I asked another colored woman to let me into her house, and she let me. Next day I had nothing to eat. After that I asked a white lady to give me some medicine for my babe; it was low and I could get nothing for it. The lady was kind; she gave me medicine for my babe, but it died and the lady buried it; I was not able to bury it. My babe lived nearly two weeks after that night, and then it died.

DOCUMENT 104:
Thirteenth, Fourteenth, and Fifteenth Amendments to the United States Constitution, 1865–1870.

Extensive debates over slavery and the meaning of freedom resulted in three postwar amendments to the Constitution that guaranteed civic and political participation of African Americans, though women were still prohibited from voting until the passage of the Nineteenth Amendment on August 18, 1920.

Thirteenth Amendment (December 6, 1865)
Section 1.Neither slavery nor involuntary servitude, except as a punishment for crime whereof the party shall have been duly convicted, shall exist within the United States, or any place subject to their jurisdiction.

Section 2.Congress shall have power to enforce this article by appropriate legislation.

Fourteenth Amendment (July 9, 1868)
Section 1. All persons born or naturalized in the United States, and subject to the jurisdiction thereof, are citizens of the United States and of the state wherein they reside. No state shall make or enforce any law which shall abridge the privileges or immunities of citizens of the United States; nor shall any state deprive any person of life, liberty, or property, without due process of law; nor deny to any person within its jurisdiction the equal protection of the laws.

Section 2. Representatives shall be apportioned among the several states according to their respective numbers, counting the whole number of persons in each state, excluding Indians not taxed. But when the right to vote at any election for the choice of electors for President and Vice President of the United States, Representatives in Congress, the executive and judicial officers of a state, or the members of the legislature thereof, is denied to any of the male inhabitants of such state, being twenty-one years of age, and citizens of the United States, or in any way abridged, except for participation in rebellion, or other crime, the basis of representation therein shall be reduced in the proportion which the number of such male citizens shall bear to the whole number of male citizens twenty-one years of age in such state.

Section 3. No person shall be a Senator or Representative in Congress, or elector of President and Vice President, or hold any office, civil or military, under the United States, or under any state, who, having previously taken an oath, as a member of Congress, or as an officer of the United States, or as a member of any state legislature, or as an executive or judicial officer of any state, to support the Constitution of the United States, shall have engaged in insurrection or rebellion against the same, or given aid or comfort to the enemies thereof. But Congress may by a vote of two-thirds of each House, remove such disability.

Section 4. The validity of the public debt of the United States, authorized by law, including debts incurred for payment of pensions and bounties for services in suppressing insurrection or rebellion, shall not be questioned. But neither the United States nor any state shall assume or pay any debt or obligation incurred in aid of insurrection or rebellion against the United States, or any claim for the loss or emancipation of any slave; but all such debts, obligations and claims shall be held illegal and void.

Section 5. The Congress shall have power to enforce, by appropriate legislation, the provisions of this article.

Fifteenth Amendment (February 3, 1870)
Section 1. The right of citizens of the United States to vote shall not be denied or abridged by the United States or by any state, on account of race, color, or previous condition of servitude.

Section 2. The Congress shall have power to enforce this article by appropriate legislation.

DOCUMENT 105:

An Act to Establish A Bureau For The Relief Of Freedmen And Refugees, March 3, 1865. *Statutes at Large, Treaties, and Proclamations of the United States of America,* vol. 13 (Boston: Little, Brown, and Company, 1866).

The Freedmen's Bureau, led by Major General Oliver O. Howard, was established by the War Department in 1865 to assist formerly enslaved men and women with food, clothing, health care, education, legal assistance, and employment. The South's loss in the Civil War freed more than four million people who struggled to make sense of their newfound freedom. The records left by the bureau from 1865 to 1872 offer a rich glimpse into this tumultuous time in American history. The bureau's greatest successes came in the area of education, as more than one thousand schools were built for African Americans, many either led by or influenced by women. It was strongly opposed by conservative Southern politicians and disbanded by President U. S. Grant in 1872.

Be it enacted . . . , That there is hereby established in the War Department, to continue during the present war of rebellion, and for one year thereafter, a bureau of refugees, freedmen, and abandoned lands, to which shall be committed, as hereinafter provided, the supervision and management of all abandoned lands, and the control of all subjects relating to refugees and freedmen from rebel states, or from any district of country within the territory embraced in the operations of the army, under such rules and regulations as may be prescribed by the head of the bureau and approved by the President. The said bureau shall be under the management and control of a commissioner to be appointed by the President, by and with the advice and consent of the Senate . . . .

SEC. 2. *And be it further enacted,* That the Secretary of War may direct such issues of provisions, clothing, and fuel, as he may deem needful for the immediate and temporary shelter and supply of destitute and suffering refugees and freedmen and their wives and children, under such rules and regulations as he may direct.

SEC. 3. *And be it further enacted,* That the President may, by and with the advice and consent of the Senate, appoint an assistant commissioner for each of the states declared to be in insurrection, not exceeding ten in number, who shall, under the direction of the commissioner, aid in the execution of the provisions of this act; . . . And any military officer may be detailed and assigned to duty under this act without increase of pay or allowances. . . .

SEC. 4. *And be it further enacted,* That the commissioner, under the direction of the President, shall have authority to set apart, for the use of loyal refugees and freedmen, such tracts of land within the insurrectionary states as shall have been abandoned, or to which the United States shall have acquired title by confiscation or sale, or otherwise, and to every male citizen, whether refugee or freedman, as aforesaid, there shall be assigned not more than forty acres of such land, and the person to whom it was so assigned shall be protected in the use and enjoyment of the land for the term of three years at an annual rent not exceeding six per centum upon the value of such land, as it was appraised by the state authorities in the year eighteen hundred and sixty, for the purpose of taxation, and in case no such appraisal can be found, then the rental shall be based upon the estimated value of the land in said year, to be ascertained in such manner as the commissioner may by regulation prescribe. At the end of said term, or at any time during said term, the occupants of any parcels so assigned may purchase the land and receive such title thereto as the United States can convey, upon paying therefor the value of the land, as ascertained and fixed for the purpose of determining the annual rent aforesaid.

DOCUMENT 106:
Photograph, Glimpses of Freedmen.

Courtesy Library of Congress LC-USZ62-37860.

The Freedmen's Bureau's most lasting legacy came in the area of education, shown here in a drawing by James E. Taylor (1839–1901) that was printed in Frank Leslie's *Illustrated Newspaper.* It shows a group of African American women sewing, learning a trade that will help in their transfer from slavery to freedom.

Document 106

DOCUMENT 107:
Margaret Ann Meta Morris Grimball, Journal of Meta Morris Grimball, South Carolina, December 1860– February 1866, Call #975, Manuscripts Department.

Courtesy of the Southern Historical Collection, University of North Carolina at Chapel Hill.

Margaret, a descendent of Lewis Morris, who signed the Declaration of Independence, was born in 1810. At the age of twenty, she married John Berkeley Grimball, a rice plantation owner in South Carolina. Margaret's diary, kept from before until after the Civil War, documents daily life and the major national events of this period. During the war, the family lived in Spartanburg, South Carolina, and later lost their plantation in 1870 because they could no longer afford the mortgage. The excerpt, written during Reconstruction, offers Margaret's perspective on the former slaves' love for their masters, as well as the reduced circumstances of the former slaveholders. As a white woman, her perspective on the affection between races warrants careful review.

February 20th 1866.

I read over my journal this morning and determined to finish it by making a note of the events of the Summer just passed. In April Arthur came home from the Army in North Carolina being sent to a hospital in Raleigh, and there being no room for him in the over crowded building, he was allowed to proceed home, to recruit, having had a severe attack of fever. In June Berkley & Harry arrived, the war being over, both Armys Lees & Johnstons having surrendered, & the Southern States overwhelmed, & conquered.

The boys found us most happy to see them, but with an empty corn box, & no money, that could be so called; we sent about, & did as others, sold dresses and ornaments, and bought bacon, & corn, the servants continued with us & Patty who had lived with me for 36 years, and always behaved with the most examplary propriety, being a skillful seamstress, tailoress, Mantuamaker, & washer & ironer, proposed herself to work out; wash & iron for us & support her 2 children & herself, the children waiting on us. This she did faithfully until she left us the 10th January, being sent for by her son & Husband. When she could she sold articles for us, going at all times, & would take nothing for her trouble. She frequently brought me grist, Molasses, & flour, which she said was my share of what she made. The old Mauma has acted throughout with the most perfect consideration, she was terribly mortified by Elizabeth being a teacher, & Gabriella, & Charlotte keeping a little School. She said to the Kenedys, "You see dem going long so; but dey has plenty of gould and silver in de bank; and dey is such an old family.—"

When Patty came to take leave of me she said "My dear Mistress, My dear Mistress", with a great appearance of feeling, & brought a little oven in her hand, a present to the young ladies, they had often borrowed it from her during the war to bake cakes in their room. I asked her if she could not take it with her, she said "Oh, yes mam, but I always termined to give it to the young ladies when I went away," and then she sent them a little clothes horse to dry their muslins on. I am thankful amid the wreck of all to have this example of affection and duty to always remember. 3 days before she went one of the servants asked her if she was going to bake for her journey, no she said I am going to wash my mistresses clothes, & so she did leaving every thing clean, tubs &c.

The old Mauma is living at Mrs Hankels her own choice, she has behaved with uniform kindness. Always when she got any thing nice she brought it to Lotty or Ella and they took it from her & seemed to enjoy it coming out of her pocket, wrapped in a piece of clean cloth, or a scrap of brown paper. During the hardest part of the war she was living at Mrs Irwins, and as they kept a plentiful table, & fed her well for her services, she saved some of her dinner every day for Harry, & he with the apetite of a growing boy, scarcely satisfied, went every night to see her, & eat her present to him.—

. . . We have engaged a family of our own former slaves as our hired servants, a man Josey, his wife Amy & daughter Delia for $16 per Month. The man $10, the girl & woman $6, they do so far very well.—

DOCUMENT 108:
Mattie J. Jackson, *The Story of Mattie J. Jackson; Her Parentage—Experience of Eighteen Years in Slavery— Incidents During the War—Her Escape from Slavery. A True Story* (New York: Sentinel Office, 1866), 10–13.

Courtesy Documenting the American South, University Library, The University of North Carolina at Chapel Hill.

Mattie Jackson was born around 1846 in St. Louis to enslaved parents, but escaped in 1863 to Indianapolis via the Underground Railroad. The memoir, edited by Dr. L. S. Thompson, tells the complicated story of the various family members' attempts to escape and reunite with each other. This excerpt focuses on the end of the Civil War and how it shaped social relations between slaves and masters.

THE SOLDIERS, AND OUR TREATMENT DURING THE WAR.

Soon after the war commenced the rebel soldiers encamped near Mr. Lewis' residence, and remained there one week. They were then ordered by General Lyons to surrender, but they refused. There were seven thousand Union and seven hundred rebel soldiers. The Union soldiers surrounded the camp and took them and exhibited them through the city and then confined them in prison. I told my mistress that the Union soldiers were coming to take the camp. She replied that it was false, that it was General Kelly coming to re-enforce Gen. Frost. In a few moments the alarm was heard. I told Mrs. L. the Unionists had fired upon the rebels. She replied it was only the salute of Gen. Kelley. At night her husband came home with the news that Camp Jackson was taken and all the soldiers prisoners. Mrs. Lewis asked how the Union soldiers could take seven hundred men when they only numbered the same. Mr. L. replied they had seven thousand. She was much astonished, and cast her eye around to us for fear we might hear her. Her suspicion was correct; there was not a word passed that escaped our listening ears. My mother and myself could read enough to make out the news in the papers. The Union soldiers took much delight in tossing a paper over the fence to us. It aggravated my mistress very much. My mother used to sit up nights and read to keep posted about the war. In a few days my mistress came down to the kitchen again with another bitter complaint that it was a sad affair that the Unionists had taken their delicate citizens who had enlisted and made prisoners of them—that they were babes. My mother reminded her of taking Fort Sumpter and Major Anderson and serving them the same and that turn about was fair play. She then hastened to her room with the speed of a deer, nearly unhinging every door in her flight, replying as she went that the Niggers and Yankees were seeking to take the country. One day, after she had visited the kitchen to superintend some domestic affairs, as she pretended, she became very angry without a word being passed, and said—"I think it has come to a pretty pass, that old Lincoln, with his long legs, an old rail splitter, wishes to put the Niggers on an equality with the whites; that her children should never be on an equal footing with a Nigger. She had rather see them dead." As my mother made no reply to her remarks, she stopped talking, and commenced venting her spite on my companion servant. On one occasion Mr. Lewis searched my mother's room and found a picture of President Lincoln, cut from a newspaper, hanging in her room. He asked her what she was doing with old Lincoln's picture. She replied it was there because she liked it. He then knocked her down three times, and sent her to the trader's yard for a month as punishment. My mistress indulged some hopes till the victory of New Orleans, when she heard the famous Union song sang to the tune of Yankee Doodle:

> The rebels swore that New Orleans never should be taken,
> But if the Yankees came so near they should not save their bacon.
> That's the way they blustered when they thought they were so handy,
> But Farragut steamed up one day and gave them Doodle Dandy
>
> Ben. Butler then was ordered down to regulate the city;
> He made the rebels walk a chalk, and was not that a pity?
> That's the way to serve them out—that's the way to treat them,
> They must not go and put on airs after we have beat them.
>
> He made the rebel banks shell out and pay the loyal people,
> He made them keep the city clean from pig's sty to church steeple.
> That's the way Columbia speaks, let all men believe her;
> That's the way Columbia speaks instead of yellow fever.

He sent the saucy women up and made them treat us well

He helped the poor and snubbed the rich; they thought he was
     the devil.

Bully for Ben. Butler, then, they thought he was so handy;

Bully for Ben Butler then,—Yankee Doodle Dandy.

The days of sadness for mistress were days of joy for us. We shouted
and laughed to the top of our voices. My mistress was more enraged than
ever—nothing pleased her. One evening, after I had attended to my usual
duties, and I supposed all was complete, she, in a terrible rage, declared I
should be punished that night. I did not know the cause, neither did she.
She went immediately and selected a switch. She placed it in the corner
of the room to await the return of her husband at night for him to whip
me. As I was not pleased with the idea of a whipping I bent the switch in
the shape of W, which was the first letter of his name, and after I had
attended to the dining room my fellow servant and myself walked away
and stopped with an aunt of mine during the night. In the morning we
made our way to the Arsenal, but could gain no admission. While we were
wandering about seeking protection, the girl's father overtook us and persuaded us to return home. We finally complied. All was quiet. Not a word
was spoken respecting our sudden departure. All went on as usual. I was
permitted to attend to my work without interruption until three weeks
after. One morning I entered Mrs. Lewis' room, and she was in a room
adjoining, complaining of something I had neglected. Mr. L. then enquired
if I had done my work. I told him I had. She then flew into a rage and told
him I was saucy, and to strike me, and he immediately gave me a severe
blow with a stick of wood, which inflicted a deep wound upon my head.
The blood ran over m clothing, which gave me a frightful appcarance. Mr.
Lewis then ordered me to change my clothing immediately. As I did not
obey be became more enraged, and pulled me into another room and
threw me on the floor, placed his knee on my stomach, slapped me on the
face and beat me with his fist, and would have punished me more had not
my mother interfered. He then told her to go away or he would compel
her to, but she remained until he left me. I struggled mightily, and stood
him a good test for a while, but he was fast conquering me when my
mother came. He was aware my mother could usually defend herself
against one man, and both of us would overpower him, so after giving his

wife strict orders to take me up stairs and keep me there, he took his carriage and drove away. But she forgot it, as usual. She was highly gratified with my appropriate treatment, as she called it, and retired to her room, leaving me to myself. I then went to my mother and told her I was going away. She bid me go, and added "May the Lord help you." I started for the Arsenal again and succeeded in gaining admittance and seeing the Adjutant. He ordered me to go to another tent, where there was a woman in similar circumstances, cooking. When the General found I was there he sent me to the boarding house. I remained there three weeks, and when I went I wore the same stained clothing as when I was so severely punished, which has left a mark on my head which will ever remind me of my treatment while in slavery. Thanks be to God, though tortured by wrong and goaded by oppression, the hearts that would madden with misery have broken the iron yoke.

DOCUMENT 109:
Civil Rights Act of 1866, 14 Stat. 27–30, April 9, 1866.

The Civil Rights Act granted formerly enslaved men and women civil rights, especially in the areas of employment and housing. The act had three main parts that applied equally to men and women— it extended citizenship to all persons born in the United States, defined citizenship as colorblind, and made it illegal to discriminate on the basis of race, color, or prior condition of slavery or involuntary servitude. The Radical Republicans passed the act over President Andrew Johnson's veto. The act is still in effect today.

CHAP. XXXI.
An Act to protect all Persons in the United States in their Civil Rights, and furnish the Means of their Vindication.

Be it enacted by the Senate and House of Representatives of the United States of America in Congress assembled, That all persons born in the United States and not subject to any foreign power, excluding Indians not taxed, are hereby declared to be citizens of the United States; and such citizens, of every race and color, without regard to any previous condition of slavery or involuntary servitude, except as a punishment for crime whereof the party shall have been duly convicted, shall have the same right, in every State and Territory in the United States, to make and enforce contracts, to sue, be parties, and give evidence, to inherit, purchase, lease, sell, hold, and convey real and personal property, and to full and equal benefit of all laws and proceedings for the security of person and property, as is enjoyed by white citizens, and shall be subject to like punishment, pains, and penalties, and to none other, any law, statute, ordinance, regulation, or custom, to the contrary notwithstanding.

Sec. 2. *And be it further enacted,* That any person who, under color of any law, statute, ordinance, regulation, or custom, shall subject, or cause to be subjected, any inhabitant of any State or Territory to the deprivation of any right secured or protected by this act, or to different punishment, pains, or penalties on account of such person having at any time been held in a condition of slavery or involuntary servitude, except as a punishment for crime whereof the party shall have been duly convicted, or by reason of his color or race, than is prescribed for the punishment of white persons, shall be deemed guilty of a misdemeanor, and, on conviction, shall be punished by fine not exceeding one thousand dollars, or imprisonment not exceeding one year, or both, in the discretion of the court.

Sec. 3. *And be it further enacted,* That the district courts of the United States, within their respective districts, shall have, exclusively of the courts of the several States, cognizance of all crimes and offences committed against the provisions of this act, and also, concurrently with the circuit courts of the United States, of all causes, civil and criminal, affecting persons who are denied or cannot enforce in the courts or judicial tribunals of the State or locality where they may be any of the rights secured to them by the first section of this act; and if any suit or prosecution, civil or criminal, has been or shall be commenced in any State court, against any such person, for any cause whatsoever, or against any officer, civil or military, or other person, for any arrest or imprisonment, trespasses, or wrongs done or committed by virtue or under color of authority derived from this act or the act establishing a Bureau for the relief of Freedmen and Refugees, and all acts amendatory thereof, or for refusing to do any act upon the ground that it would be inconsistent with this act, such defendant shall have the right to remove such cause for trial to the proper district or circuit court in the manner prescribed by the "Act relating to habeas corpus and regulating judicial proceedings in certain cases," approved March three, eighteen hundred and sixty-three, and all acts amendatory thereof. The jurisdiction in civil and criminal matters hereby conferred on the district and circuit courts of the United States shall be exercised and enforced in conformity with the laws of the United States, so far as such laws are suitable to carry the same into effect; but in all cases where such laws are not adapted to the object, or are deficient in the provisions necessary to furnish suitable remedies and punish offences against law, the common law, as modified and changed by the constitution and statutes of the State wherein the court having jurisdiction of the cause, civil or criminal, is held, so far as the same is not inconsistent with the Constitution and laws of the United States, shall be extended to and govern said courts in the trial and disposition of such cause, and, if of a criminal nature, in the infliction of punishment on the party found guilty.

Sec. 4. *And be it further enacted,* That the district attorneys, marshals, and deputy marshals of the United States, the commissioners appointed by the circuit and territorial courts of the United States, with powers of arresting, imprisoning, or bailing offenders against the laws of the United States, the officers and agents of the Freedmen's Bureau, and every other officer who may be specially empowered by the President of the United States, shall be, and they are hereby, specially authorized and required, at the expense of the United States, to institute proceedings against all and every person who shall violate the provisions of this act, and cause him or them to be arrested and imprisoned, or bailed, as the case may be, for trial before such court of the United States or territorial court as by this act has cognizance of the offence. And with a view to affording reasonable protection to all persons in their constitutional rights of equality before the law, without distinction of race or color, or previous condition of slavery or involuntary servitude, except as a punishment for crime, whereof the party shall have been duly convicted, and to the prompt discharge of the duties of this act, it shall be the duty of the circuit courts of the United States and the superior courts of the Territories of the United States, from time to time, to increase the number of commissioners, so as to afford a speedy and convenient means for the arrest and examination of persons charged with a violation of this act; and such commissioners are hereby authorized and required to exercise and discharge all the powers and duties conferred on them by this act, and the same duties with regard to offences created by this act, as they are authorized by law to exercise with regard to other offences against the laws of the United States.

Sec. 5. *And be it further enacted,* That it shall be the duty of all marshals and deputy marshals to obey and execute all warrants and precepts issued under the provisions of this act, when to them directed; and should any marshal or deputy marshal refuse to receive such warrant or other process when tendered, or to use all proper means diligently to execute the same, he shall, on conviction thereof, be fined in the sum of one thousand dollars, to the use of the person upon whom the accused is alleged to have committed the offense. And the better to enable the said commissioners to execute their duties faithfully and efficiently, in conformity with the Constitution of the United States and the requirements of this act, they are hereby authorized and empowered, within their counties respectively, to appoint, in writing, under their hands, any one or more suitable persons, from time to time, to execute all such warrants and other process as may be issued by them in the lawful performance of their respective duties; and the persons so appointed to execute any warrant or process as aforesaid shall have authority to summon and call to their aid the bystanders or posse comitatus of the proper county, or such portion of the land or naval forces of the United States, or of the militia, as may be necessary to the performance of the duty with which they are charged, and to insure a faithful observance of the clause of the Constitution which prohibits slavery, in conformity with the provisions of this act; and said warrants shall run and be executed by said officers anywhere in the State or Territory within which they are issued.

Sec. 6. *And be it further enacted,* That any person who shall knowingly and willfully obstruct, hinder, or prevent any officer, or other person charged with the execution of any warrant or process issued under the provisions of this act, or any person or persons lawfully assisting him or them, from arresting any person for whose apprehension such warrant or process may have been issued, or shall rescue or attempt to rescue such person from the custody of the officer, other person or persons, or those lawfully assisting as aforesaid, when so arrested pursuant to the authority herein given and declared, or shall aid, abet, or assist any person so arrested as aforesaid, directly or indirectly, to escape from the custody of the officer or other person legally authorized as aforesaid, or shall harbor or conceal any person for whose arrest a warrant or process shall have been issued as aforesaid, so as to prevent his discovery and arrest after notice or knowledge of the fact that a warrant has been issued for the apprehension of such person, shall, for either of said offences, be subject to a fine not exceeding one thousand dollars, and imprisonment not exceeding six months, by indictment and conviction before the district court of the United States for the district in which said offense may have been committed, or before the proper court of criminal jurisdiction, if committed within any one of the organized Territories of the United States.

Sec. 7. *And be it further enacted,* That the district attorneys, the marshals, their deputies, and the clerks of the said district and territorial courts shall be paid for their services the like fees as may be allowed to them for similar services in other cases; and in all cases where the proceedings are before a commissioner, he shall be entitled to a fee of ten dollars in full for his services in each case, inclusive of all services incident to such arrest and examination. The person or persons authorized to execute the process to be issued by such commissioners for the arrest of offenders against the provisions of this act shall be entitled to a fee of five dollars for each person he or they may arrest and take before any such commissioner as aforesaid, with such other fees as may be deemed reasonable by such commissioner for such other additional services as may be necessarily performed by him or them, such as attending at the examination, keeping the prisoner in custody, and providing him with food and lodging during his detention, and until the final determination of such commissioner, and in general for performing such other duties as may be required in the premises; such fees to be made up in conformity with the fees usually charged by the officers of the courts of justice within the proper district or county, as near as may be practicable, and paid out of the Treasury of the United States on the certificate of the judge of the district within which the arrest is made, and to be recoverable from the defendant as part of the judgment in case of conviction.

Sec. 8. *And be it further enacted,* that whenever the President of the United States shall have reason to believe that offences have been or are likely to be committed against the provisions of this act within any judicial district, it shall be lawful for him, in his discretion, to direct the judge, marshal, and district attorney of such district to attend at such place within the district, and for such time as he may designate, for the purpose of the more speedy arrest and trial of persons charged with a violation of this act; and it shall be the duty of every judge or other officer, when any such requisition shall be received by him, to attend at the place and for the time therein designated.

Sec. 9. *And be it further enacted,* that it shall be lawful for the President of the United States, or such person as he may empower for that purpose, to employ such part of the land or naval forces of the United States, or of the militia, as shall be necessary to prevent the violation and enforce the due execution of this act.

Sec. 10. *And be it further enacted,* That upon all questions of law arising in any cause under the provisions of this act a final appeal may be taken to the Supreme Court of the United States.

SCHUYLER COLFAX,
Speaker of the House of Representatives

LAFAYETTE S. FOSTER,
President of the Senate, pro tempore.

In the Senate of the United States, April 6, 1866.

The President of the United States having returned to the Senate, in which it originated, the bill entitled "An act to protect all persons in the United States in their civil rights, and furnish the means of their vindication," with his objections thereto, the Senate proceeded, in pursuance of the Constitution, to reconsider the same; and,
Resolved, That the said bill do pass, two-thirds of the Senate agreeing to pass the same.

Attest:

J. W. Forney,
Secretary of the Senate.
In the House of Representatives U.S. April 9th, 1866.

The House of Representatives having proceeded, in pursuance of the Constitution, to reconsider the bill entitled, "An act to protect all persons in the United States in their civil rights, and furnish the means of their vindication," returned to the Senate by the President of the United States, with his objections, and sent by the Senate to the House of Representatives, with the message of the President returning the bill:

Resolved, That the bill do pass, two-thirds of the House of Representatives agreeing to pass the same.

Attest:

Edward McPherson, Clerk,
by Clinton Lloyd, Chief Clerk.

DOCUMENT 110:
Excerpt, Lucy A. Delaney, *From Darkness Cometh the Light or Struggles for Freedom* (St. Louis: J. T. Smith, c. 1891), 33–51.

Courtesy Documenting the American South, University Library, The University of North Carolina at Chapel Hill.

Lucy Delaney was born in 1830 in St. Louis to a free woman who was later kidnapped in Illinois and sold into slavery to Major Taylor Berry. Though scheduled to be manumitted upon Berry's death, the family ignored the will, and Lucy and her family remained enslaved. The family was further fragmented when Lucy's sister fled to Canada, and her father was sold to a plantation in Mississippi. This memoir focuses much on the attempts that Lucy's mother made to prove that she was free. The final section focuses on Lucy's life after slavery and the reuniting of her family, making it a particularly valuable first-person account. This excerpt focuses on Lucy's mother's efforts to legally seek her freedom once again, and illustrates a key theme of self-respect for African American women.

CHAPTER IV.

On the morning of the 8th of September, 1842, my mother sued Mr. D. D. Mitchell for the possession of her child, Lucy Ann Berry. My mother, accompanied by the sheriff, took me from my hiding-place and conveyed me to the jail, which was located on Sixth Street, between Chestnut and Market, where the Laclede Hotel now stands, and there met Mr. Mitchell, with Mr. H. S. Cox, his brother in-law.

Judge Bryant Mullanphy read the law to Mr. Mitchell, which stated that if Mr. Mitchell took me back to his house, he must give bond and security to the amount of two thousand dollars, and furthermore, I should not be taken out of the State of Missouri until I had a chance to prove my freedom. Mr. H. S. Cox became his security and Mr. Mitchell gave bond accordingly, and then demanded that I should be put in jail.

"Why do you want to put that poor young girl in jail?" demanded my lawyer. "Because," he retorted, "her mother or some of her crew might run her off, just to make me pay the two thousand dollars; and I would like to see her lawyer, or any other man, in jail, that would take up a d—nigger case like that."

"You need not think, Mr. Mitchell," calmly replied Mr. Murdock, "because my client is colored that she has no rights, and can be cheated out of her freedom. She is just as free as you are, and the Court will so decide it, as you will see."

However, I was put in a cell, under lock and key, and there remained for seventeen long and dreary months, listening to the

> "—foreign echoes from the street,
> Faint sounds of revel, traffic, conflict keen—
> And, thinking that man's reiterated feet
>
> Have gone such ways since e'er the world has been,
> I wondered how each oft-used tone and glance
> Retains its might and old significance."

My only crime was seeking for that freedom which was my birthright! I heard Mr. Mitchell tell his wife that he did not believe in slavery, yet, through his instrumentality, I was shut away from the sunlight, because he was determined to prove me a slave, and thus keep me in bondage. Consistency, thou art a jewel!

At the time my mother entered suit for her freedom, she was not instructed to mention her two children, Nancy and Lucy, so the white people took advantage of this flaw, and showed a determination to use every means in their power to prove that I was not her child.

This gave my mother an immense amount of trouble, but she had girded up her loins for the fight, and, knowing that she was right, was resolved, by the help of God and a good lawyer, to win my case against all opposition.

After advice by competent persons, mother went to Judge Edward Bates and begged him to plead the case, and, after fully considering the proofs and learning that my mother was a poor woman, he consented to undertake the case and make his charges only sufficient to cover his expenses. It would be well here to give a brief sketch of Judge Bates, as many people wondered that such a distinguished statesman would take up the case of an obscure negro girl.

Edward Bates was born in Belmont, Goochland county, Va., September, 1793. He was of Quaker descent, and inherited all the virtues of that peace-loving people. In 1812, he received a midshipman's warrant, and was only prevented from following the sea by the influence of his mother, to whom he was greatly attached. Edward emigrated to Missouri in 1814, and entered upon the practice of law, and, in 1816, was appointed prosecuting lawyer for the St. Louis Circuit. Toward the close of the same year, he was appointed Attorney General for the new State of Missouri, and in 1826, while yet a young man, was elected representative to congress as an anti-Democrat, and served one term. For the following twenty-five years, he devoted himself to his profession, in which he was a shining light. His probity and uprightness attracted to him a class of people who were in the right and only sought justice, while he repelled, by his virtues, those who traffic in the miseries or mistakes of unfortunate people, for they dared not come to him and seek counsel to aid them in their villainy.

In 1847, Mr. Bates was delegate to the Convention for Internal Improvement, held in Chicago, and by his action he came prominently before the whole country. In 1850, President Fillmore offered him the portfolio of Secretary of War, which he declined. Three years later, he accepted the office of Judge of St. Louis Land Court.

When the question of the repeal of the Missouri Compromise was agitated, he earnestly opposed it, and thus became identified with the "free labor" party in Missouri, and united with it, in opposition to the admission of Kansas under the Lecompton Constitution. He afterwards became a prominent antislavery man, and in 1859 was mentioned as a candidate for the presidency. He was warmly supported by his own State, and for a time it seemed that the opposition to Governor Seward might concentrate on him. In the National Republican Convention, 1860, he received forty-eight votes on the first ballot, but when it became apparent that Abraham Lincoln was the favorite, Mr. Bates withdrew his name. Mr. Lincoln appointed Judge Bates Attorney General, and while in the Cabinet he acted a dignified, safe and faithful part. In 1864, he resigned his office and returned to his home in St. Louis, where he died in 1869, surrounded by his weeping family.

> "—loved at home, revered abroad.
>
> Princes and lords are but the breath of kings;
>
> 'An honest man's the noblest work of God.'"

On the 7th of February, 1844, the suit for my freedom began. A bright, sunny day, a day which the happy and care-free would drink in with a keen sense of enjoyment. But my heart was full of bitterness; I could see only gloom which seemed to deepen and gather closer to me as I neared the courtroom. The jailer's sister-in-law, Mrs. Lacy, spoke to me of submission and patience; but I could not feel anything but rebellion against my lot. I could not see one gleam of brightness in my future, as I was hurried on to hear my fate decided.

Among the most important witnesses were Judge Robert Wash and Mr. Harry Douglas, who had been an overseer on Judge Wash's farm, and also Mr. MacKeon, who bought my mother from H. S. Cox, just previous to her running away.

Judge Wash testified that "the defendant, Lucy A. Berry, was a mere infant when he came in possession of Mrs. Fannie Berry's estate, and that he often saw the child in the care of its reputed mother, Polly, and to his best knowledge and belief, he thought Lucy A. Berry was Polly's own child."

Mr. Douglas and Mr. MacKeon corroborated Judge Wash's statement. After the evidence from both sides was all in, Mr. Mitchell's lawyer, Thomas Hutchinson, commenced to plead. For one hour, he talked so bitterly against me and against my being in possession of my liberty that I was trembling, as if with ague, for I certainly thought every-body must believe him; indeed I almost believed the dreadful things he said, myself, and as I listened I closed my eyes with sickening dread, for I could just see myself floating down the river, and my heart-throbs seemed to be the throbs of the mighty engine which propelled me from my mother and freedom forever!

Oh! what a relief it was to me when he finally finished his harangue and resumed his seat! As I never heard anyone plead before, I was very much alarmed, although I knew in my heart that every word he uttered was a lie! Yet, how was I to make people believe? It seemed a puzzling question!

Judge Bates arose, and his soulful eloquence and earnest pleading made such an impression on my sore heart, I listened with renewed hope. I felt the black storm clouds of doubt and despair were fading away, and that I was drifting into the safe harbor of the realms of truth. I felt as if everybody *must* believe *him,* for he clung to the truth, and I wondered how Mr. Hutchinson could so lie about a poor defenseless girl like me.

Judge Bates chained his hearers with the graphic history of my mother's life, from the time she played on Illinois banks, through her trials in slavery, her separation from her husband, her efforts to become free, her voluntary return to slavery for the sake of her child, Lucy, and her subsequent efforts in securing her own freedom. All these incidents he lingered over step by step, and concluding, he said:

"Gentlemen of the jury, I am a slave-holder myself, but, thanks to the Almighty God. I am above the base principle of holding any a slave that has as good right to her freedom as this girl has been proven to have; she was free before she was born; her mother was free, but kidnapped in her youth, and sacrificed to the greed of negro traders, and no free woman can give birth to a slave child, as it is in direct violation of the laws of God and man!"

At this juncture he read the affidavit of Mr. A. Posey, with whom my mother lived at the time of her abduction; also affidavits of Mr. and Mrs. Woods, in corroboration of the previous facts duly set forth. Judge Bates then said:

"Gentleman of the jury, here I rest this case, as I would not want any better evidence for one of my own children. The testimony of Judge

Wash is alone sufficient to substantiate the claim of Polly Crockett Berry to the defendant as being her own child."

The case was then submitted to the jury, about 8 o'clock in the evening, and I was returned to the jail and locked in the cell which I had occupied for seventeen months, filled with the most intense anguish.

CHAPTER V.

"There's a joy in every sorrow,

There's a relief from every pain;

Though to-day 'tis dark to-morrow

HE will turn all bright again."

Before the sheriff bade me good night he told me to be in readiness at nine o'clock on the following morning to accompany him back to court to hear the verdict. My mother was not at the trial. She had lingered many days about the jail expecting my case would be called, and finally when called to trial the dear, faithful heart was not present to sustain me during that dreadful speech of Mr. Hutchinson. All night long I suffered agonies of fright, the suspense was something awful, and could only be comprehended by those who have gone through some similar ordeal.

I had missed the consolation of my mother's presence, and I felt so hopeless and alone! Blessed mother! how she clung and fought for me. No work was too hard for her to undertake. Others would have flinched before the obstacles which confronted her, but undauntedly she pursued her way, until my freedom was established by every right and without a questioning doubt!

On the morning of my return to Court, I was utterly unable to help myself. I was so overcome with fright and emotion,—with the alternating feelings of despair and hope—that I could not stand still long enough to dress myself. I trembled like an aspen leaf; so I sent a message to Mrs. Lacy to request permission for me to go to her room, that she might assist me in dressing. I had done a great deal of sewing for Mrs. Lacy, for she had showed me much kindness, and was a good Christian. She gladly assisted me, and under her willing hands I was soon made ready, and, promptly at nine o'clock, the sheriff called and escorted me to the courthouse.

On our way thither, Judge Bates overtook us. He lived out a short distance in the country, and was riding on horseback. He tipped his hat to me as politely as if I were the finest lady in the land, and cried out, "Good morning Miss Lucy, I suppose you had pleasant dreams last night!" He seemed so bright and smiling that I was inbued with renewed hope; and when he addressed the sheriff with "Good morning Sir." I don't suppose the jury was out twenty minutes were they?" and the sheriff replied "oh! no, sir," my heart gave a leap, for I was sure that my fate was decided for weal or woe.

I watched the judge until he turned the corner and desiring to be relieved of suspense from my pent-up anxiety, I eagerly asked the sheriff if I were free, but he gruffly answered that "he didn't know." I was sure he did know, but was too mean to tell me. How could he have been so flinty, when he must have seen how worried I was.

At last the courthouse was reached and I had taken my seat in such a condition of helpless terror that I could not tell one person from another. Friends and foes were as one, and vainly did I try to distinguish them. My long confinement, burdened with harrowing anxiety, the sleepless night I had just spent, the unaccountable absence of my mother, had brought me to an indescribable condition. I felt dazed, as if I were no longer myself. I seemed to be another person—an on looker—and in my heart dwelt a pity for the poor, lonely girl, with down-cast face, sitting on the bench apart from anyone else in that noisy room. I found myself wondering where Lucy's mother was, and how she would feel if the trial went against her; I seemed to have lost all feeling about it, but was speculating what Lucy would do, and what her mother would do, if the hand of Fate was raised against poor Lucy! Oh! how sorry I did feel for myself!

At the sound of a gentle voice, I gathered courage to look upward, and caught the kindly gleam of Judge Bates' eyes, as he bent his gaze upon me and smilingly said, "I will have you discharged in a few minutes, Miss Lucy!"

Some other business occupied the attention of the Court, and when I had begun to think they had forgotten all about me, Judge Bates arose and said calmly, "Your Honor, I desire to have this girl, Lucy A. Berry, discharged before going into any other business."

Judge Mullanphy answered "Certainly!" Then the verdict was called for and rendered, and the jurymen resumed their places. Mr. Mitchell's lawyer jumped up and exclaimed:

"Your Honor, my client demands that this girl be remanded to jail. He does not consider that the case has had a fair trial, I am not informed as to what course he intends to pursue, but I am now expressing his present wishes?"

Judge Bates was on his feet in a second and cried: "For shame! is it not enough that this girl has been deprived of her liberty for a year and a half, that you must still pursue her after a fair and impartial trial before a jury, in which it was clearly proven and decided that she had every right to freedom? I demand that she be set at liberty at once!"

"I agree with Judge Bates," responded Judge Mullanphy, "and the girl may go!"

Oh! the overflowing thankfulness of my grateful heart at that moment, who could picture it? None but the good God above us! I could have kissed the feet of my deliverers, but I was too full to express my thanks, but with a voice trembling with tears I tried to thank Judge Bates for all his kindness.

As soon as possible, I returned to the jail to bid them all good-bye and thank them for their good treatment of me while under their care. They rejoiced with me in my good fortune and wished me much success and happiness in years to come.

I was much concerned at my mother's prolonged absence, and was deeply anxious to meet her and sob out my joy on her faithful bosom. Surely it was the hands of God which prevented mother's presence at the trial, for broken down with anxiety and loss of sleep on my account, the revulsion of feeling would have been greater than her over-wrought heart could have sustained.

As soon as she heard of the result, she hurried to meet me, and hand in hand we gazed into each others eyes and saw the light of freedom there, and we felt in our hearts that we could with one accord cry out: "Glory to God in the highest, and peace and good will towards men."

Dear, dear mother! how solemnly I invoke your spirit as I review these trying scenes of my girlhood, so long agone! Your patient face and neatly-dressed figure stands ever in the foreground of that checkered time; a figure showing naught to an on-looker but the common place virtues of an honest woman!

Never would an ordinary observer connect those virtues with aught of heroism or greatness, but to me they are as bright rays as ever emanated from the lives of the great ones of earth, which are portrayed on historic pages—to me, the qualities of her true, steadfast heart and noble soul become "a constellation, and is tracked in Heaven straightway."

DOCUMENT 111:
Photograph, School Saint Helena Island, South Carolina, 1862.

Courtesy Library of Congress, LC—USZ62—40893.

This Freedmen's School, established on one of the Sea Islands in 1862, was typical in size and design. African American and white teachers, often women, came from the North to help educate former slaves. They were encouraged to find multigenerational classrooms brimming with enthusiastic students. Many organizations helped fund such schools, providing literacy for more than 150,000 freedmen, women, and children.

DOCUMENT 112:
Excerpt, Eliza Moore Chinn McHatton Ripley, *From Flag to Flag: A Woman's Adventure and Experiences in the South during the War, in Mexico, and in Cuba* (New York: D. Appleton and Company, 1889), 58.

Courtesy Documenting the American South, University Library, The University of North Carolina at Chapel Hill.

Eliza Ripley was born in Kentucky in 1832, moved to New Orleans, and later married and moved to Baton Rouge. During the Civil War, she and her husband, James A. McHatton, traveled to Mexico and later to Cuba. In Cuba, they operated a sugar plantation and enjoyed elite white society among other displaced Southerners. Her memoir documents an idyllic life on Arlington Plantation to their difficult travel to Mexico, with their dwindling resources. The memoir ends with her return to the United States. This short excerpt focuses on the end of the Civil War and an incident involving her mother's laundress, Aunt Hannah.

SEA-ISLAND SCHOOL, No. 1.—ST. HELENA ISLAND. ESTABLISHED APRIL, 1862.

TEACHERS { MISS LAURA M. TOWNE,
           ELLEN MURRAY,
           MRS. HARRIOT W. RUGGLES.   Supported by the Pennsylvania Branch.

EDUCATION AMONG THE FREEDMEN.

Pennsylvania Branch of the American Freedman's Union Commission.

PENNSYLVANIA FREEDMEN'S RELIEF ASSOCIATION,
No. 711 Sansom Street.

To the Friends of Education among the Freedmen.

As we enter upon our work for another year, we wish to present a statement of our plans and wants to the people.

The various organizations throughout the country having the education of the Freedmen in charge, have provided schools for 150,000 persons, in care of fourteen hundred teachers. The expense of supporting these schools has been borne by voluntary contributions.

It is frequently asked, Does not the Government accomplish this work through the "Freedmen's Bureau?" The simple answer is, No! The "Bureau" has no authority to employ teachers. The representatives of the "Bureau," from the honored Commissioner

Document 111

CHAPTER VII.
SECOND VISIT OF THE ENEMY—MIDNIGHT FLIGHT— FAREWELL TO ARLINGTON.

. . . Old "Aunt Hannah" (that was my mother's laundress long before I was born, and who had been given a cabin to herself to sun away her half-blind and grumbling old age) stood in her little cabin-door, as straight as an arrow; she always complained of *rheumatiz,* and I don't think I ever saw her straight before; but there she stood, with the air of one suddenly elevated to an exalted position, and waved me a "Good-by, madam—I b'ar you no malice."

DOCUMENT 113:
Excerpt, Caroline Elizabeth Thomas Merrick, *Old Times in Dixie Land: A Southern Matron's Memories* (New York: Grafton Press, 1901), 80–82 and 176–78.

Courtesy Documenting the American South, University Library, The University of North Carolina at Chapel Hill.

Born in Louisiana in 1825, Caroline Thomas married Edwin T. Merrick, who eventually became the chief justice of Louisiana. After the Civil War, she and her family moved to New Orleans, where Caroline became active in the women's rights movement. This 1901 memoir focuses on her childhood and years as a young wife; it also includes a defense of slavery and a description of the Civil War and its aftermath. One notable theme throughout the memoir is the contributions of white women to the war effort and their marginalization afterward. These two excerpts focus on her perspectives on the Reconstruction South and a paternalistic speech she gave at a Women's Christian Temperance Union booth at the World Exposition in New Orleans in 1885. Julia Ward Howe (1819–1910), mentioned in the speech, was a noted abolitionist and women's rights activist best remembered for writing "Battle Hymn of the Republic."

CHAPTER VIII.
HOW WOMAN CAME TO THE RESCUE.

. . ."I saw a late article in the *Chicago Times* in which the writer said: 'You had better be a poor man's dog than a Southerner now.' If our negroes are idle and impudent we are not allowed to send them away. If we have crops waiting in the fields for gathering, the hands are all given by the semi-military government 'passes to *go*,' though we pay wages; and (weakly or humanely?) buy food, furnish doctors and wait on the sick, very much in the old way, simply because nature refuses to snap the ties of a lifetime on the authority of new conditions. I have it in mind to make Myrtle Grove a very disagreeable place to some of the most trifling, so that they will get into the humor to hunt a new home.

"General Price said: 'We played for the negro, and the Yankees fairly won the stake, with Cuffy's help.' Let them have him and *keep* him! Your father has just had a settlement with his freedmen. They are extremely dissatisfied with the result. Though they acknowledge every item on their accounts, furnished at New Orleans wholesale prices, it is a disappointment not to have a large sum of money for their year's labor—that, too, after an extravagance of living we have not dared to allow ourselves, and an idleness for which we are like sufferers, as the crop was planted on shares. I am convinced the negroes are too much like children to understand or be content with the share system.

"I have a good cook, but she has a *cavaliere servente,* besides her own husband and children, to provide for out of my storeroom, which she does in my presence very often—though it is not in the bond. I *am* impatient when she takes the butter given her for pastry and substitutes lard; yet I cannot withhold my admiration when I see her double the recipe in order that her own table may be graced with a soft-jumble as good as mine. Somebody has said: 'By means of fire, blood, sword and sacrifice you have been separated from your black idol.' It looks to me as if he is hung around our necks like the Ancient Mariner's albatross. You ridicule President Johnson's idea of loaning us farming implements. You must not forget who burned ours. We need money, for we have to pay the four years' taxes on our freed negroes!

"There is bad blood between the races. Those familiar with conditions here anticipate that the future may witness a servile war—a race war—result of military drilling, arming and haranguing the negro for political ends. Secession was a mistake for which you and I were not responsible. But even if our country was wrong, and we knew it at the time—which we did not—we were right in adhering to it. The best people in the South were true to our cause; only the worthless and unprincipled, with rare exceptions, went over to the enemy. We must bear our trials with what wisdom and patience we may be able to summon until our status is fully defined. I cannot but feel, however, that if war measures had ceased with the war, if United States officers on duty here, and the Government at Washington, had shown a friendly desire to bury past animosities and to

start out on a real basis of reunion, we should have become a revolution-
ized, reconstructed people by this time. But certain it is that the enemy—
authorities and 'scalawag '—friends, who now cruelly oppress the whites
and elevate the negro over us—are hated as the ravaging armies never
were, and a true union seems farther off than ever."

CHAPTER XVI.
MRS. JULIA WARD HOWE
AND THE BLESSED COLORED PEOPLE.

. . . Some interesting exercises took place during one afternoon of the
Exposition. Mrs. Julia Ward Howe addressed the colored people in a
gallery devoted to their exhibit. There was a satisfactory audience, chiefly
of the better classes of the race. Mrs. Howe had asked me to accompany
her, and when I assented some one said: "Well, you are probably the only
Southern woman here who would risk public censure by speaking to a
negro assembly." Mrs. Howe told them how their Northern friends had
labored to put the colored people on a higher plane of civilization, and
how Garrison had been dragged about the streets of Boston for their sake,
and urged that they show themselves worthy of the great anti-slavery leaders who had fought their battles. Her address was extremely well received.
I was then invited to speak. I told them: "The first kindly face I ever looked
into was one of this race who called forth the sympathy of the world in
their days of bondage. Among the people you once called masters you
have still as warm, appreciative friends as any in the world. Some of us
were nurtured at your breasts, and most of us when weaned took the first
willing spoonful of food from your gentle, persuasive hands; and when
our natural protectors cast us off for a fault, for reproof, for punishment,
you always took us up and comforted us. Can we ever forget it?

"Have you not borne the burdens of our lives through many a long
year? When troubles came did you not take always a full share? Well do
I remember, as a little child, when I saw my beloved mother die at the
old plantation home. The faithful hands from the fields assembled
around the door, and at her request Uncle Caleb Harris knelt by her bed-
side and prayed for her recovery—if it was God's will. How the men and
women and children wept! And after she was laid in the earth my infant
brother, six months old, was given entirely to the care of Aunt Rachel,

who loved him as her own life even into his young manhood, and to the day of her death. And who can measure your faithfulness during the late war when all our men had gone to the front to fight for their country? Your protection of the women and children of the South in those years of privation and desolation; your cultivation of our fields that fed us and our army; your care of our soldier boys on the field of battle, in camp and hospital, and the tender loyalty with which you—often alone— brought home their dead bodies so that they might be laid to sleep with their fathers, has bound to you the hearts of those who once owned you, in undying remembrance and love.

"I do not ask you to withhold any regard you may have for those who labored to make you free. Be as grateful as you can to the descendants of the people who first brought you from Africa—and then sold you 'down South' when your labor was no longer profitable to themselves. But remember, now you are free, whenever you count up your friends never to count out the women of the South. They too rejoice in your emancipation and have no grudges about it; and would help you to march with the world in education and true progress. As we have together mourned our dead on earth let us rejoice together in all the great resurrections now and hereafter." At the close, many colored people with tearful eyes extended a friendly hand, and Mrs. Howe too did the same.

DOCUMENT 114:
Excerpt, Susie King Taylor, *Reminiscences of My Life in Camp with the 33d United States Colored Troops late 1st S.C. Volunteers* (Boston: The Author, 1902), 9–11.

Courtesy Library of Congress.

Born into slavery in 1848 in Georgia, Taylor attended a school in Savannah and later opened one for African Americans while still a teenager on St. Simons Island. The excerpt is focused on her work there during the Civil War. After marrying Sergeant Edward King of the South Carolina Volunteers, Taylor traveled with his regiment and worked in various jobs, from nurse to laundress. This memoir focuses mainly on her life during the war, offering important details about disease, military campaigns, deserters, and the status of black soldiers. After the war, she returned to Savannah, where her husband died in 1866, and she moved to Boston and remarried in 1879. The final portion of the book focuses on life in Jim Crow America.

II
MY CHILDHOOD

. . . After we were all settled aboard and started on our journey, Captain Whitmore, commanding the boat, asked me where I was from. I told him Savannah, Ga. He asked if I could read; I said, "Yes!" "Can you write?" he next asked. "Yes, I can do that also," I replied, and as if he had some doubts of my answers he handed me a book and a pencil and told me to write my name and where I was from. I did this; when he wanted to know if I could sew. On hearing I could, he asked me to hem some napkins for him. He was surprised at my accomplishments (for they were such in those days), for he said he did not know there were any negroes in the South able to read or write. He said, "You seem to be so different from the other colored people who came from the same place you did." "No!" I replied, "the only difference is, they were reared in the country and I in the city, as was a man from Darien, Ga., named Edward King." That seemed to satisfy him, and we had no further conversation that day on the subject.

In the afternoon the captain spied a boat in the distance, and as it drew nearer he noticed it had a white flag hoisted, but before it had reached the Putumoka he ordered all passengers between decks, so we could not be seen, for he thought they might be spies. The boat finally drew alongside of our boat, and had Mr. Edward Donegall on board, who wanted his two servants, Nick and Judith. He wanted these, as they were his own children. Our captain told him he knew nothing of them, which was true, for at the time they were on St. Simon's, and not, as their father supposed, on our boat. After the boat left, we were allowed to come up on deck again.

III
ON ST. SIMON'S ISLAND
· 1862

NEXT morning we arrived at St. Simon's, and the captain told Commodore Goldsborough about this affair, and his reply was, "Captain

Whitmore, you should not have allowed them to return; you should have kept them." After I had been on St. Simon's about three days, Commodore Goldsborough heard of me, and came to Gaston Bluff to see me. I found him very cordial. He said Captain Whitmore had spoken to him of me, and that he was pleased to hear of my being so capable, etc., and wished me to take charge of a school for the children on the island. I told him I would gladly do so, if I could have some books. He said I should have them, and in a week or two I received two large boxes of books and testaments from the North. I had about forty children to teach, beside a number of adults who came to me nights, all of them so eager to learn to read, to read above anything else. Chaplain French, of Boston, would come to the school, sometimes, and lecture to the pupils on Boston and the North.

DOCUMENT 115:

Excerpt, Louise Wigfall Wright, *A Southern Girl in '61: The War-Time Memories of a Confederate Senator's Daughter* (New York: Doubleday, Page, and Company, 1905), 15–18.

Courtesy Documenting the American South, University Library, The University of North Carolina at Chapel Hill.

Born in 1846 in Rhode Island, Wright's father was a politician, who represented Texas in the U.S. Senate beginning in 1859. A supporter of the Confederacy, her father moved the family to follow his career, and Louisa was educated in Washington, D.C., and Richmond, Virginia. She married Judge D. Giraud Wright, and with access to elite white Southern society, Wright's memoir offers a unique perspective on the war—social events, politics, and military campaigns. This excerpt from the second chapter focuses on her perspective of enslaved men and women, whom she calls "lazy and idle." During part of the war, Wright was in Atlanta. She relocated to Macon when the city fell, then to Richmond, Virginia, Raleigh, North Carolina, and finally back to Texas with other refugees. The book was published in 1905 and is strongly sympathetic to the "Lost Cause."

CHAPTER II.
FROM VILLAGE TO CITY LIFE

. . . There have been volumes written about the negro, generally by persons who knew nothing, by practical experience, of the subject of which they wrote. They theorized, from a false basis, on a condition of things which existed only in their imaginations; and they built up a fabric, which, in these later days, has tumbled down about their ears, and bids fair, in its fall, to work havoc, in more directions than one. It may be that out of the dirt and débris, a new structure will be erected in time; but that time is certainly not yet. Now I do not propose to theorize on the subject. I merely wish to relate two or three facts, to the truth of which I can bear witness—facts that exhibit the character of the negro, as shown during the War, under the then existing conditions of slavery.

When my parents left home in the autumn of 1860 to go to Washington, they anticipated returning in a few months. We had a faithful woman, named Sarah, whose family had belonged to ours for two generations. Before our departure the silver was packed away and the key given to Sarah. For nearly four years we were absent. During that time the house was occupied, on several occasions, as headquarters, by Generals of our own army in command at Marshall, permission of course being given. Sarah, for the credit of the establishment, as she told us afterwards, produced the silver and had it constantly in use. When we returned, not a single piece was missing; though, in the meantime the War had ended, and she was free to come and go as she chose, and could easily, in the lawlessness of the time, have decamped with her prize, with no one to gainsay her. When, on our return home after weeks of waiting in fear and anxiety for my father's safety, at last tidings were brought us that he was in our neighborhood—it was to Sarah that we confided the fact, and through her connivance, under cover of night, he entered his home. It was Sarah who watched with us and stood on guard through the long weary hours while we sat together and talked over the plans for the future—and it was Sarah who saw in the early dawn that the coast was clear for her master—her master no longer—to make his escape from his foes!

Then again there was Henry, my brother's body servant during the War. In looking back it seems strange that officers in the army, at a time when they were barely existing on a third of a pound of bacon a day and a little corn meal, should have decreased their slender store by sharing it with servants. But those were the good old days and the good old ways, and I, for one, would never have changed them! Now one of my father's admirers in Texas had sent to him at Richmond a very beautiful Mexican saddle, heavily mounted in silver, and he, caring little for such vanities and always delighting to give to his children, promptly transferred the valuable present to my brother. Henry's pride in his young master's grandeur was unbounded, and he polished the handsome silver mountings with unwearied zeal, and I doubt if the suggestion ever occurred to his simple mind as to how sensible it would be to convert a portion of those jingling chains and buckles into some good digestible article to appease the ever-present hunger of both master and man. After General Johnston's surrender, and when my brother determined to make his way across the river to join Kirby Smith, he had to part from Henry. That Henry should leave him voluntarily never occurred to either of them. He left him at a point in Alabama and told him to wait with the horse and famous saddle until he should receive orders to come. And there he remained for weeks, faithful and obedient. When at last my brother wrote for him he sold the horse and the saddle, according to his orders, and with the proceeds made his way home, where he appeared one day to give an account of his adventures and expenditures. Can these instances of faithful service be matched in any negro to-day, after nearly forty years of freedom?

The negro in slavery before and during the War, was lazy and idle— he will always be that—but he was simple, true and faithful. What he has become since his emancipation from servitude is a queer comment on the effect of the liberty bestowed upon him. But that is going very far afield and away from our subject.

DOCUMENT 116:
Excerpt, Emma J. Smith Ray and Lloyd P. Ray, *Twice Sold, Twice Ransomed; Autobiography of Mr. and Mrs. L. P. Ray* (Chicago: The Free Methodist Publishing House, 1926), 18–22.

Emma Smith was born in Missouri in 1859 and was sold with her mother in Arkansas. During the Civil War, General John Charles Fremont, without authorization from Abraham Lincoln, declared slaves in Arkansas free. Shortly thereafter, Emma was forced back into slavery and later freed at the end of the Civil War. Told from a first-person perspective, this autobiography was published in 1926, and this excerpt focuses on the episode involving General Fremont.

I can not remember how long we were south; I don't think it was long, perhaps a few months. It was somewhere in Arkansas. There soon came a regiment of Union soldiers through Arkansas, commanded by General Fremont, and they took us back to Spring-field, under their protection, so I had the opportunity of singing to the Confederate soldiers going to Arkansas, and to the Union soldiers coming back.

I had a sister born on the way down to Arkansas when we stopped at the Bethphage camping ground. My mother named her Priscilla Bethphage. Priscilla was a very sad child, sick and delicate, being melancholy all her days.

When we arrived at Springfield, we went right back to our old owners; like so many chickens, we had nowhere else to go. But we did not stay there very long because General Fremont commanded every slave owner to give up all slaves who wanted to leave their masters. This was before the Emancipation Proclamation, and for this order General Fremont lost his position as Military Commander. We all left with great rejoicing. We had no place to live; we did not know how to provide for ourselves.

A neighboring slave owner, in sympathy with the north, let us (my father and mother, two sisters and myself) live in an old log cabin not far from our old home. My three brothers ran away from the Boyd family leaving my oldest sister on the plantation alone. She was the only slave left on the place. Around the fire at night, she had heard the other slaves talking about running away, and our mother had told her that she could run away and come to her. It was not very long before she started at night after getting the chores done, traveling at night, creeping through the underbrush. She had to come about two and one-half miles from the plantation into town. As she had heard them talking about the "underground railroad" and run-away negroes going north, it gave her a little idea of what to do. When the slaves ran away, the only thing they knew to do was to follow the north star. My sister came to us in the log cabin.

I remember hearing the slaves talk about getting to Canada over the "underground railroad," with the help of sympathetic northerners.

I never go across to the British side now, but I feel like lifting my heart in gratitude to God. It takes me back to the days of slavery, when our poor fathers and mothers prayed so earnestly to see that land and never had the opportunity and yet I, their offspring, reaped the fruit of their faith and prayers. God surely works in a mysterious way, His wonders to perform. Amen! Hallelujah!

My sister's liberty was short-lived, because the old master and the two daughters came after her. We were all happy, playing on the floor in the log cabin. The old mistress came to the door and said, "I have come after my nigger." My sister screamed and started for the back door, but some one was there to catch her. We children cried and our mother begged and prayed but our sister was taken back and they put a ball and chain on her and kept her chained down until she was subdued and would run away no more. But in a few days she was back again; this time mother ran with her to some Union sympathizer near by, and they kept her until the Proclamation was issued.

When the glad tidings came that we were freed, and the war was over, such rejoicing and weeping and shouting among the slaves was never heard before, unless it was the time that the Ark of the Covenant was brought back to the children of Israel. Great numbers of the slaves left their masters immediately. They had no shelter, but they dug holes in the ground, made dug-outs, brush houses, with a piece of board here and there, whenever they could find one, until finally they had a little village called "Dink-town," looking more like an Indian village than anything else. There they sang and prayed and rejoiced. Later on, the soldiers began to come through, returning from the war. They brought many negroes with them who were searching for members of their families. I remember my mother, with me holding on to her skirts, standing watching the soldiers as they passed in their blue suits, and the colored people all shouting "Hurrah for Marse Abe," and cheering the Union boys as they passed. That was a glad day. That certainly was a year of jubilee for the poor black slave. They had heard about the Liberation from Bondage of the Children of Israel from the Egyptians and their prayers were always to the Almighty God, and the God of Abraham, Isaac and Jacob that they too some day might be delivered, and now it had actually come. Oh! what joy!

My father was the only colored man that could write. Slaves were not allowed to learn to read and write, under penalty of flogging, but my father was a house servant and had stolen his education from the young masters as they said over their lessons. He was kept up for hours at night, and sometimes almost all night, writing letters trying to find out where loved ones were. Some had been run south, some were sold away, and they could not tell their names, only the first names. Mothers were hunting children, and husbands hunting wives; they kept my father very busy.

It was also very hard upon the slave owners, as there were none of the white women that knew anything about work, and they were left without a single servant. It was hard for both blacks and whites to become used to the change, for the slaves had no idea how to earn a living. Some of the slaves that had good masters never left, but stayed on the plantations the rest of their lives.

It was not long until my brothers came home and we were all gathered together. Soon after that came the assassination of Abraham Lincoln. That brought great sorrow over all the land, and especially to the blacks. I remember the village of huts where the negroes lived; every one would have a little piece of black cloth hung on it. They could not afford crepe, but it was merely a piece of old black pants, or coat, or anything in order to show their bereavement and their sorrow, that one so great had been taken from them; they loved him as their friend and deliverer. I heard them speak so much about "Marse Abraham" in their prayers, and sermons, and talk, and about "resting in Abraham's bosom" that I thought for a long time that Abraham Lincoln, and Abraham in the Bible, were the same man, until I began to go to Sunday-school and learned the difference.

DOCUMENT 117:
Excerpt, Interview, Nicey Kinney. Manuscript Slave
Narrative Collection, Federal Writers' Project (Washington,
D.C.: Library of Congress, 1930), Georgia Narratives, pt.
3, pp. 22–31.

Courtesy Library of Congress.

In this testimony taken in the 1930s, Nicey Kinney remembered
her work on a small farm and expresses deep affection for her master and mistress, suggesting that close bonds sometimes formed
under slavery despite the brutal conditions and harsh labor. The
interviewer frequently edited and modified the original language
of the speaker.

A narrow path under the large water oaks led through a well-kept yard
where a profusion of summer flowers surrounded Nicey Kinney's two-
story frame house. The porch floor and a large portion of the roof had
rotted down, and even the old stone chimney at one end of the structure
seemed to sag. The middle-aged mulatto woman who answered the
door shook her head when asked if she was Nicey Kinney. "No, mam,"
she protested, "but dat's my mother and she's sick in bed. She gits
mighty lonesome lyin' dar in de bed and she sho does love to talk. Us
would be mighty proud if you would come in and see her."

Nicey was propped up in bed and, although the heat of the
September day was oppressive, the sick woman wore a black shoulder
cape over her thick flannel nightgown; heavy quilts and blankets were
piled close about her thin form, and the window at the side of her bed
was tightly closed. Not a lock of her hair escaped the nightcap that
enveloped her head. The daughter removed an empty food tray and
announced, "Mammy, dis lady's come to see you and I 'spects you is
gwine to lak her fine 'cause she wants to hear 'bout dem old days dat
you loves so good to tell about." Nicey smiled, "I'se so glad you come
to see me," she said, "'cause I gits so lonesome; jus' got to stay here in
dis bed, day in and day out. I'se done wore out wid all de hard wuk I'se
had to do, and now I'se a aged 'oman, done played out and sufferin' wid
de high blood pressur', But I kin talk and I does love to bring back dem
good old days a-fore the war."

Newspapers had been pasted on the walls of Nicey's room. In one corner an enclosed staircase was cut off from the room by a door at the head of the third step; the space underneath the stair was in use as a closet. The marble topped bureau, two double beds, a couple of small tables, and some old chairs were all of a period prior to the current century. A pot of peas was perched on a pair of "firedogs" over the coals of a wood fire in the open fireplace. One the bed of red coals a thick iron pan held a large pone of cornbread, and the tantalizing aroma of coffee attention to the steaming coffeepot on a trivet on one corner of the hearth. Nicey's daughter turned the bread over and said, "Missy, I jus' bet you ain't never seed nobody cookin' dis way. Us is got a stove back in de kitchen, but our somepin t'eat seems to taste better fixed dis 'way; it brings back dem old days when us was chillun and all of us was at home wid mammy." Nicey grinned. "Missy," she said, "Annie—dat's dis gal of mine here—laughs at de way I laks dem old ways of livin', but she's jus' as bad 'bout 'em as I is, 'specially 'bout dat sort of cookin'; somepin t'eat cooked in dat old black pot is sho good.

"Marse Gerald Sharp and his wife, Miss Annie, owned us and, Child, dey was grand folks. Deir old house was 'way up in Jackson County 'twixt Athens and Jefferson. Dat big old plantation run plumb back down to de Oconee River. Yes, mam, all dem rich river bottoms was Marse Gerald's.

"Mammy's name was Ca'line and she b'longed to Marse Gerald, but Marse Hatton David owned my daddy—his name was Phineas. De David place warn't but 'bout a mile from our plantation and daddy was 'lowed to stay wid his fambly most evvy night; he was allus wid us on Sundays. Marse Gerald didn't have no slaves but my mammy and her chillun, and he was sho mighty good to us.

"Marse Gerald had a nice four-room house wid a hall all de way through it. It even had two big old fireplaces on one chimbly. No, mam, it warn't a rock chimbly; dat chimbly was made out of home-made bricks. Marster's fambly had deir cookin' done in a open fireplace lak evvybody else for a long time and den jus' 'fore de big war he bought a stove. Yes, mam, Marse Gerald bought a cook stove and us felt plumb rich 'cause dere warn't many folks dat had stoves back in dem days.

"Mammy lived in de old kitchen close by de big house 'til dere got to be too many of us; den Marse Gerald built us a house jus' a little piece off from de big house. It was jus' a log house, but Marster had all dem cracks chinked tight wid red mud, and he even had one of dem franklin-backed chimblies built to keep our little cabin nice and warm. Why, Child, ain't you never seed none of dem old chimblies? Deir backs sloped out in de middle to throw out de heat into de room and keep too much of it from gwine straight up de flue. Our beds in our cabin was corded jus' lak dem up at de big house, but us slept on straw ticks and, let me tell you, dey sho slept good atter a hard day's wuk.

"De bestest water dat ever was come from a spring right nigh our cabin and us had long-handled gourds to drink it out of. Some of dem gourds hung by de spring all de time and dere was allus one or two of 'em hangin' by de side of our old cedar waterbucket. Sho', us had a cedar bucket and it had brass hoops on it; dat was some job to keep dem hoops scrubbed wid sand to make 'em bright and shiny, and dey had to be clean and pretty all de time or mamy would git right in behind us wid a switch. Marse Gerald raised all dem long-handled gourds dat us used 'stid of de tin dippers folks has now, but dem warn't de onliest kinds of gourds he growed on his place. Dere was gourds mos' as big as water buckets, and dey had short handles dat was bent whilst de gourds was green, so us could hang 'em on a limb of a tree in de shade to keep the water cool for us when us was wukin' in de field durin' hot weather.

"I have never done much field wuk 'til de war come on, 'cause Mistress was larnin' me to be a housemaid. Marse Gerald and Miss Annie never had no chillun 'cause she warn't no bearin' 'oman, but dey was both mighty fond of little folks. On Sunday mornin's mammy used to fix us all up nice and clean and take us up to de big house for Marse Gerald to play wid. Dey was good christian folks and tuk de mostest pains to larn us chillun how to live right. Marster used to 'low as how he had done paid $500 for Ca'line but he sho wouldn't sell her for no price.

"Evvything us needed was raised on dat plantation 'cept cotton. Nary a stalk of cotton was growed dar, but jus' de same our clothes was made out of cloth dat Mistess and my mammy wove out of thread us chillun spun, and Mistess tuk a heap of pains makin' up our dresses. Durin' de war evvybody had to wear homespun, but dere didn't nobody have no better or prettier dresses dan ours, 'cause Mistess knowed more'n anybody 'bout dyein' cloth. When time come to make up a batch of clothes Mistess would say, "'Ca'line holp me git up my things for dyein', 'and us would fetch dogwood bark, sumach, poison ivy, and sweetgum bark. The poison ivy made the best black of anything us ever tried, and Mistess could dye the prettiest sort of purpole wid sweetgum bark. Cop'ras was used to keep de colors from fadin', and she knowed so well how to handle it dat you could wash cloth what she had dyed all day long and it wouldn't fade a speck.

"Marster was too old to go do de war, so he had to stay home and he sho seed dat us done our wuk raisin' somepin t'eat. He had us plant all our cleared ground, and I sho has done some hard wuk down in dem old bottom lands, plowin', hoein', pullin' corn and fodder, and I'se even cut cordwood and split rails. Dem was hard times and evvybody had to wuk.

"Sometimes Marse Gerald would be away a week at a time when he went to court at Jefferson, and de very last thing he said 'fore he driv off allus was, 'Ca'line, you and de chillun take good care of Mistess.' He most allus fetched us new shoes when he come back, 'cause he never kept no shoemaker man on our place, and all our shoes was store-bought. Dey was jus' brogans wid brass toes, but us felt powerful dressed up when we got 'em on, 'specially when dey was new and de brass was bright and shiny. Dere was nine of us chillun, four boys and five gals. Us gals had plain cotton dresses made wid long sleeves and wore big sun-bonnets. What would gals say now if dey had to wear dem sort of clothes and do wuk lak what us done? Little boys didn't wear nothin' but long shirts in summertime, but come winter evvybody had good warm clothes made out of wool off Marse Gerald's own sheep, and boys, even little tiny boys, had britches in winter.

"Did you ever see folks shear sheep, Child? Well, it was a sight in dem days. Marster would tie a sheep on de scaffold, what he had done built for dat job, and den he would have me set on de sheep's head whilst he cut off de wool. He sont it to de factory to have it carded into bats and us chillun spun de thread at home and mammy and Mistess wove it into cloth for our winter clothes. Nobody warn't fixed up better on church days dan Marster's Niggers and he was sho proud of dat.

"Us went to church wid our white folks 'cause dere warn't no colored churches dem days. None of de churches 'round our part of de country had meetin' evvy Sunday, so us went to three diffunt meetin' houses. On de fust Sunday us went to Captain Crick Baptist church, to Sandy Crick Presbyterian church on second Sundays, and on third Sundays meetin' was at Antioch Methodist church whar Marster and

Mistess was members. Dey put me under de watchkeer of deir church when I was a mighty little gal, 'cause my white folks so b'lieved in de church and livin' for God; de larnin' dat dem two good old folks gimme is done stayed right wid me all through life, so far, and I aims to live by it to de end. I didn't sho 'nough jine up wid no church 'til I was done growed up and had left Marse Gerald; den I jined de Cedar Grove Baptist church and was baptized dar, and dar's whar I b'longs yit.

"Marster was too old to wuk when dey sot us free, so for a long time us jus' stayed dar and run his place for him. I never seed none of dem Yankee sojers but one time. Marster was off in Jefferson and while I was down at de washplace I seed 'bout 12 men come ridin' over de hill. I was so skeered and when I run and told Mistess she made us all come inside her house and lock all de doors. Dem Yankee mens 'jus' rode on through our yard down to de river and stayed dar a little while; den dey turned around and rid back through our yard and on down de big road, and us never seed 'em no more.

"Soon atter dey was sot free Niggers started up churches of dey own and it was some sight to see and hear 'em on meetin' days. Dey would go in big crowds and sometimes dey would go to meetin's a fur piece off. Dey was all fixed up in deir Sunday clothes and dey walked barfoots wid deir shoes across deir shoulders to keep 'em from gittin' dirty. Jus' 'fore dey got to de church dey stopped and put on deir shoes and en dey was ready to git together to hear de preacher.

"Folks don't know nothin' 'bout hard times now, 'specially young folks; dey is on de gravy train and don't know it, but dey is headed straight for 'struction and perdition; dey's gwine to land in dat burin' fire if dey don't mind what dey's about. Jus' trust in de Lord, Honey, and cast your troubles on Him and He'll stay wid you, but if you turns your back on Him, den you is lost, plumb gone, jus' as sho as shelled corn.

"When us left Marse Gerald and moved nigh Athens he got a old Nigger named Egypt, what had a big fambly, to live on his place and do all de wuk. Old Marster didn't last long atter us was gone. One night he had done let his farm hands have a big cornshuckin' and had seed dat dey had plenty of supper and liquor to go wid it and, as was custom dem days, some of dem Niggers got Old Marster upon on deir shoulders and toted him up to de big house, singin' as dey went along. He was jus' as gay as dey was, and joked de boys. When dey put him down on de big house porch he told Old Mistess he didn't want no supper 'cept a little coffee and bread, but he strangled on de fust bite. Mistess sont for de doctor but he was too nigh gone, and it warn't long 'fore he had done gone into de glory of de next world. He was 'bout 95 years old when he died and he had sho been a good man. One of my nieces and her husband went dar atter Marse Gerald died and tuk keer of Mistess 'til she went home to glory too.

"Mammy followed Old Mistess to glory in 'bout 3 years. Us was livin' on de Johnson place den, and it wasn't long 'fore me and George Kinney got married. A white preacher married us but us didn't have no weddin' celebration. Us moved to de Joe Langford place in Oconee County, but didn't stay dar but one year; den us moved 'crost de crick into Clarke County and atter us farmed dar 9 years, us moved on to dis here place whar us has been ever since. Plain old farmin' is de most us is ever done, but George used to make some mighty nice cheers to sell to de white folks. He made 'em out of hick'ry what he seasoned jus' right and put rye split bottoms in 'em. Dem cheers lasted a lifetime; when dey got dirty you jus' washed 'em good and sot 'em in de sun to dry and dey was good as new. George made and sold a lot of rugs and mats dat he made out of plaited shucks. Most evvybody kep' a shuck footmat 'fore deir front doors. Dem sunhats made out of shucks and bulrushes was mighty fine to wear in de field when de sun was hot. Not long atter all ten of our chillun was borned, George died out and left me wid dem five boys and five gals.

DOCUMENT 118:
Testimony of Witness Before the Joint Congressional Committee, KKK Hearings, vol. 5, South Carolina Court Proceedings, December 19 and 30, 1871; and Vol. 9 Testimony before the joint committee of Mississippi Legislature to investigate the Meridian riot, March 21, 1871.

The KKK, first founded in Tennessee in 1865 at the end of the Civil War, embraced violence and terror as a way to control race relations. Numerous state governments during Reconstruction passed laws against the KKK, and the U.S. Congress passed the first of four

Force Acts in 1870. A congressional committee, comprised of twenty-one members of the U.S. House of Representatives and the U.S. Senate, held hearings about the Klan's activities. The final report filled thirteen volumes and advocated strong federal control over such vigilante groups. In this excerpt, several women from Mississippi and South Carolina are interviewed about their experiences.

TESTIMONY OF WITNESSES BEFORE THE JOINT CONGRESSIONAL COMMITTEE

Spartanburg, South Carolina

WITNESS: HARRIET HERNANDEZ

QUESTION: How old are you?

ANSWER: Going on thirty-four years.

QUESTION: Are you married or single?

ANSWER: Married.

QUESTION: Did the Ku-Klux ever come to your house at any time?

ANSWER: Yes, sir; twice.

QUESTION: Go on to the second time; you said it was two months afterwards?

ANSWER: Two months from Saturday night last. They came in; I was lying in bed. Says he, "Come out here, sir; Come out here, sir!" They took me out of bed; they would not let me get out, but they took me up in their arms and toted me out—me and my daughter Lucy. He struck me on the forehead with a pistol, and here is the scar above my eye now. Says he, "Damn you, fall!" I fell. Says he, "Damn you, get up!" I got up. Says he, "Damn you, get over this fence!" and he kicked me over when I went to get over; and then he went to a brush pile, and they laid us right down there, both together. They laid us down twenty yards apart, I reckon. They had dragged and beat us along. They struck me right on the top of my head, and I thought they had killed me; and I said, "Lord o' mercy, don't don't kill my child!" He gave me a lick on the head, and it liked to have killed me; I saw stars. He threw my arm over my head so I could not do anything with it for three weeks, and there are great knots on my wrist now.

QUESTION: What did they say this was for?

ANSWER: They said, "You can tell your husband that when we see him we are going to kill him."

QUESTION: Did they say why they wanted to kill him?

ANSWER: They said, "He voted the radical ticket, didn't he?" I said, "Yes, that very way."

QUESTION: When did your husband get back after this whipping? He was not at home, was he?

ANSWER: He was lying out; he couldn't stay at home, bless your soul! . . . He had been afraid ever since last October.

QUESTION: Is that the situation of the colored people down there to any extent?

ANSWER: That is the way they all have to do—men and women both.

QUESTION: What are they afraid of?

ANSWER: Of being killed or whipped to death.

QUESTION: What has made them afraid?

ANSWER: Because men that voted radical tickets they took the spite out on the women when they could get at them.

Columbia, S.C.

WITNESS: HARRIET SIMRIL

QUESTION: Who is your husband?

ANSWER: Sam Simmons.

QUESTION: Where do you live?

ANSWER: At Clay Hill in York County.

QUESTION: Has your husband lived there a good many years?

ANSWER: Yes, sir.

QUESTION: Do you know what politics he is?

ANSWER: He is a radical.

QUESTION: Did the Ku-Klux ever visit your house?

ANSWER: Yes, sir; they came on him three times. . . . The first time they come my old man was at home. They hollered out, "open the door," and he got up and opened the door. . . . These young men walked up and they took my old man out after so long; and they wanted him to join this democratic ticket; and after that they went a piece above the house and hit him about five cuts with the cowhide.

QUESTION: Do you know whether he promised to be a democrat or not?

ANSWER: He told them he would rather quit all politics, if that was the way they was going to do with him.

QUESTION: What did they do to you?

ANSWER: . . . They came back after the first time on Sunday night after my old man again, and this second time the crowd was bigger. . . . They called for him, and I told them he wasn't here. . . . They asked me where was my old man? I told them I couldn't tell; when he went away he didn't tell me where he was going. They searched about in the house a long time, and staid with me an hour that time. . . .

QUESTION: What did they do to you?

ANSWER: Well, they were spitting in my face and throwing dirt in my eyes; and when they made me blind they busted open my cupboard, and they eat all my pies up, and they took two pieces of meat . . . and after awhile they took me out of doors and told me all they wanted was my old man to join the democratic ticket; if he joined the democratic ticket they would have no more to do with him; and after they had got me out of doors, they dragged me out into the big road, and they ravished me out there.

QUESTION: How many of them?

ANSWER: There were three.

QUESTION: One right after the other?

ANSWER: Yes, sir.

QUESTION: Threw you down on the ground?

ANSWER: Yes, sir, they throwed me down.

QUESTION: Do you know who the men were who ravished you?

ANSWER: Yes, sir, I can tell who the men were; there was Ches McCollum, Tom McCollum, and this big Jim Harper. . . .

QUESTION: What was your condition when they left you?

ANSWER: After they had got done with me I had no sense for a long time. I laid there, I don't know how long. . . .

QUESTION: Have the Ku-Klux ever come to you again?

ANSWER: . . . They came back . . . but I was never inside the house.

QUESTION: Did your husband lay out at night?

ANSWER: Yes, sir; and I did too—took my children, and when it rained thunder and lightning. . . .

QUESTION: Did they burn your house down?

ANSWER: Yes, sir; I don't know who burnt it down, but the next morning I went to my house and it was in ashes. . . .

Meridian, Miss.

WITNESS: ELLEN PARTON

I reside in Meridian; have resided here nine years; occupation, washing and ironing and scouring; Wednesday night was the last night they came to my house; by "they" I mean bodies or companies of men; they came on Monday, Tuesday and Wednesday; on Monday night they said they came to do us no harm; on Tuesday night they said they came for the arms; I told them there was none, and they said they would take my word for it; on Wednesday night they came and broke open the wardrobe and trunks, and committed rape upon me; there were eight of them in the house; I do not know how many there were outside; they were white men . . . I called upon Mr. Mike Slamon, who was one of the crowd, for protection; I said to him, "Please protect me tonight, you have known me a long time;" this man covered up his head then; he had a hold of me at this time; Mr. Slamon had an oil-cloth and put it before his face, trying to conceal himself, and the man that had hold me told me not to call Mr. Slamon's name anymore; he then took me in the dining room, and told me I had to do just what he said; I told him I could do nothing of that sort; that was not my way, and he replied, "by God, you have got to," and then threw me down; this man had a black eye, where someone had beaten him; he had a black velvet cap on; after he got through with me he came through the house and said he was after the Union Leagues; I yielded to him because he had a pistol drawn; when he took me down he hurt me of course; I yielded to him on that account; he . . . hurt me with his pistol. . . .

Columbia, S.C.

WITNESS: HARRIET POSTLE
EXAMINATION BY MR. CORBIN:

I live in the eastern part of York County . . . on Mr. James Smith's plantation; I am about thirty years old; my husband is a preacher; I have a family of six children; the oldest is about fourteen; the Ku-Klux visited me last spring . . . I was asleep when they came; they made a great noise and waked me up, and called out for Postle; my husband heard them and jumped up, and I thought he was putting on his clothes, but when I got up I found he was gone; they kept on hallooing for Postle and knocking at the door; I was trying to get on my clothes, but I was so frightened I did not get on my clothes at all . . . [they] began to come into the house, and my oldest child got out and ran under the bed; one of them saw him and said, "There he is; I see him;" and with that three of them pointed their pistols under the bed; I then cried out, "It is my child;" they told him to come out . . . my child came out from under the bed . . . and . . . commenced hallooing and crying, and I begged them not to hurt my child . . . one of them ran the child back against the wall, and ground a piece of skin off as big as my hand. I then took a chair and sat it back upon a loose plank, and sat down upon it; one of the men stepped up; seeing the plank loose, he just jerked the chair and threw me over, while my babe was in my arms, and I fell with my babe to the floor, when one of them clapped his foot upon the child, and another had his foot on me; I begged him, for the Lord's sake, to save my child; I went and picked up my babe, and when I opened the door and looked I saw they had formed a line; they asked me if Postle was there; I said no; they told me to make up a light, but I was so frightened I could not do it well, and I asked my child to make it up for me; then they asked me where my husband was; I told them he was gone; they said, "He is here somewhere;" I told them he was gone for some meal; they said he was there somewhere, and they called me a damned liar; one of them said: "He is under the house;" then one of them comes to me and says: "I am going to have the truth to-night; you are a damned, lying bitch, and you are telling a lie;" and he had a line, and commenced putting it over my neck; said he; "you are telling a lie; I know it; he is here;" I told them again he was gone; when he had the rope round my head he said, "I want you to tell where your husband is;" . . . I commenced hallooing, and says he, "We are men of peace, but you are telling a damned lie . . . ;" and the one who had his foot on my body mashed me badly but not so badly as he might have done, for I was seven or eight months gone in travail; then I got outside of the house and sat down with my back against the house, and I called the little ones to me, after they were all dreadfully frightened; they said my husband was there, and that they would shoot into every crack; and they did shoot all over the place, and there are bullet-holes there and bullet-marks on the hearth yet; at this time there were some in the house and some outside, and says they to me: "We're going to have the truth out of you, you damned lying bitch; he is somewhere about here;" said I, "He is gone;" with that he clapped his hands on my neck, and with one hand put the line over my neck . . . and with that he beat my head against the side of the house till I had no sense hardly left; but I still had hold of my babe.

QUESTION: Did you recognize anybody?

ANSWER: Yes, sir; I did; I recognized the first man that came into the house; it was Dr. Avery (pointing to the accused). I recognized him by his performance, and when he was entangling the line round my neck; as I lifted my hand to keep the rope off my neck, I caught his lame hand; it was his left hand that I caught, his crippled hand; I felt it in my hand, and I said to myself right then, "I know you;" And I knew Joe Castle and James Matthews—the old man's son; I didn't know anyone else; I suppose there was about a dozen altogether there. . . . they said to me that they rode thirty-eight miles that night to see Old Abe Broomfield and preacher Postle; they said that they had heard that preacher Postle had been preaching up fire and corruption; they afterward found my husband under the house, but I had gone to the big house with my children to take them out of the cold, and I did not see them pull him out from the house.

K.K.K. Hearings, Vol. 5, South Carolina Court
Proceedings, December 19 and 30, 1871; and Vol. 9,
Testimony before the joint committee of Mississippi
Legislature to investigate the Meridian riot, March 21, 1871.

DOCUMENT 119:
Suffrage conferred by the Fourteenth Amendment.
Woman's suffrage in the Supreme Court of the District
of Columbia, in general term, October, 1871. Sara J.
Spencer vs. The Board of registration, and Sarah E.
Webster vs. The judges of election. Argument of the
counsel for the plaintiffs. With the opinions of the court.
Reported by J. O. Clephane.

Courtesy Library of Congress, Rare Book and Special Collections Division, National American Woman Suffrage Association Collection.

Sarah E. Webster and Sara J. Spencer both filed cases in Washington, D.C., District Court arguing that the Fourteenth Amendment granted them the right to vote. Their arguments were published in a pamphlet, though the Supreme Court of the District of Columbia denied their claim. Women, both African American and white, would have to wait until the passage of the Nineteenth Amendment in 1920, half a century later, to enjoy full enfranchisement.

Opinion

Chief Justice Cartter then delivered the opinion of the court, sustaining the demurrer, which is as follows:

These cases, involving the same questions, are presented together.

As shown by the plaintiffs' brief, the plaintiffs claim the elective franchise under the first section of the fourteenth amendment of the Constitution.

The fourth paragraph of the regulations of the Governor and Judges of the District, made registration a condition precedent to the right of voting at the election of April 20th, 1871.

The plaintiffs, being otherwise qualified, offered to register, and were refused. They then tendered their ballots at the polls, with evidence of qualification and offer to register, &c., when their ballots were rejected under the seventh section of the act providing a government for the District of Columbia.

Mrs. Spencer brings her suit for this refusal of registration, and Mrs. Webster for the rejection of her vote, under the second and third sections of the act of May 31, 1870.

The seventh section of the organic act above referred to, limits the right to vote to "all male citizens," but it is contended that in the presence of the Fourteenth Amendment, the word *male* is without effect, and the act authorizes "all citizens" to exercise the elective franchise.

The question involved in the two actions which have been argued, and which, for the purposes of judgment, may be regarded as one, is, whether the plaintiffs have a right to exercise within this jurisdiction, the elective franchise. The letter of the law controlling the subject, is to be found in the seventh section of the act of February 21, 1871, entitled, "An act to provide a government for the District of Columbia," as follows:

And be it further enacted, That all male citizens of the United States, above the age of twenty-one years, who shall have been actual residents of said District for three months prior to the passage of this act, except such as are *non compos mentis,* and persons convicted of infamous crimes, shall be entitled to vote at said election, in the election district or precinct in which he shall then reside, and shall have so resided for thirty days immediately preceding said election, and shall be eligible to any office within the said district, and for all subsequent elections, twelve months prior residence shall be required to constitute a voter; but the Legislative Assembly shall have no right to abridge or limit the right of suffrage.

It will be seen by the terms of this act that females are not included within its privileges. On the contrary, by implication, they are excluded. We do not understand that it is even insisted in argument that authority for the exercise of the franchise is to be derived from law. The position taken is, that the plaintiffs have a right to vote, independent of the law; even in defiance of the terms of the law. The claim, as we understand it, is, that they have an inherent right, resting in nature, and guaranteed by the Constitution in such wise that it may not be defeated by legislation. In virtue of this natural and constitutional right, the plaintiffs ask the court to overrule the law, and give effect to rights lying behind it, and rising superior to its authority.

The Court has listened patiently and with interest to ingenious argument in support of the claim, but have failed to be convinced of the correctness of the position, whether on authority or in reason. In all periods, and in all countries, it may be safely assumed that no privilege has been held to be more exclusively within the control of conventional power than the privilege of voting, each State in turn regulating the subject by the sovereign political will. The nearest approach to the natural right to vote, or govern—two words in this connection signifying the same thing—is to be found in those countries and governments that assert the hereditary right to rule. The assumption of Divine right would be a full vindication of the natural right contended for here, provided it did not involve the hereditary obligation to obey.

Again, in other States, embracing the Republics, and especially our own, including the States which make up the United States, this right has been made to rest upon the authority of political power, defining who may be an elector, and what shall constitute his qualification; most

States in the past period declaring property as the familiar basis of a right to vote; others, intelligence; others, more numerous, extending the right to all male persons who have attained the age of majority.

While the conditions of the right have varied in several States, and from time to time been modified in the same State, the right has uniformly rested upon the express authority of the political power, and been made to revolve within the limitations of express law.

Passing from this brief allusion to the political history of the question to the consideration of its inherent merits, we do not hesitate to believe that the legal vindication of the natural right of all citizens to vote, would, at this stage of popular intelligence, involve the destruction of civil government. There is nothing in the history of the past that teaches us otherwise. There is little in current history that promises a better result. The right of all men to vote is as fully recognized in the population of our large centres and cities as can well be done, short of an absolute declaration that all men shall vote, irrespective of qualifications. The result in these centres is political profligacy and violence verging upon anarchy. The influences working out this result are apparent in the utter neglect of all agencies to conserve the virtue, integrity and wisdom of government, and the appropriation of all agencies calculated to demoralize and debase the integrity of the elector. Institutions of learning, calculated to bring them up to their state of political citizenship, and indispensable to the qualifications of the mind and morals of the responsible voter, are postponed to the agency of the dramshop and gambling hell; and men of conscience and capacity are discarded, to the promotion of vagabonds to power.

This condition demonstrates that the right to vote ought not to be, and is not, an absolute right. The fact that the practical working of the assumed right would destructive of civilization is decisive that the right does not exist.

Has it become a constitutional right, under the provisions of the Fourteenth and Fifteenth Amendments of the Constitution, which provide as follows:

Fourteenth Amendment, section 1.—"All persons, born or naturalized in the United States, and subject to the jurisdiction thereof, are citizens of the United States, and of the State wherein they reside. No State shall make or enforce any law which shall abridge the privileges or immunities of citizens of the United State."

Fifteenth amendment, section 1.—"The right of citizens of the United States to vote shall not be denied or abridged by the United States, or by any State, on account of race, color or previous condition of servitude."

Section 2.—"The Congress shall have power to enforce this article by appropriate legislation."

It will be seen by the first clause of the Fourteenth Amendment, that the plaintiffs, in common with all other persons born in the United States, are citizens thereof, and, if to make them citizens is to make them voters, the plaintiffs may, of right, vote. It will be inferred from what has already been said, that to make a person a citizen is not to make him or her a voter. All that has been accomplished by this Amendment to the Constitution, or by its previous provisions, is to distinguish them from aliens, and make them capable of becoming voters.

In giving expression to my own judgment, this clause does advance them to full citizenship, and clothes them with the capacity to become voters. The provision ends with the declaration of their citizenship. It is a constitutional provision that does not execute itself. It is the creation of a constitutional condition that requires the supervision of legislative power in the exercise of legislative discretion to give it effect. The constitutional capability of becoming a voter created this Amendment lies dormant, as in the case of an infant, until made effective by legislature action. Congress, the legislative power of this jurisdiction, as yet, has not seen fit to carry the inchoate right into effect, as is apparent in the law regulating the franchise of this District. When that shall have been done it will be the pleasure of this court to administer the law as they find it. Until this shall be done, the consideration of fitness and unfitness, merit and demerit, are considerations for the law-making power. The demurrer in these cases is sustained.

After the reading of the opinion of the court by Chief Justice Cartter, Mr. Riddle, counsel for the plaintiffs, in open court, prayed an appeal to the Supreme Court of the United States.

Timeline

1619—In August, approximately "twenty and odd" blacks arrive in Jamestown, Virginia, on a Dutch ship and are sold as slaves.

1652—Rhode Island passes the first law against slavery in North America.

1656—Elizabeth Key sues for and gains her freedom. Her mother was enslaved, and her father was a white planter. She claims that her father's status and baptism entitle her to freedom.

1661—Virginia legally recognizes slavery.

1662—The Virginia House of Burgesses passes a law that children born to slave women follow the condition of the mother. This law contradicts English common law that holds that the father's status determines that of the child.

1663—A law in Maryland holds that a free white woman, and her children, loses her freedom if she marries a black slave.

1668—A Virginia law holds that free black women are to be taxed, while white female servants are exempt. The same law also holds that "Negro women, though permitted to enjoy their freedome" do not have the same rights as "the English."

1688—A Germantown, Pennsylvania, Society of Friends protests slavery, creating one of the first antislavery documents.

1739—A rebellion erupts in Stono, South Carolina.

1753—Phillis Wheatley, a slave in Boston, published *Poems on Various Subjects.*

c. 1797—Noted abolitionist, minister, and lecturer Isabella Van Wagener (known as Sojourner Truth) is born.

1789—The U.S. Constitution is adopted, sanctioning slavery without ever mentioning the term. Representation is based on three-fifths of "other persons," the slave trade is extended for two more decades, and sections are included to address the issues of runaway slaves.

1793—Eli Whitney's patent of the cotton gin helps expand cotton production and slavery throughout the American South.

1800—More than one million African Americans live in the United States, 18.9 percent of the population. That number does not distinguish between enslaved and free.

1802—Thomas Jefferson is first accused in the *Richmond Recorder* of keeping "as his concubine, one of his own slaves." That woman was Sally Hemings.

1807—The U.S. Congress bans the importation of slaves to the United States, but does not end slavery.

1822—The west African country of Liberia is established by the Colonization Society.

1825—Frances Wright establishes Nashoba plantation near Memphis, Tennessee, where she purchased slaves who would be allowed to become educated, purchase their freedom through their own labor, and then when freed move out of the United States. The project failed in 1829, and she removed the remaining slaves to Haiti.

1829—Sarah Moore Grimké publishes "Epistle to the Clergy to the Southern States," an antislavery tract.

1831—Abolitionist William Lloyd Garrison establishes his influential newspaper, *The Liberator,* in Boston. That same year, Nat Turner leads a slave rebellion in Southampton, Virginia. The Underground Railroad begins to help thousands of women, men, and children gain freedom in Canada or the northern United States.

1832—In Salem, Massachusetts, African American women found the Female Anti-Slavery Society.

1833—William Lloyd Garrison establishes the American Anti-Slavery Society. That same year, the Female Anti-Slavery Society is founded in Philadelphia. Lucretia Mott serves as the first president. Lydia Marie Child publishes *An Appeal in Favor of the Class of Americans Called Africans.* Oberlin Collegiate Institute becomes the first coeducational institution to accept African American students.

1836—"Appeal to the Christian Women of the South" is published by Angelina Grimké.

1839—For the first time, women are permitted to vote at the American Anti-Slavery Society convention.

1840—London's World Anti-Slavery Convention refuses to seat or allow female delegates to speak, prompting Lucretia Mott and Elizabeth Cady Stanton to organize the first women's rights convention in Seneca Falls, New York, in 1848.

1847—Frederick Douglass begins publication of his newspaper, *The North Star.*

1848—The Women's Rights Convention is held in Seneca Falls and includes numerous antislavery notables. Sixty-eight women and thirty-two men sign the Declaration of Sentiments.

1849—Harriet Tubman escapes slavery only to become active in the Underground Railroad, returning nineteen times to the South to rescue more than three hundred other slaves.

1850—The Fugitive Slave Act is passed.

1851—Sojourner Truth delivers her now-famous "Ar'n't I a Woman" speech in Akron, Ohio, at a women's rights convention.

1852—*Uncle Tom's Cabin* is published by the noted abolitionist Harriet Beecher Stowe.

1854—Francis Ellen Watkins Harper publishes *Poems on Miscellaneous Subjects,* which includes "Bury Me in a Free Land."

1856—Wilberforce College is founded to educate African Americans in Ohio.

1857—*Dred Scott v. Sanford* is passed.

1859—Harriet Wilson publishes the first novel by an African American woman, *Our Nig; Or Sketches from the Life of a Free Black.*

1861—The Civil War begins. Harriet Jacobs publishes *Incidents in the Life of a Slave Girl.*

1862—Mary Jane Patterson becomes the first African American woman to graduate from an American college (Oberlin).

1863—The Emancipation Proclamation is signed by President Abraham Lincoln. Fanny Kemble publishes *Journal of a Residence on a Georgia Plantation,* and Susie King Taylor publishes *In Reminiscences of My Life in Camp: Civil War Nurse.*

1865—With General Robert E. Lee's surrender at Appomattox, Virginia, the Civil War ends. The same year, the Freedman's Bureau is established and the Thirteenth Amendment, abolishing slavery, is adopted. Charlotte Forten, an African American woman from the North, publishes *Life on the Sea Islands,* about her work teaching former slaves.

1866—The Civil Rights Act is passed on April 9. It extended citizenship to all persons born in the United States, defined citizenship as colorblind, and made it illegal to discriminate on the basis of race, color, or prior condition of slavery or involuntary servitude. The Radical Republicans pass the act over President Andrew Johnson's veto. The act is still in effect today.

1868—The Fourteenth Amendment is passed, granting African Americans U.S. citizenship.

1869—Sarah Bradford publishes *Harriet Tubman: The Moses of Her People.*

1870—The Fifteenth Amendment is passed, extending the vote regardless of "race, color, or previous condition of servitude." This did not extend to African American women or white women.

1875—The Civil Rights Act outlawing discrimination in public accommodations is passed; *Plessy v. Ferguson* in 1896 would ultimately invalidate the provisions of the act.

1877—President Rutherford B. Hayes removes federal troops from the South on May 1, effectively ending Reconstruction.

Questions for Consideration

1. How were enslaved women's lives shaped by Article IV, Section II of the U.S. Constitution, Las Siete Partidas, and the Code Noir (all in chapter 1), documents that do not explicitly focus on their status? What do such documents reveal about the experiences of women under slavery?

2. What does the petition filed by Ruthey Ann Hansley (in chapter 1) suggest about women's power and how it is shaped by assumptions about race and gender? What does this document reveal about the lives of enslaved women?

3. What does Lucy Andrews's petition to return to slavery illustrate about the daily lives of freedwomen?

4. Select five documents that focus on the status of quadroons, octoroons, and freedwomen. How did their daily lives differ and what opportunities did they enjoy?

5. What strategies did enslaved women use to overcome the worst abuses of slavery and build strong communities?

6. Compare the Vilet Lester and J. W. Loguen letters. What forces shaped the relationships between these white and formerly enslaved women?

7. What did Abigail Adams's perspective on slavery reveal about the contradictions in the Founding Fathers' vision for the new nation?

8. What role did religion play in ameliorating the worst elements of slavery for both white and African American women?

9. What opportunities did the abolitionist movement offer white and black women, and how was the movement shaped by assumptions about race and gender?

10. What accounted for the different perspectives on slavery of Catharine Beecher and Angelina Grimké?

11. How were enslaved women's efforts to resist or escape slavery affected by their gender and family relationships?

12. How did the abolitionist movement influence, motivate, or impede the suffragist movement?

13. How were freedwomen positioned and to what degree were they accepted in Northern and Southern society?

14. What do the documents written by enslaved or freewomen, such as the one by Martha Harrison, reveal about the affection between whites and blacks? Compare that to white women's views of the same relationships. How do these perspectives change after slavery ends?

15. What role do women, both black and white, play in the Civil War?

16. What is important about the symbolic power of figures such as Sojourner Truth or Harriet Tubman? How were they used by the abolitionist movement to further their cause?

17. What role did education play in defining freedom? Compare documents written by African American and white women.

18. What kind of violence was directed at women during and after the Civil War?

19. In what ways were assumptions about race changed by the end of slavery, and in what ways were racist ideologies continued into the era of Reconstruction?

20. How has the scholarship on women and slavery since the 1970s reshaped the study of women's history that often focused narrowly on the experiences of middle-class women in New England?

Classroom and Research Activities

Activity #1

Charlotte Forten, in her letter to *The Liberator* featured in chapter 5, argues that African American women deserve to be educated to equip them to educate their own children. Compare her argument with that made by Linda Kerber in *Women of the Republic: Intellect and Ideology in Revolutionary America* (Chapel Hill: University of North Carolina Press, 1997). Analyze the two perspectives and identify other moments in women's history where activists made similar cases to advocate for increased rights or access to education.

Activity #2

Journalists and writers employed by the Works Progress Administration interviewed more than two thousand former slaves from 1936 to 1938 during the New Deal. This has created one of the richest and most valuable archives for scholars interested in the daily lives of slaves. Select five narratives with formerly enslaved women and examine how they define and make sense of their newfound freedom. The WPA narratives are available on the following Web sites:

The African-American Experience in Ohio, 1850–1920
http://dbs.ohiohistory.org/africanam/mss/gr7999.cfm

American Slave Narratives: An Online Anthology
http://xroads.virginia.edu/~HYPER/wpa/wpahome.html

"Been Here So Long": Selections from the WPA Slave
Narratives
http://newdeal.feri.org/asn/asn00.htm

Born in Slavery: Slave Narratives from Federal Writers'
Project, 1936–38
http://memory.loc.gov/ammem/snhtml/snhome.html

Slave Narratives: Black Autobiography in Nineteenth-
Century America
http://www.yale.edu/ynhti/curriculum/units/1985/5/85.
05.02.x.html

Slave Narratives: Constructing U.S. History Through
Analyzing Primary Sources
http://edsitement.neh.gov/view_lesson_plan.asp?id=364

Unchained Memories: Readings from the Slave Narratives
http://www.hbo.com/docs/programs/unchained_
memories/index.html

For a printed version, see George P. Rawick, ed., *The American Slave: A
Composite Autobiography* (Westport, CT: Greenwood Press, 1972–79).

Activity #3

Margaret Garner's story is one of the most heart-wrenching examples
of resistance during slavery. Review the image of her in chapter 4 of this
collection and research additional details about her life and attempts to
gain freedom for her family in Kentucky in 1856. Compare the facts of
Garner's story to Toni Morrison's Pulitzer Prize–winning novel *Beloved*
(1987) said to be based on her account. Finally, read Mark Reinhart's
essay, "Who Speaks for Margaret Garner? Slavery, Silence and the Politics
of Ventriloquism," *Critical Inquiry* 29 (Autumn 2002): 81–119 (available
on JSTOR), and Stefanie Sievers, *Liberating Narratives: The Authorization
of Black Female Voices in African American Women Writers' Novels of Slavery*
(Piscataway, NJ: Transaction Publishers, 1999 (annotated in this volume).

Activity #4

Examine how slavery has been displayed and interpreted at historic sites and via the web in the past twenty years. First, review the following online exhibitions:

> "The African-American Experience at Colonial Williamsburg"
> http://www.history.org/Almanack/life/Af_amer/aalife.cfm

> "Slavery—The Peculiar Institution" at the Library of Congress
> http://memory.loc.gov/ammem/aaohtml/exhibit/aopart1.html

> "To Labor for Another" at Monticello
> http://www.monticello.org/jefferson/dayinlife/plantation/home.html

> "Lest We Forget: The Triumph Over Slavery, The Schomburg Center for Research in Black Culture
> http://digital.nypl.org/lwf/flash.html

Then read James Oliver Horton and Lois Horton, eds., *Slavery and Public History: The Tough Stuff of American Memory* (New York: New Press, 2006) and consider how women's experiences have been portrayed in comparison to men's experiences. Are women's lives central to the exhibitions' discussions of work, family and community life, resistance, and freedom?

Activity #5

Read two contemporary novels focused on slavery: Margaret Walker's *Jubilee* and Sherley Anne Williams's *Dessa Rose*. Consider the questions posed by Stefanie Sievers in her book *Liberating Narratives: The Authorization of Black Female Voices in African American Women Writers' Novels of Slavery* (Piscataway, NJ: Transaction Publishers, 1999), 5: "How can the past be 'known' at all in a meaningful way? Which theories of historical knowledge have so far shaped public consciousness? What kind of historical information is available at any given time? Can novelistic discourse express an understanding of history that differs from the kind of understanding supported by traditional historiography, and thus help to change perceptions? Which historical and literary pre-texts does each writer choose to engage in? How do these choices relate to her (self-) positioning within and vis-à-vis various sociocultural groups? How does she authorize her revisionary narrative?"

Activity #6

The historian Anne Firor Scott argued in her book *The Southern Lady: From Pedestal to Politics, 1830–1930* (Chicago: University of Chicago Press, 1970) that white women had a softening influence on the institution of slavery, motivated by their empathy for enslaved women. Do the documents in this collection support Scott's thesis? Consider how the historian Elizabeth Fox-Genovese responded to Scott's conclusions in her work *Within the Plantation Household: Black and White Women of the Old South* (Chapel Hill: University of North Carolina Press, 1988).

ANNOTATED BIBLIOGRAPHY

Books and Monographs

Andrews, William L., ed. *Six Women's Slave Narratives*. Oxford and New York: Oxford University Press, 1988.

> This collection, drawn from the New York Public Library's Schomburg Center for Research in Black Culture, includes a foreword by Henry Louis Gates Jr. and an introduction by William L. Andrews. The *six* narratives include *The History of Mary Prince, A West Indian Slave* (1831); *The Narrative of Asa-Asa, A Captured African; Memoir of Old Elizabeth, a Coloured Woman* (1863); *The Story of Mattie J. Jackson* (1866), edited by Dr. L. S. Thompson; *From the Darkness Cometh the Light or Struggles for Freedom* (c. 1891) by Lucy A. Delaney; *A Slave Girl's Story* (1898) by Kate Drumgoold; and *Memories of Childhood's Slavery Days* (1909) by Annie L. Burton. As Andrews argues in the introduction, "The six black women's stories reprinted in the book represent most of the major themes and narrative forms that appear in Afro-American women's autobiographies from the nineteenth to early twentieth centuries.

Bleser, Carol, ed. *In Joy and in Sorrow: Women, Family, and Marriage in the Victorian South*, 1830–1900. Oxford: Oxford University Press, 1992.

> This edited collection, with an introduction by C. Vann Woodward and a foreword by Ann Firor Scott, features the most important historians in the field at the time: Eugene Genovese, Catherine Clinton, Elizabeth Fox-Genovese, Carol Bleser, Drew Gilpin Faust, James Roark, Michael Johnson, Brenda Stevenson, Bertram Wyatt-Brown, Jacqueline Jones, Peter Bardaglio, and more. Bleser focuses on the book's central theme "not only that slavery crippled the lives of slaves, free blacks, and the poor whites before the civil war, but that the institution damaged the lives of the husbands, wives, and children of the Old South's planter elite, supposedly the principal beneficiaries of the peculiar institution" (xii).

Bynum, Victoria. *Unruly Women: The Politics of Social and Sexual Control in the Old South* Chapel Hill: University of North Carolina Press, 1991.

> Bynum examines the lives of black and white women prior to and after the Civil War in North Carolina who were isolated from plantation society. She culls through a range of sources, including manuscripts and legal records, to detail the daily experiences of largely voiceless and politically powerless women. As a result, Bynum's women appear to be agents of their own fate, even as they are abused and marginalized by patriarchy, classism, and racism.

Campbell, Gwyn, Suzanne Miers, and Joseph C. Miller, eds. *Women and Slavery: The Modern Atlantic.* Athens: Ohio University Press, 2007.

This volume, like *More Than Chattel,* published a decade before, seeks to introduce new scholarship on women's roles in slavery. The focus on the female slave's centrality to the global economy is detailed in the introduction. The book is then divided into five sections: The Reproductive Biology of Sugar Slavery; Women's Initiatives Under Slavery; Rebuilding Lives in the Caribbean: Emancipation and Its Aftermath; Representing Women's Slavery: Masters' Fantasies and Memoirs in Fiction; Historical Reflections on Slavery and Women. It is an especially useful collection of new work in the field.

Clinton, Catherine. *The Plantation Mistress.* New York: Pantheon, 1984.

Catherine Clinton's volume focuses attention on elite white women's experiences during slavery to recover it from myth. Published in 1983, her focus on the American South is in direct response to what she calls the "New Englandization" of women's history. Her focus on plantation women from 1790 to 1835 illustrates the intense and complex labor that often oppressed white women. Understanding the intersection between gender and race pushes her perilously close to arguing that white women suffered as much or more than slave women, a point that Elizabeth Fox-Genovese takes up in her volume, *Within the Plantation Household* five years later.

Clinton, Catherine, and Nina Silber, eds. *Divided Houses: Gender and the Civil War.* New York: Oxford University Press, 1992.

This invaluable collection of eighteen essays examines how women's lives were shaped by the Civil War. Clinton and Silber have assembled respected scholars who argue that assumptions about gender and sexuality are central to understanding this pivotal moment in American history. Of particular interest are the articles focused on women's agency and how that shaped the causes and ultimately the legacy of the war.

Dunbar, Erica Armstrong. *A Fragile Freedom: African American Women and Emancipation in the Antebellum City.* New Haven, CT: Yale University Press, 2008.

Dunbar's study of ordinary, working-class free black women in Philadelphia is an important contribution to African American history that often focused on the elite families in this city. She offers a useful survey of colonial and Revolutionary, then moves to discuss how black women moved out of slavery (which did not end in Pennsylvania until 1847) to find themselves indentured. Despite their struggle to control their own labor, they built strong communities centered mainly on the church. In one of the most useful sections, Dunbar pays particular attention to the relationship between African American abolitionists and their white counterparts that often interfered with their organizations and educational institutions. Whites, even those trying to end slavery, were not immune to racism.

Fleischman, Jennifer. *Mastering Slavery: Memory, Family, and Identity in Women's Slave Narratives.* New York: New York University Press, 1996.

This monograph, focused on slave narratives, is particularly useful for scholars interested in race and the struggle for freedom prior to the Civil War. Fleischner focuses primarily on the psychological toll slavery took on individuals, a topic rarely considered by historians and one that might generate some discomfort. She considers narratives by white and black women, giving the volume a sense of balance. Particular attention is paid to the complexity of writing slave narratives for multiple audiences, especially Northern whites.

Fox-Genovese, Elizabeth. *Within the Plantation Household: Black and White Women of the Old South.* Chapel Hill: University of North Carolina Press, 1988.

Elizabeth Fox-Genovese details the complex and evolving world of the plantation household and boldly argues that the common ideology of domesticity that unified women in New England's middle classes—a topic well covered by women's historians such as Nancy Cott—did not translate into a Southern context. Class, economics, race, and even regional variations keep Fox-Genovese from generalizing about her topic. While white women could claim gender as a core identity, black women were pulled between gender and race and conventions that were beyond their control. An especially valuable part of this book is the bibliography and footnotes, which serve as essential reading for anyone interested in the history of the American South.

Gaspar, Barry, and Darlene Clark Hine. *More Than Chattel: Black Women and Slavery in the Americas.* Bloomington: Indiana University Press, 1996.

This edited volume presents useful comparison of slavery in Brazil, the Caribbean, and the United States and is essential reading for anyone interested in how the field evolved in the mid-1990s. The opening essay by Claire Robertson, "Africa in the Americas? Slavery and Women, the Family and the Gender Division of Labor," offers a broad overview that will appeal to scholars interested in work, family, and labor. The following two thematic sections—"Life and Labor" and "More Than Chattel"—address a range of topics, including patriarchy, sexuality, and the role of African traditions in efforts to resists.

Jones, Jacqueline. *Labor of Love, Labor of Sorrow: Black Women, Work, and the Family from Slavery to the Present.* New York: Basic Books, 1985.

Jacqueline Jones's study of African American work and family life won the 1986 Bancroft Prize in American History. In her sweeping study of black women from slavery to the 1980s, Jones argues that African American women inhabited a unique subculture, one not shared entirely by men or white women. She grounds her analysis in understanding women's labor, and her first two chapters are the most useful for those interested in understanding women's roles in slavery and Reconstruction.

Morgan, Jennifer L. *Laboring Women: Reproduction and Gender in New World Slavery.* Philadelphia: University of Pennsylvania Press, 2004.

> This volume, part of the press's Early American Studies series, examines English colonies in the West Indies and North America and the myriad ways in which they were connected. Morgan's main purpose is detailed in the introduction: "By situating the study of slavery and reproduction in both the Caribbean and the American South, I intend to suggest that women's reproductive identity—and by that I mean both the experience of childbirth and perhaps more important, the web of expectations about childbirth held by both black men and women and those who enslaved them—itself provides the comparative frame rather than the crop being cultivated or the size of the household in which one labored." The book is then divided into six chapters, followed by an epilogue and a bibliography.

Morrissey, Marietta. *Slave Women in the New World: Gender Stratification in the New World.* Lawrence: University Press of Kansas, 1989.

> A professor of sociology at the University of Toledo, Morrissey examines enslaved women's work at home for their families and in the fields and households controlled by whites. She goes on to examine how health and reproduction shape their experience of bondage and establishment of kinship networks. Finally, the volume details how white attitudes toward enslaved women as workers and mothers often conflicted.

Morton, Patricia, ed. *Discovering the Women in Slavery: Perspectives on the American Past.* Athens: University of Georgia Press, 1996.

> This collection of essays by a range of historians is divided into two main sections, "Making the Case for Women and Slavery" and "Worlds of Women and Slavery." Morton details her purpose in the introduction: "By presenting studies that examine slavery and women's histories together, this collection hopes to contribute to the placing of women's history in slavery history. This is both to emphasize the rich contribution of southern women's history to discovering the women in the Old South's peculiar institution" and "to focus more attention on the slavery experience of women outside the American South." Essays address a range of topics, from the empowerment of women in Appalachia during the Civil War to German immigrant slaveholding women in the Old South. The introduction is an especially useful survey of the historiography of slavery in the past fifty years.

Sievers, Stefanie. *Liberating Narratives: The Authorization of Black Female Voices in African American Women Writers' Novels of Slavery.* Piscataway, NJ: Transaction Publishers, 1999.

> This slim volume analyzes three novels that address women and slavery and their lives in the nineteenth century, Margaret Walker's *Jubilee* (1966), Sherley Anne William's *Dessa Rose* (1986), and Toni Morrison's *Beloved* (1987). Sievers discusses her selection in the introduction, "This selection of texts is neither meant to suggest a clearly definable sub-genre within African American women's writing, nor a clear-

cut distinction between narratives with historical and those with contemporary settings. Rather, the three texts occupy . . . different positions on a continuum of fictional texts that all negotiate the implications of historical understanding for contemporary black and female identities. Sievers's introduction and first chapter, entitled "Critical Concepts," introduces readers to the relevant literary criticism.

Spear, Jennifer M. *Race, Sex, and Social Order in Early New Orleans*. Baltimore: Johns Hopkins University Press, 2009.

> Spear offers a careful analysis and close reading of the experience of the formation of racial identities as mediated by gender in New Orleans. This volume, part of the press's Early America: History, Context Culture series, examines the experience of Native American and French women, as well as African American women, enslaved and free. In a review of the book, Daniel Usner of Vanderbilt University observes: "By focusing on everyday practice as well as on law and policy, Jennifer Spear vividly explains how free people of color became a significant social group in colonial New Orleans. She takes full advantage of tangibly special circumstances—regional economic conditions, governance by multiple regimes, and rich archival records—to replace stale assumptions about the Crescent City's peculiar society with fresh insights into its comparative importance in early American history."

White, Deborah Gray. *Ar'n't I a Woman: Female Slaves in the Plantation South*. New York: Norton, 1999.

> Deborah Gray White's important 1985 volume was one of the first to focus squarely on the experience of enslaved women. Early on, White points out that "African-American women were close to invisible in historical writings . . . because few historians saw them as important contributors to America's social, economic, or political development" (3). White debunks the various stereotypes of black women, the Mammy and Jezebel, and focuses careful attention of the life cycle of the female slave and the structure of the slave family. White's volume is a benchmark in the field, having sold nearly a quarter of a million copies. Darlene Clark Hine, in a 2007 review for the *Journal of American History,* wrote that White "clearly mapped the terrain, planting the seeds that two decades later bore abundant and glorious fruit."

Online Resources

Africa and Slavery—African History on the Internet
http://library.stanford.edu/depts/ssrg/africa/history/hislavery.html

> This invaluable Web site is a comprehensive annotated bibliography of a range of Web-based resources useful for scholars interested in all aspects of the history of slavery in a global context. There are numerous sites related to women, including Women in World History compiled by the Center for History and New Media at George Mason University.

The African American: A Journey from Slavery to Freedom
http://www.liu.edu/cwis/CWP/library/aaslavry.htm

> Organized by the library at Long Island University, this site includes articles and essays related to slavery, profiling notable figures in African American history such as Dred Scott and Harriet Tubman.

The African-American Mosaic, Library of Congress
http://www.loc.gov/exhibits/african/intro.html

> This Web site features an online exhibition produced in conjunction with the publication of *The African-American Mosaic: A Library of Congress Resource Guide for the Study of Black History and Culture.* The Mosaic is the first resource guide published that focuses exclusively on the Library of Congress's African American collections. Pay particular attention to the Library of Congress Prints and Photographs division for images related to slavery. There are also useful links on this site to other resources at the Library of Congress: for the K–12 classroom at http://www.loc.gov/teachers/classroommaterials/presentationsandactivities/

African Americans and the End of Slavery in Massachusetts
http://www.masshist.org/endofslavery/

> The Massachusetts Historical Society site includes 117 manuscripts focused on African American life from the late seventeenth century to 1780, the year slavery was abolished in the Massachusetts Constitution.

African American Women On-Line Archival Collections, Duke University Libraries, Rare Book, Manuscript, and Special Collections Library
http://library.duke.edu/specialcollections/collections/digitized/african-american-women/

> Duke University's collection features numerous primary documents related to women's experiences under slavery in the United States. This Web site was rated among the top humanities Web sites by the National Endowment for the Humanities.

African American World, Public Broadcasting System
http://www.pbs.org/wnet/aaworld

> This site, billed as "your guide to African American history and culture," provides a broad overview of African American history and sections on art, society, and civil rights. There is a timeline, a useful guide for teachers, a resource section, and profiles of notable personalities.

Africans in America, Public Broadcasting System
http://www.pbs.org/wgbh/aia/rb_index_hd.html

> This Web site, a companion to the six-hour PBS series Africans in America, has
> a wealth of primary documents focused on slavery from the fifteenth century to
> the Civil War. This particular link goes directly to primary documents supporting
> the series. The whole site is organized into four chronological sections.

Afro-American Sources in Virginia: A Guide to Manuscripts
http://www.upress.virginia.edu/plunkett/mfp.html

> This Web site, published by the University of Virginia Press, features a guide pub-
> lished in 1994 created by Michael Plunkett. There are 130 collections that address
> slavery in some fashion.

The Atlantic Slave Trade and Slave Life in the Americas: A Visual Record
http://hitchcock.itc.virginia.edu/Slavery

> This project, funded by the Virginia Foundation for the Humanities and organ-
> ized by the Digital Media Lab at the University of Virginia, includes 1,235 images
> related to slavery.

Avery Research Center for African American History and Culture
http://avery.cofc.edu/collections.htm

> Founded in 1985, the Avery Research Center for African American History and
> Culture at the College of Charleston features archival and museum collections
> on this site, largely related to South Carolina and the city of Charleston.

The Church in the Southern Black Community, 1780–1925, University of North
    Carolina
http://memory.loc.gov/ammem/award99/ncuhtml/csbchome.html

> These primary documents, drawn from the libraries at the University of North
> Carolina at Chapel Hill, examine the role of Protestant Christianity played in
> African American life. The site is easily searched by keyword.

Digital History, University of Houston
http://www.digitalhistory.uh.edu/do_history/slavery/index.cfm

> This Web site, divided into five sections, includes a range of Web-based resources
> and research questions related to slavery, though few focus on women. The site
> was designed by the College of Education and the Department of History at the
> University of Houston and is intended for use in K–12 schools and colleges.

Freedmen's Bureau Online
http://www.freedmensbureau.com

> This Web site is organized by state and is searchable by the type of document. It includes materials related to marriages, labor, and contracts, as well as crimes during Reconstruction. It also includes links to other sites related to the bureau.

The Gilder Lehrman Center for the Study of Slavery, Resistance, and Abolition at Yale University
http://www.yale.edu/glc/archive/subject.htm

> Directed by Dr. David Blight, the Gilder Lehrman Center's Web site features a wealth of primary documents related to slavery, largely from the Yale Center for International and Area Studies. Of particular interest is the section "Slavery and Freedom in American History and Memory" and the online documents.

Guide to African American Documentary Collections in North Carolina
http://www.upress.virginia.edu/epub/pyatt/nchome.html

> Published by the University of Virginia Press, this Web site is edited by Timothy D. Pyatt, and compiled by Linda Simmons Henry and Lisa Parker. It was the result of the North Carolina African American Archives Group, under the direction of Dean Benjamin F. Speller Jr., School of Library and Information Science, North Carolina Central University Grant.

Making of America, Cornell University
http://digital.library.cornell.edu/m/moa/

> This site includes primary sources from the Cornell University Library Making of America Collection from the antebellum period through Reconstruction. Funded by the Andrew W. Mellon Foundation, there are 267 monographs available and more than 100,000 journal articles from the nineteenth century.

National Underground Railroad Freedom Center
http://www.freedomcenter.org

> This site includes educational activities related to a range of topics related to slavery as well as information about places and people affiliated with the Underground Railroad. Click on the "Underground Railroad" tab for the most comprehensive information, including a timeline.

Reconstruction: The Second Civil War, Public Broadcasting System
http://www.pbs.org/wgbh/amex/reconstruction/

> Accompanying the PBS series by the same name, part of The American Experience, this user-friendly site includes primary sources and teaching materials related to the postwar era. It is arranged by themes and topics and includes a comprehensive teacher's guide focused on history, geography, economics, and civics.

The Rise and Fall of Jim Crow
www.pbs.org/wnet/jimcrow

> This is one of the most comprehensive sites online on this topic, with numerous essays, links to other sites, and resources for teachers. It was originally created in support of the PBS series The Rise and Fall of Jim Crow produced by Thirteen/WNET New York and sponsored by the New York Life Insurance Company. The series aired in 2002.

Slavery and the Making of America, Public Broadcasting System
http://www.pbs.org/wnet/slavery/resources/online.html

> This Web site provides a wealth of information about slavery in America, divided into four categories: print resources, online resources, television and film resources, and resources for children.

Slaves and the Courts, 1740–1860, Library of Congress
http://memory.loc.gov/ammem/sthtml/

> This site features more than one hundred books and pamphlets focused on African American life in the colonies. Most of the documents are from the Law Library and the Rare Book and Special Collections Division of the Library of Congress. The legal cases are mostly from America, though a few were tried in Great Britain. The documents present a wide range of voices, a minority of which are women.

Slave Trade Archives, UNESCO
http://portal.unesco.org/ci/en/ev.php-
URL_ID=8780&URL_DO=DO_TOPIC&URL_SECTION=201.html

> Begun in 1999, the Slave Trade Archives Project provides primary documents related to the transatlantic slave trade and slavery throughout the world and is part of the UNESCO Memory of the World project.

Third Person, First Person, Slave Voices from the Duke University Special Collections Library
http://scriptorium.lib.duke.edu/slavery/

> This site is the result of an exhibition on view at the Perkins Library at Duke University in 1995. It is not a large collection of documents and only a few relate to women's experiences.

The Time of the Lincolns
http://www.pbs.org/wgbh/amex/lincolns/

> This site was created for the PBS series, Abraham Lincoln and Mary Lincoln: A House Divided. Pay particular attention to the section on "Slavery and Freedom" and "A Woman's World."

University of North Carolina, Chapel Hill, Documenting the American South
http://docsouth.unc.edu/

> One of the most useful sites on the Web, Documenting the American South (known as DocSouth) includes texts, images, and audio related to southern history, literature, and culture. Users can view fourteen thematic collections that include a range of materials, many related to women and slavery.

University of North Carolina, Greensboro, The Digital Library on American Slavery
http://library.uncg.edu/slavery_petitions/about.aspx

> This Web site features eighteenth- and nineteenth-century documents that focus on 150,000 individuals, including slaves, free people of color, and whites. Users can search by name, by subject, by year, or by state.

University of Virginia, Virginia Center for Digital History
http://www.vcdh.virginia.edu/index.php?page=About

> Established in the College of Arts and Sciences at the University of Virginia in 1998 by Edward Ayres and William G. Thomas III, the VCDH sponsors numerous digital projects for K–12 audiences and the general public, including ones focused on women and slavery.

"Voices from the Days of Slavery," Library of Congress
http://memory.loc.gov/ammem/collections/voices/

> This site features interviews completed between 1932 and 1975 in nine Southern states. Twenty-three interviewees, born between 1823 and the early 1860s, discuss a range of topics, including family life and the meaning of freedom.

Voyages: The Trans-Atlantic Slave Trade Database
http://www.slavevoyages.org/tast/index.faces

> The Trans-Atlantic Slave Trade Database gathers information from archives and libraries with holdings related to the Atlantic world, including several decades of research by historians, librarians, curriculum specialists, cartographers, computer programmers, and Web designers with scholars of the slave trade from universities in Europe, Africa, South America, and North America. The project is sponsored by the National Endowment for the Humanities and the Emory University Digital Library Research Initiative.

Works Progress Administration (WPA) Slave Narratives

> The Works Progress Administration of the New Deal sponsored a Federal Writers' Project to gather oral histories with former slaves in the 1930s. The following Web sites feature selected sources from this project.

The African-American Experience in Ohio, 1850–1920
http://dbs.ohiohistory.org/africanam/mss/gr7999.cfm

American Slave Narratives: An Online Anthology
http://xroads.virginia.edu/~HYPER/wpa/wpahome.html

"Been Here So Long": Selections from the WPA Slave Narratives
http://newdeal.feri.org/asn/asn00.htm

Born in Slavery: Slave Narratives from the Federal Writers' Project, 1936–38
http://memory.loc.gov/ammem/snhtml/snhome.html

Slave Narratives: Black Autobiography in Nineteenth-Century America
http://www.yale.edu/ynhti/curriculum/units/1985/5/85.05.02.x.html

Slave Narratives: Constructing U.S. History Through Analyzing Primary Sources
http://edsitement.neh.gov/view_lesson_plan.asp?id=364

Unchained Memories: Readings from the Slave Narratives
http://www.hbo.com/docs/programs/unchained_memories/index.html

INDEX

ABOUT THE AUTHORS

CATHERINE M. LEWIS is a professor of history and interim executive director of Museums, Archives and Rare Books at Kennesaw State University. She is also a guest curator and special projects coordinator for the Atlanta History Center. She completed a B.A. in English and history with honors at Emory University and a M.A. and Ph.D. in American Studies at the University of Iowa. She has curated more than twenty-five exhibitions throughout the nation and has authored, coauthored, or coedited eight books, including *The Changing Face of Public History: The Chicago Historical Society and the Transformation of An American History Museum* (2005) and *Don't Ask What I Shot: How Eisenhower's Love of Golf Helped Shape 1950s America* (2007). She has coedited with Dr. J. Richard Lewis two additional documentary collections with the University of Arkansas Press: *Race, Politics, and Memory: A Documentary History of the Little Rock School Crisis* (2007) and *Jim Crow America: A Documentary History* (2009).

J. RICHARD LEWIS is president of JRL Educational Services, Inc. He completed his B.A. in English at Mercer University, his M.A. in English at Florida State University, and his Ph.D. in curriculum and instruction at the University of Maryland. He spent his career as an educator and administrator in Florida, Maryland, and Virginia. He has served as a visiting faculty member at Western Maryland College and Johns Hopkins University. He retired as the director of Success for All and as a researcher at Johns Hopkins University in 2001. He has served as a desegregation consultant for the Miami Desegregation Assistance Center, the Urban Education Center and Milwaukee Public Schools, the Cincinnati Desegregation Assistance Center at the University of Cincinnati, and Memphis State University, among others. He has coedited with Dr. Catherine M. Lewis two additional documentary collections with the University of Arkansas Press: *Race, Politics, and Memory: A Documentary History of the Little Rock School Crisis* (2007) and *Jim Crow America: A Documentary History* (2009).